TEACHING, NO GREATER CALL

A Resource Guide for Gospel Teaching

Published by
The Church of Jesus Christ of Latter-day Saints
Salt Lake City, Utah

Comments and Suggestions

Your comments and suggestions about this book would be appreciated. Please submit them to:

Curriculum Planning
50 East North Temple Street, Floor 24
Salt Lake City, UT 84150-3200 USA
E-mail: cur-development@ldschurch.org

Please list your name, address, ward, and stake. Be sure to give the title of the book. Then offer your comments and suggestions about the book's strengths and areas of potential improvement.

English approval: 8/98

Cover, Page 3:	*Jesus in the Synagogue at Nazareth*, by Greg K. Olsen. © by Greg K. Olsen.
Page 1:	*Sermon on the Mount*, by Carl Bloch. Used by permission of the National Historic Museum at Frederiksborg in Hillerød.
Page 5:	*Lovest Thou Me More Than These?* by David Lindsley. © by David Lindsley.
Page 22:	*Pioneer Garden*, by Valoy Eaton. © by Valoy Eaton.
Page 29:	*Jesus and the Samaritan Woman*, by Carl Bloch. Used by permission of the National Historic Museum at Frederiksborg in Hillerød.
Page 31:	*Storytime in Galilee*, by Del Parson. © by Del Parson.
Page 33:	*Woman Touching the Hem of the Savior's Garment*, by Judith Mehr. © by Judith Mehr.
Page 35:	*The Good Shepherd*, by Del Parson. © by Del Parson.

HOW TO USE
THIS RESOURCE GUIDE

Who should use this resource guide?

This resource guide is for all who teach the gospel, including:

- Parents.
- Classroom teachers.
- Priesthood and auxiliary leaders.
- Home teachers and visiting teachers.

What does this resource guide contain?

Teaching, No Greater Call contains guidelines and suggestions related to teaching, as shown in the following outline:

Part A
Your Call to Teach

This part of the book explains the importance of gospel teaching in God's plan. It also includes helps on how individuals can prepare to teach the gospel.

Part B
Basic Principles of Gospel Teaching

This part of the book helps build a foundation for all gospel teaching.

Part C
Teaching Different Age-Groups

This part of the book provides information and suggestions for teaching the gospel to children, youth, and adults.

Part D
Teaching in the Home

This part of the book provides help for parents to teach the gospel to their children. It also includes suggestions for home teachers and visiting teachers.

Part E
Teaching in Leadership Settings

This part of the book helps priesthood and auxiliary leaders understand their vital responsibility to teach.

Part F
Methods of Teaching

This part of the book describes a variety of different methods that teachers can use to enrich lesson presentations.

Part G
The Teaching the Gospel Course

This part of the book includes twelve lessons that prepare individuals to teach the gospel. The lessons are designed to be taught as part of an organized class. They may also be studied individually or as a family.

How should this resource guide be used?

Teaching, No Greater Call is designed as a resource guide rather than a book to be read cover to cover. It is intended to be used as:

- A personal study guide.
- A resource for teacher improvement meetings.
- The manual for the Teaching the Gospel course.
- A resource for leaders as they work with teachers in their organizations.

To gain the greatest benefit from the book, teachers should:

- Review the items listed in the table of contents.
- Study the articles that address their particular interests or needs at the time.

For example, parents may want to make better use of teaching moments to help their children grow spiritually. Part D, "Teaching in the Home," includes an article titled

"Teaching Moments in Family Life," which discusses how to recognize teaching moments and teach principles that children are ready to learn. Teachers may want to include a greater variety of teaching methods in their lessons. The articles in Part B under "Use Effective Methods" provide helpful ideas on how to select and use different teaching methods.

As teachers use *Teaching, No Greater Call* in this way, it will become an important resource in their ongoing efforts to improve their teaching.

Superseded Publications

This book replaces the following publications:
- All previous versions of *Teaching—No Greater Call*
- *The How Book for Teaching Children*
- *Primary Sharing Time Resource Manual*

List of Items Referenced

An alphabetical list of the Church-produced materials that are referenced in this publication is provided below. The item numbers are provided below rather than in the text of this publication.

"Activities" section of the *Church Handbook of Instructions* (35710)

Book of Mormon Stories (35666)

Children's Songbook (35324 and 35395)

Church Handbook of Instructions, Book 2: Priesthood and Auxiliary Leaders (35209)

Church Materials Catalog (published annually with a new item number each year)

Family Home Evening Resource Book (31106)

Gospel Art Picture Kit (34730)

Gospel Principles (31110)

"Gospel Teaching and Leadership" section of the *Church Handbook of Instructions* (35903)

How to Teach a Song to Children (53005)

Hymns (see the *Church Materials Catalog* for a complete listing of item numbers)

Improving Gospel Teaching: A Leader's Guide (35667)

Index to Periodicals of The Church of Jesus Christ of Latter-day Saints (see the *Church Materials Catalog* for the current item number)

"Music" section of the *Church Handbook of Instructions* (35714)

My Achievement Days booklet (35317)

Primary Leader Training videocassette (53008)

Primary Video Collection (53179)

Scripture Stories (31120)

Teaching Guidebook (34595)

Teach the Child videocassette (53677)

Visual Aids Cutouts (complete collection: 08456; single sets: 33239, 33242 through 33250)

CONTENTS

A

YOUR CALL TO TEACH

THE IMPORTANCE OF GOSPEL TEACHING IN GOD'S PLAN

As teachers you stand upon the highest peak in education, for what teaching
can compare in priceless value and in far-reaching effect with that
which deals with man as he was in the eternity of yesterday,
as he is in the mortality of today, and as he will be in
the forever of tomorrow. Not only time but eternity is your field.

President J. Reuben Clark Jr.

1

NO GREATER CALL

Speaking in general conference, Elder Jeffrey R. Holland said: "We are *so* grateful to all who teach. We love you and appreciate you more than we can say. We have great confidence in you." He continued: "To teach effectively and to feel you are succeeding is demanding work indeed. But it is worth it. We can receive 'no greater call.' . . . For each of us to 'come unto Christ,' to keep His commandments and follow His example back to the Father, is surely the highest and holiest purpose of human existence. To help others do that as well—to teach, persuade, and prayerfully lead them to walk that path of redemption also—surely that must be the second most significant task in our lives. Perhaps that is why President David O. McKay once said, 'No greater responsibility can rest upon any man [or woman], than to be a teacher of God's children'" (in Conference Report, Apr. 1998, 30–31; or *Ensign,* May 1998, 25).

The Role of Teaching in Heavenly Father's Plan

To be able to fully exercise our agency in righteousness, we must learn of the Savior and the doctrines of His gospel. Because of this, gospel teaching has always played an essential role in Heavenly Father's plan for His children.

In the premortal spirit world, we "received [our] first lessons . . . and were prepared to come forth in the due time of the Lord to labor in his vineyard for the salvation of the souls of men" (D&C 138:56). After Adam and Eve were cast out of the Garden of Eden, the Lord sent angels to teach them the plan of redemption (see Alma 12:27–32). He later commanded Adam and Eve to "teach these things freely" to their children (see Moses 6:57–59).

In every dispensation of the gospel, the Lord has directed the teaching of the plan of redemption. He has sent angels (see Mosiah 3:1–4; Moroni 7:29–32; Joseph Smith—History 1:30–47), called prophets (see Amos 3:7), provided the scriptures (see D&C 33:16), and helped people know the truth by the power of the Holy Ghost (see 1 Nephi 10:19; Moroni 10:5). He has commanded His followers to teach the gospel to their family members (see Deuteronomy 6:5–7; Mosiah 4:14–15; D&C 68:25–28), to other members of the Church (see D&C 88:77–78, 122), and to those who have not yet received the fulness of the gospel (see Matthew 28:19–20; D&C 88:81).

Of the importance of gospel teaching in the Church, Elder Gordon B. Hinckley said: "Fundamental to the very program of the Church is the teaching of the gospel to the membership of the Church. In fulfillment of the obligation which was laid upon the Church in its inception, there has developed within the Church a system of great teaching organizations—the priesthood quorums, both Melchizedek and Aaronic, the far-flung church school system, and the auxiliaries . . . , all of which play so important a part in the education of our people" (in Conference Report, Oct. 1962, 72–73).

Every Member a Teacher

When the resurrected Savior taught the Nephites, He said: "Hold up your light that it may shine unto the world. Behold I am the light which ye shall hold up— that which ye have seen me do" (3 Nephi 18:24). In this instruction the Lord made no distinction among those who heard His voice. All were commanded to teach.

The same is true today. The responsibility to teach the gospel is not limited to those who have formal callings as teachers. As a

member of The Church of Jesus Christ of Latter-day Saints, you have the responsibility to teach the gospel. As a parent, son, daughter, husband, wife, brother, sister, Church leader, classroom teacher, home teacher, visiting teacher, coworker, neighbor, or friend, you have opportunities to teach. Sometimes you can teach openly and directly by the things you say and the testimony you bear. And you always teach by example.

The Lord said, "This is my work and my glory—to bring to pass the immortality and eternal life of man" (Moses 1:39). As you think of the role of gospel teaching in the salvation and exaltation of God's children, can you imagine a duty more noble or sacred? It calls for your diligent efforts to increase your understanding and improve your skills, knowing that the Lord will magnify you as you teach in the way He has commanded. It is a labor of love—an opportunity to help others exercise their agency righteously, come unto Christ, and receive the blessings of eternal life.

2

NOURISHING THE SOUL

On the shore of the Sea of Galilee, the resurrected Lord asked Peter three times, "Lovest thou me?" Each time Peter's reply was the same: "Thou knowest that I love thee." To Peter's declaration the Lord responded: "Feed my lambs. . . . Feed my sheep. . . . Feed my sheep" (John 21:15–17).

The Lord's instruction to Peter applies to all who have been called to His service. President Gordon B. Hinckley wrote: "There is hunger in the land, and a genuine thirst—a great hunger for the word of the Lord and an unsatisfied thirst for things of the Spirit. . . . The world is starved for spiritual food. Ours is the obligation and the opportunity to nourish the soul" ("Feed the Spirit, Nourish the Soul," *Ensign,* Oct. 1998, 2; see also Amos 8:11–12).

The Gospel of Jesus Christ: Lasting Nourishment for the Soul

Just as we need nourishing food to survive physically, we need the gospel of Jesus Christ to survive spiritually. Our souls are nourished by whatever speaks of Christ and leads us to Him, whether it is written in the scriptures, spoken by latter-day prophets, or taught by other humble servants of God. The Savior Himself said, "I am the bread of life: he that cometh to me shall never hunger; and he that believeth on me shall never thirst" (John 6:35).

Teaching that is nourishing to the soul uplifts others, builds their faith, and gives them confidence to meet life's challenges. It motivates them to forsake sin and to come to Christ, call on His name, obey His commandments, and abide in His love (see D&C 93:1; John 15:10).

Some Teaching Does Not Nourish the Soul

Many topics are interesting, important, and even relevant to life and yet not nourishing to the soul. It is not our commission to teach such topics. Instead, we are to edify others and teach them principles that pertain to the kingdom of God and the salvation of mankind.

Teaching that stimulates the intellect without speaking to the spirit cannot nourish. Nor can anything that raises doubts about the truth of the restored gospel or the need to commit ourselves to it with all our heart, might, mind, and strength.

Elder Bruce R. McConkie counseled: "Teach the doctrines of salvation; supply spiritual food; bear testimony of our Lord's divine Sonship—anything short of such a course is unworthy of a true minister who has been called by revelation. Only when the Church is fed the bread of life are its members kept in paths of righteousness" (*Doctrinal New Testament Commentary,* 3 vols. [1966–73], 2:178).

The Challenge of Nourishing Others

Some people may not seem interested in hearing the principles of the gospel. You should prayerfully search for a way to teach them those principles anyway. You should always remember the goal to help others be "nourished by the good word of God" (Moroni 6:4).

Those you teach may be like the Samaritan woman who met Jesus at Jacob's Well. When Jesus first spoke to her, she did not know who He was. However, He knew her. He was aware of her cares, responsibilities, worries, and concerns. He knew of her need for the "living water" that only He could give. He began by asking her for a drink of water. Then He told her, "Whosoever drinketh of this water shall thirst again: But whosoever drinketh of the water that I shall give him shall never

President Spencer W. Kimball related:

"Some years ago we visited a country where strange ideologies were taught and 'pernicious doctrines' were promulgated every day in the schools and in the captive press. Every day the children listened to the doctrines, philosophies, and ideals their teachers related.

"Someone said that 'constant dripping will wear away the hardest stone.' This I knew, so I asked about the children: 'Do they retain their faith? Are they not overcome by the constant pressure of their teachers? How can you be sure they will not leave the simple faith in God?'

"The answer amounted to saying 'We mend the damaged reservoir each night. We teach our children positive righteousness so that the false philosophies do not take hold. Our children are growing up in faith and righteousness in spite of the almost overwhelming pressures from outside.'

"Even cracked dams can be mended and saved, and sandbags can hold back the flood. And reiterated truth, renewed prayer, gospel teachings, expression of love, and parental interest can save the child and keep him on the right path" (Faith Precedes the Miracle [1972], 113–14).

thirst; but the water that I shall give him shall be in him a well of water springing up into everlasting life." Her interest quickened. She took a sincere interest in what He had to teach her. When He testified that He was the Messiah, she believed Him and went and testified of Him among her people. (See John 4:1–30.)

Sister Susan L. Warner, who served as second counselor in the Primary general presidency, shared the following experience: "In our family we have tried to hold early-morning scripture study. But we were often frustrated when one son complained and had to be coaxed out of bed. When he finally came, he would often put his head right down on the table. Years later, while serving his mission, he wrote home in a letter: 'Thank you for teaching me the scriptures. I want you to know that all those times I acted like I was sleeping, I was really listening with my eyes closed.'"

Sister Warner continued: "Parents and teachers, our efforts to help our children establish a heritage of rich spiritual memories are never wasted. Sometimes the seeds we plant may not bear fruit for years, but we may take comfort in the hope that someday the children we teach will remember how they have 'received and heard' the things of the Spirit. They will remember what they know and what they have felt. They will remember their identity as children of Heavenly Father, who sent them here with a divine purpose" (in Conference Report, Apr. 1996, 109; or Ensign, May 1996, 79).

If you teach youth, you may sometimes think that they do not want to talk about doctrines and principles of the gospel. You may be tempted to simply be friendly to them, keeping them entertained and talking with them about their social activities and their experiences at school. This would be a serious mistake. President J. Reuben Clark Jr. said:

"The youth of the Church are hungry for things of the Spirit; they are eager to learn the gospel, and they want it straight, undiluted. . . .

"These students as they come to you are spiritually working on toward a maturity which they will early reach if you but feed them the right food. . . .

" . . . You do not have to sneak up behind [them] and whisper religion in [their] ears; you can come right out, face to face, and talk with [them]. You do not need to disguise religious truths with a cloak of worldly things; you can bring these truths to [them] openly, in their natural guise. . . . There is no need for gradual approaches, for 'bedtime' stories, for coddling, for patronizing" (The Charted Course of the Church in Education, rev. ed. [pamphlet, 1994], 3, 6, 9).

One Church member was called to teach the 12- and 13-year-olds in Sunday School. Her husband later recorded that she had spoken with him at length about what would be the "right food" for those she would be teaching, even if they "might demand a more entertaining 'dessert' portion." He wrote of the experience she had as she nourished the souls of the youth in her class:

"She taught them the food of nourishment and growth, encouraging them to bring their scriptures and to consider the grand doctrines of the kingdom.

"Such a shift took time, but more important, it took trust that the students really needed and wanted the nourishment of the gospel and that the presentation of the food through the scriptures and the Spirit really was what would sustain them. Over the next few months a gradual change took place wherein the students began to bring their scriptures regularly, began to discuss the gospel more freely and willingly, and began to sense the wonder of the message.

"Parents began asking [her] what was happening in the class, why their children were insisting on taking scriptures to church, and even, kiddingly, how to answer the questions being posed by their children at the Sunday dinner table concerning the doctrines and principles of the gospel taught that day in class. The students were craving the gospel, because they had a teacher who . . . understood . . . what food

was nourishing and the way it needed to be presented" (Jerry A. Wilson, *Teaching with Spiritual Power* [1996], 26–27).

If you teach little children, you know that it can be a challenge to teach them the gospel. But little children want and need to hear gospel truths. They will respond to your efforts to present warm, varied, and enthusiastic gospel lessons. A Primary teacher shared the following experience:

"Admittedly, what happened was unusual. But it showed what really mattered to the nine-year-olds I was teaching. Without realizing what they were doing, they took over the class discussion on their own. It began with Katie. She responded to a question in the lesson manual about the plan of salvation. Then she followed up with her own question. Another class member volunteered an answer that helped clarify Katie's understanding. Then John asked a question on the same topic that seemed to probe deeper than Katie's did. An answer was given, and then Carly asked a follow-up question. For the remainder of the class period, the children kept asking questions and answering them, with an interest and thoughtfulness far beyond their years. There were no disruptions or speaking out of turn. Their honest and forthright insights, occasionally supplemented by me, covered the lesson material. They were curious; they wanted answers; they were truly interested; what they said required thought and understanding. I knew then that these children of our Father in Heaven were ready and eager to learn the truths the gospel has to offer."

3

THE TEACHER'S DIVINE COMMISSION

"Teach ye diligently and my grace shall attend you, that you may be instructed more perfectly in theory, in principle, in doctrine, in the law of the gospel, in all things that pertain unto the kingdom of God, that are expedient for you to understand" (D&C 88:78).

The following is an excerpt from a talk delivered by Elder Bruce R. McConkie to the Church Sunday School Department in 1977. The entire excerpt is a direct quotation.

In all our teaching we represent the Lord and are appointed to teach His gospel. We are the Lord's agents, and as such we are empowered to say only those things which He wants said.

Agents represent their principal. They have no power of their own. They act in someone else's name. They do what they are told to do. They say what they are authorized to say—nothing more, nothing less.

We are the Lord's agents. We represent Him. "As ye are agents," He says, "ye are on the Lord's errand; and whatever ye do according to the will of the Lord is the Lord's business" (D&C 64:29).

Our business as teachers is to teach His doctrine and none other. There is no other course we can follow if we are to save souls. We have no saving power of our own. We cannot create a law or a doctrine that will redeem or resurrect or save another person. The Lord only can do these things, and we are appointed to teach what He reveals on these and all gospel doctrines.

What then, are we authorized to do in teaching the gospel? What is our divine commission? The teacher's divine commission is summarized under five headings:

1. We are commanded—it is something on which we have no choice; there are no alternative courses open to us—we are commanded to teach the principles of the gospel.

In the revelation known as "the law of the Church," the Lord says, "The elders, priests and teachers of this church shall teach the principles of my gospel" (D&C 42:12). Numerous revelations say: Preach my gospel and my word, "saying none other things than that which the prophets and apostles have written, and that which is taught them by the Comforter through the prayer of faith" (D&C 52:9).

Manifestly we cannot teach that which is unknown to us. A prerequisite to teaching the gospel is studying the gospel. Hence such divine decrees as:

"Search the scriptures" (John 5:39).

"Search these commandments" (D&C 1:37).

"[Treasure] up my word" (Joseph Smith—Matthew 1:37).

"Study my word" (D&C 11:22).

"Search the prophets" (3 Nephi 23:5).

"Ye ought to search these things. Yea, a commandment I give unto you that ye search these things diligently; for great are the words of Isaiah" (3 Nephi 23:1).

"Seek not to declare my word, but first seek to obtain my word, and then shall your tongue be loosed; then, if you desire, you shall have my Spirit and my word, yea, the power of God unto the convincing of men" (D&C 11:21).

We can read all of the standard works of the Church in one year if we proceed at the rate of about six pages a day. To do the sincere searching and the solemn pondering required will take more time.

There is knowledge and there are spiritual experiences to be gained from reading, pondering, and praying about the scriptures which can be gained in no other way. No matter how devoted and active members of the Church are in administrative matters, they will never gain the great blessings which come from scriptural study unless they pay the price of that study and thus make the written word a part of their lives.

2. We are to teach the principles of the gospel as they are found in the standard works of the Church.

In the law of the Church the Lord says: "The elders, priests and teachers of this church shall teach the principles of my gospel"—and now note this restriction—"which are [found] in the Bible and the Book of Mormon, in the which is the fulness of the gospel" (D&C 42:12).

Then the Lord speaks of the need to be guided by the Spirit, but comes back to the scriptural source of gospel truth in these words: "And all this ye shall observe to do as I have commanded concerning your teaching, until the fulness of my scriptures is given" (D&C 42:15).

When this revelation was given, the Bible and the Book of Mormon were the only scriptures available to the Latter-day Saints. Now we have also the Doctrine and Covenants and the Pearl of Great Price, and there are, of course, other revelations which shall be given in due course.

3. We are to teach by the power of the Holy Ghost.

Having commanded all teachers to teach the principles of the gospel as found in the standard works, the Lord says: "These shall be their teachings, as they shall be directed by the Spirit."

Then He gives the great directive: "And the Spirit shall be given . . . by the prayer of faith; and if ye receive not the Spirit ye shall not teach."

Along with this instruction, He gives this promise: "As ye shall lift up your voices by the Comforter, ye shall speak and prophesy as seemeth me good; For, behold, the Comforter knoweth all things, and beareth record of the Father and of the Son" (D&C 42:13–14, 16–17).

Every teacher in every teaching situation might well reason along this line:

If the Lord Jesus were here, what He would say in this situation would be perfect.

But He is not here. Instead, He has sent me to represent Him.

I should say what He would say if He were here; I should say what He wants said.

The only way I can do this is to have Him tell me what to say.

This revealed direction can come to me only by the power of His Spirit.

Therefore I must be guided by the Spirit if I am to teach in my capacity as an agent of the Lord.

These principles of teaching gospel truths by the power of the Spirit are further expounded in another revelation by means of revealed questions and answers in this way:

Question: "I the Lord ask you this question—unto what were ye ordained?" (D&C 50:13).

That is: "What is your commission? What have I empowered you to do? What authorization have you received from me?"

Answer: "To preach my gospel by the Spirit, even the Comforter which was sent forth to teach the truth" (D&C 50:14).

That is: "Your commission, your authorization, the thing you have been ordained to do is to teach my gospel, not any private views, not the philosophies of the world, but my everlasting gospel, and to do it by the power of my Spirit, all in harmony with the commandment I have heretofore given: 'If ye receive not the Spirit ye shall not teach.'"

Question: "He that is ordained of me and sent forth to preach the word of truth by the Comforter, in the Spirit of truth, doth he preach it by the Spirit of truth or some other way?" (D&C 50:17).

Before hearing the revealed answer, let us note that the Lord is here talking about teaching the gospel, the word of truth, the principles of salvation. He is not talking about the doctrines of the world and the commandments of men, the adherence to which is vain and does not lead to salvation.

The question is, when we preach the gospel, when we teach the word of truth, when we set forth the true doctrines of salvation, do we do so by the power of the Holy Ghost or in some other way? Obviously the "other way" to teach the truth is by the power of the intellect.

Now the revealed answer: "If it be by some other way it is not of God" (D&C 50:18).

Let us make this clear. Even though what we teach is true, it is not of God unless it is taught by the power of the Spirit. There is no conversion, no spiritual experience, unless the Spirit of the Lord is involved.

Question: "And again, he that receiveth the word of truth, doth he receive it by the Spirit of truth or some other way?" (D&C 50:19).

Answer: "If it be [by] some other way it is not of God" (D&C 50:20).

This is why I said at the beginning that if this presentation was to have converting power, I must present it by the power of the Spirit and you must hear and receive by that same power. Only then can "he that preacheth and he that receiveth, understand one another," so that "both are edified and rejoice together" (D&C 50:22).

4. We are to apply the gospel principles taught to the needs and circumstances of our hearers.

The gospel principles never change. They are the same in all ages. And in general the needs of people are the same in all ages. There are no problems which have befallen us except those which have been the common lot of men from the beginning. And so it is not difficult to take the principles of the everlasting word and apply them to our specific needs. The abstract truth must live in the lives of men if they are to bear fruit.

Nephi quoted from the book of Moses and the writings of Isaiah and then said, "I did liken all scriptures unto us, that it might be for our profit and learning" (1 Nephi 19:23)—meaning he applied the teachings of Moses and Isaiah to the needs of the Nephites.

5. We must testify that what we teach is true.

We are a testimony-bearing people, as we should be. Our meetings abound in the solemn assurances that the work in which we are engaged is true. We certify with fervor and conviction that Jesus is the Lord, that Joseph Smith is His prophet, and that The Church of Jesus Christ of Latter-day Saints is "the only true and living church upon the face of the whole earth" (D&C 1:30).

In all of this we do well. But we ought to do more. The inspired teacher, the one who teaches by the power of the Spirit, is expected to bear testimony that the doctrine he teaches is true.

Alma set us an example in this respect. He preached a mighty sermon on being born again. Then he said he had spoken plainly, had been commissioned so to do, had quoted the scriptures, and had taught the truth.

"And this is not all," he added. "Do ye not suppose that I know of these things myself? Behold, I testify unto you that I do know that these things whereof I have spoken are true" (Alma 5:45).

This is the crowning seal placed on gospel teaching—the personal witness of the teacher that the doctrine he has taught is true!

Who can argue with a testimony? Unbelievers may contend about our doctrine. They may wrest the scriptures to their destruction. They may explain away this or that from a purely intellectual standpoint, but they cannot overpower a testimony.

If I say this or that Messianic prophecy of Isaiah was fulfilled in this or that event in the life of our Lord, many voices are waiting to debate the issue and show that the wise men of the world think otherwise. But if I say I know by the revelations of the Holy Spirit to my soul that the Messianic utterances refer to Jesus of Nazareth, who was God's Son, what is there to debate? I have then borne personal witness on the doctrinal point being taught, and every hearer who is in tune with the same Spirit knows in his heart that what I have said is true.

Alma, having borne testimony that the things he had taught are true, then asked, "And how do ye suppose that I know of their surety?" His answer, which sets a pattern for all teachers, is: "Behold, I say unto you [that] they are made known unto me by the Holy Spirit of God. Behold, I have fasted and prayed many days that I might know these things of myself. And now I do know of myself that they are true; for the Lord God hath made them manifest unto me by his Holy Spirit; and this is the spirit of revelation which is in me" (Alma 5:45–46).

And so we have now before us an exposition of our status as the Lord's agents and of the teacher's divine commission.

We are appointed:

1. To teach the principles of the gospel

2. Out of the standard works

3. By the power of the Holy Ghost,

4. Always applying the teachings to our needs, and

5. To testify that what we have taught is true.

Now there remains but one more thing for me to say on these matters, and that is to bear testimony that the concepts here presented are true, and that if we follow them we will have power to convert and save the souls of men.

I know:

That the Lord has commanded us to teach the principles of His gospel as they are set forth in His holy scriptures;

That unless we do this by the power of His Holy Spirit, our teaching is not of God;

That He expects us to apply the principles of eternal truth to our lives;

That we should bear testimony to all who will hear that our teachings come from Him who is Eternal and will lead men to peace in this life and eternal life in the world to come.

That all of us who teach may do so according to this divine pattern, I pray, in the name of the Lord Jesus Christ, amen.

PREPARE YOURSELF SPIRITUALLY

Now these sons of Mosiah . . . had waxed strong in
the knowledge of the truth; for they were men of a sound
understanding and they had searched the scriptures
diligently, that they might know the word of God.

But this is not all; they had given themselves to much prayer,
and fasting; therefore they had the spirit of prophecy,
and the spirit of revelation, and when they taught, they taught
with power and authority of God.

Alma 17:2–3

4

SEEKING THE GIFT OF CHARITY

Toward the end of Jesus' mortal ministry, He said to His disciples, "A new commandment I give unto you, That ye love one another; as I have loved you, that ye also love one another" (John 13:34). This was an important admonition for gospel teachers then, and it is important for gospel teachers today.

The Apostle Paul emphasized the need for charity, or the pure love of Christ: "Though I speak with the tongues of men and of angels, and have not charity, I am become as sounding brass, or a tinkling cymbal. And though I have the gift of prophecy, and understand all mysteries, and all knowledge; and though I have all faith, so that I could remove mountains, and have not charity, I am nothing. And though I bestow all my goods to feed the poor, and though I give my body to be burned, and have not charity, it profiteth me nothing" (1 Corinthians 13:1–3).

If you have Christlike love, you will be better prepared to teach the gospel. You will be inspired to help others know the Savior and follow Him.

What You Can Do to Receive the Gift of Charity

Charity is a gift that you can receive as you pray to be filled with love, as you give service, and as you look for the good in others.

Pray to be filled with love. The prophet Mormon admonished: "Charity is the pure love of Christ, and it endureth forever; and whoso is found possessed of it at the last day, it shall be well with him. Wherefore, . . . pray unto the Father with all the energy of heart, that ye may be filled with this love" (Moroni 7:47–48). You may not feel the pure love of Christ immediately or all at once in answer to your prayers. But as you live righteously and continue to pray sincerely and humbly for this blessing, you will receive it.

Give service. We grow to love people as we serve them. When we set aside our own interests for the good of another in the pattern set by the Savior, we become more receptive to the Spirit. As you pray for those you teach, ponder their needs, and prepare lessons, your love for them will increase. (For other ways to serve the people you teach, see "Reaching Out to the One," pages 35–36.)

Look for the good in others. As you discover the good qualities in others, you will grow in your understanding of them as children of God. The Spirit will confirm the truth of your discoveries about them, and you will appreciate and love them more.

5

SEEKING THE SPIRIT

Elder Bruce R. McConkie said, "There is no price too high, . . . no struggle too severe, no sacrifice too great, if out of it all we receive and enjoy the gift of the Holy Ghost" (A New Witness for the Articles of Faith *[1985], 253).*

Living in a Way That Helps Us Be Receptive to the Spirit

After we have been given the gift of the Holy Ghost, what can we do to receive the companionship of the Spirit? Elder Dallin H. Oaks said, "Teaching by the Spirit requires first that we keep the commandments and be clean before God so his Spirit can dwell in our personal temples" ("Teaching and Learning by the Spirit," *Ensign,* Mar. 1997, 9).

To be "clean before God," we can remember the Savior in all we do, always acting as true disciples. We can repent of our sins. We can seek things that are "virtuous, lovely, or of good report or praiseworthy" (Articles of Faith 1:13). We can study the scriptures daily and with real intent, seeking to be "nourished by the good word of God" (Moroni 6:4). We can read good books and listen to uplifting, edifying music. We can "stand in holy places" (D&C 45:32) by attending church and partaking of the sacrament and by going to the temple as often as possible. We can serve our family members and neighbors.

Elder Boyd K. Packer taught that "spirituality, while consummately strong, reacts to very delicate changes in its environment" ("I Say unto You, Be One," *Brigham Young University 1990–91 Devotional and Fireside Speeches* [1991], 89).

We should take care to completely avoid anything that would cause us to lose the Spirit's companionship. This includes shunning conversations and entertainment that are inappropriate or light-minded. Our clothes should never be immodest. We should never injure others, even with idle talk. We should not take the name of the Lord in vain or use any other vulgar or coarse language. We should not rebel against or criticize the Lord's chosen servants.

The Blessings of Receiving the Companionship of the Spirit

Heavenly Father does not require us to be perfect before He grants to us His Spirit. He will bless us for our righteous desires and faithful efforts to do the best we can. President Ezra Taft Benson spoke of some of these blessings:

"The Holy Ghost causes our feelings to be more tender. We feel more charitable and compassionate with each other. We are more calm in our relationships. We have a greater capacity to love each other. People want to be around us because our very countenances radiate the influence of the Spirit. We are more godly in our character. As a result, we become increasingly more sensitive to the promptings of the Holy Ghost and thus able to comprehend spiritual things more clearly" ("Seek the Spirit of the Lord," *Ensign,* Apr. 1988, 4).

6

SEEKING TO OBTAIN THE WORD

In May 1829, just after the restoration of the Aaronic Priesthood, Hyrum Smith, brother of the Prophet Joseph Smith, "felt a great concern over what his own work was to be." Hyrum questioned Joseph concerning "his [own] place in the great work of restoration" (Pearson H. Corbett, *Hyrum Smith—Patriarch* [1963], 48). In response to this humble request, the Lord gave Hyrum a revelation through the Prophet. Part of this revelation applies to our preparation to teach the gospel:

"Seek not to declare my word, but first seek to obtain my word, and then shall your tongue be loosed; then, if you desire, you shall have my Spirit and my word, yea, the power of God unto the convincing of men" (D&C 11:21).

President Ezra Taft Benson said that this counsel gives us "the sequence to possessing the power of God in [our] teaching. . . . Seek first to obtain the word; then comes understanding and the Spirit, and, finally, the power to convince" (*The Gospel Teacher and His Message* [address to religious educators, 17 Sept. 1976], 5).

Learning "by Study and Also by Faith"

The Lord has told us how we should obtain His word: "Seek learning, even by study and also by faith" (D&C 88:118). We follow this command by studying the scriptures diligently, with a believing heart and a commitment to obey the principles we learn. We also follow this command when we approach scripture study with prayer and fasting.

Diligent Study

Elder Dallin H. Oaks counseled:

"Scripture reading puts us in tune with the Spirit of the Lord. . . .

"Because we believe that scripture reading can help us receive revelation, we are encouraged to read the scriptures again and again. By this means, we obtain access to what our Heavenly Father would have us know and do in our personal lives today. This is one reason Latter-day Saints believe in *daily* scripture study" ("Scripture Reading and Revelation," *Ensign,* Jan. 1995, 8).

When we study the scriptures regularly and diligently, earnestly seeking guidance from the Spirit, we will be receptive to enlightenment about how to prepare lessons. We will also be prepared to receive and follow promptings from the Spirit while we teach. As we "treasure up in [our] minds continually the words of life, . . . it shall be given [us] in the very hour that portion that shall be meted unto every man" (D&C 84:85).

Belief

Mormon counseled that we should "doubt not, but be believing" (Mormon 9:27). We should approach scripture study with this attitude. For example, Joseph Smith had a believing heart when he read James 1:5, which told him to ask God for wisdom. He did as the scripture instructed, asking the Lord which church he should join. Because of his believing attitude, he received an answer to his prayer. (See Joseph Smith—History 1:11–17.)

Obedience

We should strive to live according to the principles we study, even before we understand them completely. As we trust in what the Lord has said, our knowledge of the gospel will increase. The Lord declared, "If any man will do [the Father's] will, he shall know of the doctrine" (John 7:17).

Prayer and Fasting

Studying the scriptures is different from reading a novel, newspaper, or textbook.

We should pray before we study the scriptures each day. We should seek for the Spirit to give us understanding as we study the Lord's words.

As we pray for understanding, we should sometimes fast. Alma is a good example of someone who fasted and prayed to learn gospel truths. After testifying of the Atonement of Jesus Christ and the need to experience a mighty change of heart, he said: "Do ye not suppose that I know of these things myself? Behold, I testify unto you that I do know that these things whereof I have spoken are true. And how do ye suppose that I know of their surety? Behold, I say unto you they are made known unto me by the Holy Spirit of God. Behold, I have fasted and prayed many days that I might know these things of myself. And now I do know of myself that they are true; for

the Lord God hath made them manifest unto me by his Holy Spirit" (Alma 5:45–46). (See also "Seeking the Spirit," page 13.)

Recommitting Ourselves to a Study of the Scriptures

President Benson counseled: "Let us not treat lightly the great things we have received from the hand of the Lord! His word is one of the most valuable gifts He has given us. I urge you to recommit yourselves to a study of the scriptures. Immerse yourselves in them daily so you will have the power of the Spirit to attend you in your callings. Read them in your families and teach your children to love and treasure them" ("The Power of the Word," *Ensign,* May 1986, 82).

7

DEVELOPING A PERSONAL PLAN FOR STUDYING THE GOSPEL

Elder M. Russell Ballard said: "It is incumbent upon each of us to do everything we can to increase our spiritual knowledge and understanding by studying the scriptures and the words of the living prophets. When we read and study the revelations, the Spirit can confirm in our hearts the truth of what we are learning; in this way, the voice of the Lord speaks to each one of us" (in Conference Report, Apr. 1998, 40–41; or *Ensign*, May 1998, 32).

The following suggestions can help you develop a study plan to "increase [your] spiritual knowledge and understanding," as Elder Ballard counseled. Your plan should not be overwhelming, but it should help you be consistent in your gospel study. You may want to record your plan in a journal or notebook so you will not forget it.

What to Study

Center your gospel study on the scriptures. You may choose to study a book of scripture in its entirety, or you may focus on one or more subjects, reading what all the standard works say about them. You may combine these two methods, studying a book of scripture and focusing on topics and themes as you find them. You should also study the teachings of latter-day prophets in general conference addresses and Church magazines.

If you have a calling as a teacher, your lesson manual is an essential part of your study plan.

You should also consider including the following in your gospel study: (1) the course material for Melchizedek Priesthood and Relief Society, (2) assigned scripture passages for the Gospel Doctrine class in Sunday School, and (3) articles in Church magazines.

When to Study

If possible, set a regular time when you can study without interruption. Elder Howard W. Hunter counseled:

"Many find that the best time to study is in the morning after a night's rest has cleared the mind of the many cares that interrupt thought. Others prefer to study in the quiet hours after the work and worries of the day are over and brushed aside, thus ending the day with a peace and tranquillity that comes by communion with the scriptures.

"Perhaps what is more important than the hour of the day is that a regular time be set aside for study. It would be ideal if an hour could be spent each day; but if that much cannot be had, a half hour on a regular basis would result in substantial accomplishment. A quarter of an hour is little time, but it is surprising how much enlightenment and knowledge can be acquired in a subject so meaningful" (in Conference Report, Oct. 1979, 91–92; or *Ensign*, Nov. 1979, 64).

How to Study

Before you begin to study, pray for insight and understanding. Ponder what you read, and look for ways to apply it in your life. Learn to recognize and hearken to the promptings of the Spirit.

Consider using some or all of the following ideas to enhance your study:

- Use the helps provided in the Latter-day Saint editions of the scriptures, such as the Topical Guide, the Bible Dictionary, the excerpts from the Joseph Smith Translation, and the maps (see "Teaching from the Scriptures," pages 54–59, for suggestions).

- As you read, ask yourself, "What gospel principle is taught in this passage? How can I apply this in my life?"

- Have a notebook or journal available so you can record your thoughts and feelings. Commit yourself in writing to apply what you learn. Frequently review the thoughts you have recorded.

- Before reading a chapter of scripture, review the chapter heading. This will give you some things to look for in the chapter.

- Mark and annotate your scriptures. In the margins write scripture references that clarify the passages you are studying.

- Memorize verses that are particularly meaningful to you.

- Substitute your name in a verse of scripture to personalize it.

- After studying, offer a prayer to express thanks for what you have learned.

- Share what you learn. As you do this, your thoughts will become clearer and your power of retention will increase.

Do What You Can

One Church member tried many times to follow specific programs for scripture study, but it was always difficult for her. She later reflected:

"It seemed that with trying to raise a family and fulfill my Church responsibilities, I never completely reached the goal. I would designate a certain time and place to study each day, only to have the schedule interrupted by the needs of children who were ill or other crises typical of a growing family. During that time of my life, I never really thought of myself as someone who was good at scripture study.

"Then one day my mother was in my home. She looked at a large table which was covered with Church materials—among them my scriptures—and said, 'I love the way you are always reading your scriptures. They always seem to be open on one table or another.'

"Suddenly I had a new vision of myself. She was right. I was consistently into my scriptures, even though it was not part of a formal study program. I loved the scriptures. They fed me. There were scripture verses tacked to my kitchen walls that lifted me as I worked, scriptures I was helping my children memorize for talks they would give. I lived in a world of scripture reading, and I realized that I was being nourished abundantly."

8

LIVING WHAT YOU TEACH

Speaking to a group of gospel teachers, President Spencer W. Kimball admonished, "You will do all you teach your students to do: to fast, to bear testimony, to pay tithing, to attend all proper meetings, to attend temple sessions in due time, to keep the Sabbath holy, to give Church service ungrudgingly, to have home evenings and family prayers, to keep solvent, and be honest and full of integrity" (Men of Example [address to religious educators, 12 Sept. 1975], 7).

Personal example is one of the most powerful teaching tools we have. When we are truly converted, all our thoughts and motivations are guided by gospel principles. We testify of the truth through everything we do.

Elder Bruce R. McConkie taught that testimony includes righteous actions:

"To be valiant in the testimony of Jesus is to believe in Christ and his gospel with unshakable conviction. It is to know of the verity and divinity of the Lord's work on earth.

"But this is not all. It is more than believing and knowing. We must be doers of the word and not hearers only. It is more than lip service; it is not simply confessing with the mouth the divine Sonship of the Savior. It is obedience and conformity and personal righteousness" (in Conference Report, Oct. 1974, 45–46; or *Ensign*, Nov. 1974, 35).

The Influence of Example

Our conduct can positively influence the attitudes of those we teach. President Thomas S. Monson shared the following experience:

"At the funeral service of a noble General Authority, H. Verlan Andersen, a tribute was expressed by a son. It has application wherever we are and whatever we are doing. . . .

"The son of Elder Andersen related that years earlier, he had a special school date on a Saturday night. He borrowed from his father the family car. As he obtained the car keys and headed for the door, his father said, 'The car will need more gas before tomorrow. Be sure to fill the tank before coming home.'

"Elder Andersen's son then related that the evening activity was wonderful. . . . In his exuberance, however, he failed to follow his father's instruction and add fuel to the car's tank before returning home.

"Sunday morning dawned. Elder Andersen discovered the gas gauge showed empty. The son saw his father put the car keys on the table. In the Andersen family the Sabbath day was a day for worship and thanksgiving, and not for purchases.

"As the funeral message continued, Elder Andersen's son declared, 'I saw my father put on his coat, bid us good-bye, and walk the long distance to the chapel, that he might attend an early meeting.' Duty called. Truth was not held slave to expedience.

"In concluding his funeral message, Elder Andersen's son said, 'No son ever was taught more effectively by his father than I was on that occasion. My father not only knew the truth, but he also lived it'" (in Conference Report, Oct. 1997, 22; or *Ensign*, Nov. 1997, 18).

Our conduct can also have a negative influence. For example, when Alma's son Corianton went on a mission to teach the Zoramites, he forsook the ministry and committed grievous sins (see Alma 39:3). Alma said that many people were led astray by Corianton's actions. He told Corianton, "How great iniquity ye brought upon the Zoramites; for when they saw your conduct they would not believe in my words" (Alma 39:11).

President Heber J. Grant said, "I ask every man and woman occupying a place of responsibility whose duty it is to teach the gospel of Jesus Christ to live it and keep the commandments of God, so that their example will teach it" (*Gospel Standards*, comp. G. Homer Durham [1941], 72).

As you set an example by living what you teach:

- Your words will become vibrant with the Spirit, carrying your testimony into the hearts of those you teach (see 2 Nephi 33:1). President Joseph Fielding Smith wrote, "No man or woman can teach by the Spirit what he or she does not practice" (*Church History and Modern Revelation,* 2 vols. [1953], 1:184).

- You will help others see that the words of Christ can be followed in everyday living.

- The peace and happiness you feel from living the gospel will be evident. It will show in your countenance, in your words, and in the power of your testimony.

- Those you teach will trust you and will more readily believe what you teach.

- Your own testimony will grow. "If any man will do [my Father's] will," taught the Savior, "he shall know of the doctrine" (John 7:17). You may feel that you lack understanding of a certain principle that you are preparing to teach. However, as you prayerfully study it, strive to live it, prepare to teach it, and then share it with others, your own testimony will be strengthened and deepened.

Striving to Live the Gospel

Teaching the gospel requires more than making preparations and presentations. Elder Richard G. Scott explained:

"Your commitment to teach the precious children of our Father in Heaven is not alone the long hours you spend in preparation for each class, nor the many hours of fasting and prayer that you may become a more effective teacher. It is the commitment to a life every hour of which is purposefully lived in compliance with the teachings and example of the Savior and of his servants. It is a commitment to constant striving to be evermore spiritual, evermore devoted, evermore deserving to be the conduit through which the Spirit of the Lord may touch the hearts of those you are trusted to bring to a greater understanding of his teachings" ("Four Fundamentals for Those Who Teach and Inspire Youth," in *Old Testament Symposium Speeches, 1987,* 1).

Although you will not be perfect in everything, you can make an effort to be more perfect in living the truths you teach. You will find great strength and power in teaching gospel principles as you continually strive to live according to those principles.

9

CALLED, SET APART, AND MAGNIFIED

President Gordon B. Hinckley spoke about the meaning of the word magnify. *He said, "As I interpret it, it means to enlarge, to make more clear, to bring closer, and to strengthen." He said that when priesthood holders magnify their callings, they "enlarge the potential of [their] priesthood" (in Conference Report, Apr. 1989, 60, 63; or* Ensign, *May 1989, 46, 49).*

This applies to your calling to teach. When you magnify your calling "with all diligence . . . , by laboring with [your] might" (Jacob 1:19), you enlarge your potential to influence others for good.

Lehi's sons Jacob and Joseph provide an example for those who have been called to teach. Jacob said that he had "obtained [his] errand from the Lord." He and Joseph were consecrated, or set apart, as "priests and teachers of [the] people." Then they "did magnify [their] office unto the Lord" (Jacob 1:17–19).

Receiving the Call to Teach

If you have a calling as a teacher or leader in the Church, you can be assured that the calling is from the Lord. It was extended by one of His chosen servants, and He has said, "Whether by mine own voice or by the voice of my servants, it is the same" (D&C 1:38).

A calling is a sacred opportunity to serve. It carries with it an accountability to the Lord. It should influence the way you live, governing your decisions and motivating you to be a faithful and wise servant.

When you received a calling to teach, you may have said to yourself, "But I have not been trained to teach. I have no ability to present a lesson or lead a class discussion. There are so many who could do better than I." Perhaps others do have more teaching experience or natural ability than you. However, you are the one who has been called. The Lord will make you an instrument in His hands if you are humble, faithful, and diligent. President Thomas S. Monson taught:

"If any brother or sister feels unprepared —even incapable—of responding to a call to serve, to sacrifice, to bless the lives of others, remember this truth: 'Whom God calls, God

qualifies.' He who notes the sparrow's fall will not abandon the servant's need" ("Tears, Trials, Trust, Testimony," *Ensign,* Sept. 1997, 5).

Being Sustained and Set Apart

You will receive added strength when you are sustained by the congregation and set apart. In a setting apart, priesthood leaders lay their hands on your head and give you a charge to act in your calling. You are also given blessings to strengthen and direct you. President Spencer W. Kimball declared, "The setting apart may be taken literally; it is a setting apart from sin, apart from the carnal; apart from everything which is crude, low, vicious, cheap, or vulgar; *set apart* from the world to a higher plane of thought and activity" (*The Teachings of Spencer W. Kimball,* ed. Edward L. Kimball [1982], 478).

No formal calling to teach is complete without a setting apart by proper priesthood authority. If you have been called and sustained as a teacher but have not been set apart, contact your quorum or auxiliary leader to make the necessary arrangements to be set apart.

Magnifying Your Calling and Being Magnified by the Lord

As mentioned above, Jacob and Joseph magnified their calling to teach the people. They taught the word of God "with all diligence . . . , by laboring with [their] might" (Jacob 1:19).

As you magnify your calling to teach, the Lord will magnify you. President Ezra Taft Benson taught: "There can be no failure in the work of the Lord when [we] do [our] best. We are but instruments; this is the Lord's work. This is His Church, His gospel plan. These are His children we are working with. He will not permit us to fail if we do our part. He will magnify us even beyond our own talents and abilities when necessary. This I know. I am sure many of you have experienced it as I have. It is one of the sweetest experiences that can come to a human being" (*The Teachings of Ezra Taft Benson* [1988], 372).

IMPROVE
UPON YOUR TALENTS

The Lord has a great work for each of us to do. You may wonder
how this can be. You may feel that there is nothing
special or superior about you or your ability. . . .

The Lord can do remarkable miracles with a person of
ordinary ability who is humble, faithful, and diligent in
serving the Lord and seeks to improve himself. This is
because God is the ultimate source of power.

President James E. Faust

10

LOOKING FOR LESSONS EVERYWHERE

"And now, as ye have begun to teach the word even so I would that ye should continue to teach; and I would that ye would be diligent and temperate in all things" (Alma 38:10).

While working in his flower garden, a stake president was thinking about a talk he was to give in an upcoming stake conference. He was planning to speak about strengthening families.

His neighbor, who seemed to have a special skill for coaxing magnificent flowers to bloom, was also working in her garden. He called to her and asked, "What is your gardening secret?"

Her answer was profoundly simple. She said: "I stay close to the garden. I go into my garden every day, even when it isn't convenient. And while I'm out here, I look for little signs of possible problems, things like weeds and insects and soil conditions that are simple to correct if caught in time but that can become overwhelming if left unchecked."

The stake president was inspired to liken his neighbor's care for her garden to the care we should give our families. In his stake conference address he talked about his neighbor's garden. He observed that if we want our relationships with family members to flourish and bloom, we need to "stay close to the garden"—to spend time with family members every day, talk with them, express appreciation for them, and look for little signs of potential problems that can be resolved before they become overwhelming.

A woman who had heard the stake president's talk remembered it when she saw that a few of her plants had withered away. She had not taken time to check their progress daily. This reminded her that her children were growing up and that she should not waste the few years she had with them. Because of her stake president's teaching, she became a better parent.

The stake president had followed the example of the Savior, who often compared spiritual truths to familiar, everyday objects and activities. You can do the same. You can find lessons of life in the things you do and observe each day. As you ponder and pray about a lesson and about the people you teach, your surroundings can come alive with answers to questions and examples of gospel principles.

The following two examples show how other teachers have found lessons in their observations of everyday life:

A Primary teacher noticed a family coming to church one Sunday. She watched as a boy in the family, who was a member of her class and had sometimes been inconsiderate to other class members, helped his sister. "That's the example I need," she said to herself. "It will teach the principle and help the boy." Later she shared the example in a lesson about being kind. The children learned from the example, and the boy began to improve in his behavior toward other class members.

A father and his son were playing with building blocks. When the little boy failed in a few attempts to build large structures on top of small bases, the father saw a teaching opportunity. He explained the importance of strong, solid foundations. Then, before they continued playing, he read Helaman 5:12, which says that "it is upon the rock of our Redeemer, who is Christ, the Son of God, that [we] must build [our] foundation." Later that day, the family studied the scriptures together. In a short lesson that reinforced the passage they read, the father and son displayed the blocks and talked about the importance of building on the foundation of Christ.

Developing a Teacher's Eyes and Ears

The following suggestions can help you discover teaching ideas everywhere.

Study lessons well in advance. When you are familiar with the lessons you are going to teach, you will be more aware of everyday occurrences that you can use to teach those lessons. If you are teaching a course that has a lesson manual, it is good to have an idea of the content of the entire manual. Then you will be more likely to notice when a certain observation can be applied to a lesson that you will teach several weeks in the future.

Pray every day for help in your preparation. Ask Heavenly Father to help you be aware of things that will make your lessons vivid, memorable, and inspiring to those you teach.

Always keep in mind those you teach and the lesson you are preparing. Think about those you teach. Consider their lives, the decisions they face, and the directions they are going. Be open to teaching ideas as you do such things as study the scriptures or observe the beauties of nature. You can even find teaching ideas in activities such as cleaning your house, going to work, or going to the store. Virtually any experience can provide you with just the example, enrichment, or clarification you need for a gospel lesson.

Keeping Track of Impressions That Come

As you become more aware of teaching ideas around you, it will be helpful for you to keep track of impressions you receive. Carry a small notebook with you, and write about things that strike you as potential teaching ideas. Record insights from talks you hear or lessons in which you participate. Write about faith-promoting experiences. As you develop the habit of noting these things, you will become more and more aware of the rich teaching resources that are all around you.

Do not worry about how you might use the ideas. Just write them down. Sometimes your observations will apply to a lesson that you will soon teach, but other times you will see wonderful examples or illustrations of principles that you will not teach for weeks or even years. You may forget them if you do not record them.

You may also want to make a folder for each of the lessons you will teach in the next few months. As object lessons, comparisons, and other ideas occur to you, put a note in the appropriate folder. When the time comes to prepare a specific lesson, you may find that you have collected a treasure chest of ideas and activities to enrich the lesson.

11

MAKING A PLAN TO IMPROVE YOUR TEACHING

"Give attendance to reading, to exhortation, to doctrine. Neglect not the gift that is in thee, which was given thee by prophecy, with the laying on of the hands. . . . Meditate upon these things; give thyself wholly to them; that thy profiting may appear to all. Take heed unto thyself, and unto the doctrine; continue in them: for in doing this thou shalt both save thyself, and them that hear thee" (1 Timothy 4:13–16).

When Moroni was abridging the record of the Jaredites, he became concerned about his weakness in writing. He thought that the Gentiles who would read his words would mock them and reject them. He prayed that the Gentiles might have charity and not reject the word of God. Then the Lord gave him this promise: "Because thou hast seen thy weakness thou shalt be made strong" (Ether 12:37). The Lord also told Moroni: "If men come unto me I will show unto them their weakness. I give unto men weakness that they may be humble; and my grace is sufficient for all men that humble themselves before me; for if they humble themselves before me, and have faith in me, then will I make weak things become strong unto them" (Ether 12:27).

In your efforts to teach the gospel, you may sometimes experience feelings of inadequacy. But you can take courage in this promise from the Lord. As you humble yourself, recognize the areas in which you need His help, and exercise faith in Him, He will strengthen you and help you teach in a manner pleasing to Him.

Assessing Your Own Strengths and Weaknesses

You can start making a plan for improvement by determining how you are doing right now. You might divide this evaluation into two parts: your strengths as a teacher and your weaknesses as a teacher.

What Are My Strengths as a Teacher?

Begin by considering some of the gifts the Lord has already given you that may help you in your teaching. List these strengths in a journal or notebook or the chart on page 25. As you do so, you may want to think about the principles of teaching that are emphasized in this book, such as loving those you teach, teaching by the Spirit, teaching the doctrine, inviting diligent learning, creating a learning atmosphere, using effective methods, or preparing lessons.

Perhaps it is your patience that can help you as a teacher. Or it may be your ready smile, your concern for people, your artistic ability, your knowledge of the scriptures, your willingness to listen, your calm spirit, your habit of preparing thoroughly, or your sincere desire to teach well.

You do not need to identify a large number of your strengths; just a few will get you started. The purpose of focusing on some of your strengths is to build on them as you improve in areas where you are not as strong.

What Are My Weaknesses as a Teacher?

After considering your strengths, reflect on your recent teaching experiences. Think of the areas in which you could do better. Again, you may want to think about the principles of teaching emphasized in this book. You might want to list several things you could do better, but it is probably best to limit yourself to working on one or two things at a time. Generally speaking, we grow "line upon line, precept upon precept" (2 Nephi 28:30). We should act "in wisdom and order; for it is not requisite that a man should run faster than he has strength" (Mosiah 4:27).

When you have selected one or two areas in which you would like to improve, write them in your journal or notebook.

Making a Plan for Improvement

To decide how to improve in the area or areas you have chosen, consider the following questions:

- What can I do now to improve as a teacher?
- What skills do I need to develop?
- Who can help?
- What materials are available?

Following is an example showing how you might use these questions. In this example, a Relief Society teacher has determined that she needs to improve her ability to discern if class members understand the lessons she teaches.

What Can I Do Now to Improve as a Teacher?

The teacher decides to look through this book to get ideas of what she can do better right now. As she reads "How to Tell If They Are Learning" (page 73), she discovers that one way to assess class members' understanding is to ask them to restate principles in their own words. She decides to use this idea in the next lesson she teaches. She writes this plan in her journal.

What Skills Do I Need to Develop?

The teacher also reads that she should observe class members during lessons. She tells herself, "This is a skill that I need to develop, but it will take some practice." She writes this plan in her journal.

As she considers her plan, she realizes that she already has at least one strength that she can build on: she diligently prepares lessons. Because she is always familiar with the lesson material, she will be able to observe class members rather than focus too much on the lesson manual or her notes.

Who Can Help? What Materials Are Available?

Finally, the teacher asks herself if there are any resources she might use. She has already used this book as a resource. She thinks about other possible resources: "What about other teachers? Could I talk with the teacher

---

Use this chart (or one of your own) to make a plan to improve your teaching. In the blank spaces, write your responses to the questions.

How Am I Doing? ▪ What are my strengths as a teacher? ▪ What are my weaknesses?	
What Can I Do to Improve? ▪ What can I do now to improve as a teacher? ▪ What skills do I need to develop?	
What Resources Will I Use? ▪ Who can help? ▪ What materials are available?	

improvement coordinator or another teacher who is especially skillful at assessing class members' understanding? Could one of my leaders observe a lesson that I teach and make suggestions? Could class members give suggestions?"

Setting a Goal and Recording Your Progress

After you have made a plan for improvement, set a date by which you hope to achieve your goal. You may want to write in a journal or notebook about your progress. If you need to adjust your goal along the way, do so.

When you feel that you have made the improvement you planned, begin working on another aspect of teaching.

Qualities That Matter Most

In your continuing quest to improve as a teacher, remember the qualities that matter most.

President Harold B. Lee described a teacher who had a great influence on him when he was a child. You might use this description to guide you as you evaluate your overall effectiveness as a teacher and develop plans for improvement:

"During my childhood, the most impressive religious lessons I learned were from the Sunday School classes. Very few Sunday School teachers, however, stand out today in my memory as having made a lasting contribution to my religious education. One of these . . . had a peculiar ability, so it seemed, to burn deep into my soul the lessons of Church history, morality, and gospel truth in such a way that today, nearly forty years later, I find myself still remembering and being guided by her lessons.

"What was it that gave her the essential qualities of a successful Sunday School teacher? She was not possessed of great secular knowledge nor was she well schooled in the theories and practices of modern pedagogy. Her appearance was plain and ordinary—that of a wife and mother in a small country community where necessity demanded long hours of toil from all family members. There were three endowments which, in my opinion, made her teachings effective: first, she had the faculty of making every pupil feel that she had a personal interest in him; second, she had a knowledge of and a love for the gospel and had the ability to so aptly illustrate each lesson as to make it apply to our own lives; and third, she had an absolute faith in God and an unswerving testimony of the divinity of the restored gospel of Jesus Christ.

"There was another less obvious but . . . most vital and essential qualification for this and every other person who would be a teacher of the gospel of Jesus Christ. The Lord has declared the law of the teacher in these words: 'And the Spirit shall be given unto you by the prayer of faith; and if ye receive not the Spirit ye shall not teach' (D&C 42:14). . . .

"Such a one who prays for help in his teaching will have the power of the Holy Ghost, and his teachings will be, as Nephi declared, '[carried into] the hearts of the children of men . . . by the power of the Holy Ghost'" (*The Teachings of Harold B. Lee,* ed. Clyde J. Williams [1996], 444).

As you evaluate your strengths and weaknesses as a teacher, consider how well you reflect these "essential qualities." You may want to ponder the following questions:

- Do I show those I teach that I love them? Do I show personal interest in each of them?
- Can they feel my love for the Lord and His teachings? Do I help them see the application of those teachings in their lives?
- Can those I teach feel my testimony of the restored gospel of Jesus Christ? Can they feel my absolute faith in God?
- Do I pray in faith to teach by the power of the Holy Ghost?

Even if you are inexperienced in many technical aspects of teaching, you can focus on the qualities that matter most. You can love those you teach. You can consistently show your love for the Lord and His teachings. And you can fervently share your faith in God and your testimony of the restored gospel. You can succeed in the qualities that are most important, even while you are developing your technical skills.

With the Lord's Help, You Can Improve

As you strive to improve, the Lord's help will often come through other people. The following story, shared by a man who had served as mission president in Eastern Europe, illustrates this principle:

"During the summer of 1993, I visited one of our newly created branches. Sunday School was taught by a newly baptized member. She clearly felt uncomfortable standing before the group. Rather than risk making a mistake, she read the lesson word for word. As she kept her eyes riveted on her book, the class members shifted uncomfortably.

"After the lesson I complimented the teacher on the doctrinal accuracy of her materials and, as tactfully as I could, asked if she had considered asking a few thought-provoking questions in order to stimulate class discussion. She replied that in Europe teachers do not ask questions.

I left, wondering what we could do to help her and many other new teachers like her in a country where the Church had been established only a few years.

"In August of that year a couple was assigned to begin the Church Educational System programs in our area. We asked them to conduct what were then called teacher training sessions. One of the teachers they were to help was the teacher whose class I had visited.

"Four months later, I returned to her branch. A miracle had taken place. She stood in front of the class transformed, poised, and confident. Her carefully prepared questions elicited interested responses. She commented encouragingly on each class member's contributions. She had arranged for one class member to share a personal experience on the lesson subject and then invited others to share. Near the end, a new member bore her testimony. The teacher stopped and quietly asked, 'Did you notice the Spirit when Sister Molnar was speaking? That is the Spirit of the Lord.' As we basked in the calming and enlightening feeling we had experienced together in that rented classroom, I thanked my Heavenly Father for the couple who had taught the principles of gospel teaching to a frightened new member and helped her become one who truly deserved to be called a teacher of the gospel of Jesus Christ."

12

OBTAINING SUPPORT FROM YOUR LEADERS

Part of a priesthood or auxiliary leader's responsibility is to assist and support teachers. The quality of teaching in the Church will improve as leaders and teachers develop a supportive and caring relationship.

In priesthood and auxiliary organizations, leaders are assigned to work with specific teachers. For example, a member of a Primary presidency may be assigned to work with those who teach children ages 8 through 11. A member of an elders quorum presidency may be assigned to work with the quorum instructors.

Orientations for New Teachers

If you are a newly called teacher, your leader will meet with you, preferably before your first class. He or she will talk with you about the importance of your call and give you the materials for the class. After you have taught your first lesson, you and your leader should briefly discuss the experience.

Contacting Leaders to Counsel with Them

Contact your leader frequently to share experiences, discuss the needs of those you teach, solve problems, and seek counsel. This will provide an opportunity to review your plans for continuing improvement as a teacher.

Such contacts are most effective in person, but if necessary they may be made by telephone, mail, or some other means. You should initiate the contacts whenever you need to but at least once every three months.

When a female leader meets with a male teacher or a male leader meets with a female teacher, they should leave the door open and ask another adult to be in an adjoining room, foyer, or hall. They should avoid circumstances that might be misunderstood.

As you look forward to counseling with your leader, prepare to talk about:

- How you are feeling about your calling as a teacher.
- Experiences you have had with your class.
- Examples of how class members are responding to the lessons you teach.
- Specific needs of individual class members.
- Your goals as a teacher.
- What your leader can do to help you accomplish your goals.
- Topics that you feel should be addressed in teacher improvement meetings.

Classroom Visits

Some leaders attend the same class each week as part of their callings. Other leaders, such as members of Primary presidencies and Sunday School presidencies, are instructed to arrange with teachers to occasionally visit their classes (see *Improving Gospel Teaching: A Leader's Guide,* page 6). If a leader arranges to visit your class, you may ask him or her to simply observe the class or to help in other ways. For example, a leader may present part of the lesson, reach out to a particular class member, or assist with activities.

B

BASIC PRINCIPLES
OF GOSPEL TEACHING

LOVE THOSE YOU TEACH

Nothing is so much calculated to lead people to forsake sin
as to take them by the hand, and watch over them with tenderness.
When persons manifest the least kindness and love to me, O what
power it has over my mind, while the opposite course has a tendency to
harrow up all the harsh feelings and depress the human mind.

The Prophet Joseph Smith

1

LOVE SOFTENS HEARTS

"No one can assist in this work except he shall be humble and full of love" (D&C 12:8).

A new teacher was having problems with some misbehaving class members. She sought advice from a member of the Sunday School presidency, and he suggested that she conduct an experiment. She was to select a disruptive class member and then show that person in five different ways that she cared about him or her. A few weeks later, the leader asked the teacher how she was doing. She reported that the person she had selected had stopped misbehaving, so she was in the process of selecting another class member. After two more weeks the leader inquired again. The teacher said that she was having difficulty finding someone to work with. When he asked her a third time, she told him that she had selected three different class members, one after another, and that when she started to show that she cared about them they had ceased being disruptive. In each case, love had softened a heart.

The Power of a Teacher's Love

As we show love for those we teach, they become more receptive to the Spirit. They become more enthusiastic about learning and more open to us and others in the group. Often, they awaken to a renewed sense of their eternal worth and a greater desire for righteousness.

Elder Dallas N. Archibald of the Seventy explained:

"Proper teaching will enlarge the soul.

"For example, let us compare a child to an empty glass, and our knowledge and experience, which have accumulated over the years, to a bucketful of water. . . . We cannot pour a bucketful of water directly into a small glass. However, by using correct principles of transferring knowledge, the glass can be enlarged.

"Those principles are persuasion, long-suffering, gentleness and meekness, love unfeigned, kindness, and pure knowledge. They will enlarge the glass, which is the soul of the child, allowing that child to receive much more than the original bucketful" (in Conference Report, Oct. 1992, 34–35; or *Ensign,* Nov. 1992, 26).

A Primary teacher reported some of the rewarding experiences she and her class members had after she visited with them in their homes and expressed interest in their lives. One little boy had been reluctant to stay in class, and when he did stay, he would not participate. But after the teacher made a brief visit to his home and talked with him about his favorite things, he began looking forward to coming to Primary. Another class member had never spoken in class but talked excitedly when the teacher came to her home. After the visit, she began to participate in class. (See Norda D. Casaus, "One on One," *Ensign,* Feb. 1994, 59.)

How Christlike Love Affects Our Teaching

The Apostle Paul wrote: "Though I speak with the tongues of men and of angels, and have not charity, I am become as sounding brass, or a tinkling cymbal. And though I have the gift of prophecy, and understand all mysteries, and all knowledge; and though I have all faith, so that I could remove mountains, and have not charity, I am nothing" (1 Corinthians 13:1–2). In this dispensation the Lord has said that "no one can assist in this work except he shall be humble and full of love, having faith, hope, and charity" (D&C 12:8).

If we want to influence learners for good, we should not merely love to teach; we should love each person we teach. We should measure our success by the progress of those we teach, not by the excellence of our performance.

Love prompts us to prepare and teach differently. When we love those we teach, we pray for each of them. We do all we can to know their interests, achievements, needs, and concerns (see "Understanding Those You Teach," pages 33–34). We tailor our teaching to meet their needs, even if this takes more time and effort. We notice when they are absent and recognize them when they are present. We offer help when it is needed. We are devoted to their eternal welfare, doing all we can to promote it and doing nothing to harm it.

Many of the most important qualities of faithful and effective gospel teachers are linked with love. The prophet Mormon taught:

"Charity suffereth long, and is kind, and envieth not, and is not puffed up, seeketh not her own, is not easily provoked, thinketh no evil, and rejoiceth not in iniquity but rejoiceth in the truth, beareth all things, believeth all things, hopeth all things, endureth all things.

"Wherefore, . . . if ye have not charity, ye are nothing, for charity never faileth. Wherefore, cleave unto charity, which is the greatest of all, for all things must fail—

"But charity is the pure love of Christ, and it endureth forever; and whoso is found possessed of it at the last day, it shall be well with him" (Moroni 7:45–47).

Additional Information

For more about the importance of loving those you teach, see lesson 2 in the Teaching the Gospel course (pages 194–97).

2

UNDERSTANDING THOSE YOU TEACH

Consider the last lesson you taught. As you prepared and presented the lesson, what did you think about? Did you think about the lesson material? Did you think about those you were teaching? How much did you really know about the individuals you were teaching? If you did not know them, how might knowing at least something about each of them have made a difference in your lesson?

An Aaronic Priesthood adviser shared the following insight:

"As a deacons quorum adviser, I have learned some things about 12- and 13-year-old boys. I understand the challenges, opportunities, experiences, and questions young men that age share in common. I understand that each of these young men has recently received the priesthood and is learning what it means to exercise it worthily.

"I also know each of the deacons individually—their likes, dislikes, talents, concerns, and what is happening in their lives right now.

"As I prepare lessons and teach the boys, I try to teach gospel principles in a way that will relate to their understanding and experience. To engage one boy, I might ask a question that relates some point in the lesson to playing soccer. To help another young man participate, I might relate an experience from a recent campout that helps illustrate the application of a gospel principle. By understanding these boys, I am better able to find ways to relate each lesson to them."

Learning the Common Characteristics and Experiences of Those You Teach

Although each individual is unique, all the people you teach, whether adults, youth, or children, share many things in common. First and foremost, each is a child of Heavenly Father. Each has divine potential. Each wants to feel loved. Each wants to feel the support of others and be appreciated for his or her contributions.

In addition to these common characteristics, those you teach have probably had similar experiences. For example, many class members in an adult Gospel Doctrine class are parents who have gained significant experience and insight through raising their children. In elders quorums, many have served full-time missions. Many high priests have served in administrative positions in the ward or stake. Many of the young men and women attend the same school or similar schools.

There will always be something that those you teach have in common. You should learn about the characteristics and experiences they have in common and find ways to draw on those similarities. As you do this, those you teach will feel that your lessons are sensitive and relevant to their needs and interests. They will participate more fully and contribute more confidently.

For information about the common characteristics of different age-groups, see part C, "Teaching Different Age-Groups" (pages 107–24).

Getting to Know Each Person You Teach

Although the people you teach have many common characteristics, they come from a wide variety of backgrounds and circumstances. No two are exactly alike. They have different abilities, likes, and dislikes. They have experienced different joys, opportunities, and challenges.

When he was a regional representative, Elder Neal A. Maxwell said:

"A Church group, quorum, or classroom may contain some who are bored; some who are making an unobserved, agonizing, and crucial re-appraisal of their relationship to the Church; some who are 'single-shot' visitors who may base their future attendance and attitudes toward the Church on their experiences on a 'sample Sunday'; some whose idealism has soured; and a goodly number of . . . well-informed members who find joy and growth in a divine Church full of frail humans and who can cope with disappointments.

"To be impersonal or to use the indiscriminate . . . approach to leadership and teaching with such inevitable variety of individuals is clearly not to be 'anxiously engaged' in the leading or teaching process. Casual, insensitive leading and teaching means that the individual sees himself merely as a course or a toll-gate through which members must pass. Such leading is heedless of individual differences and devoid of meaningful, personal warmth" (" . . . A More Excellent Way" [1973], 56–57).

As you come to know and understand each person, you will be better prepared to teach lessons that speak to their individual situations. This understanding will help you to find ways to help each person participate in discussions and other learning activities (see "Reaching Out to the One," pages 35–36). You will know who will be able to handle certain questions, who might be able to contribute a faith-promoting story or personal experience, or who has had an experience that supports the purpose of a certain lesson. You will be better able to assess the responses given in discussions and adapt your lessons.

Considering Similarities and Differences As You Prepare Lessons

Think about the next lesson you will teach. Try to picture in your mind the setting and each individual who will be there. Perhaps someone who sits in the same place each week comes to mind. What do you know about that person that might help you decide which point to emphasize in the lesson? What experiences has he or she had that might help someone else better understand a gospel principle? Your knowledge of these things will influence your choices as you prepare and present lessons. This is why you need to do more than simply understand your lesson material; you need to understand the people you teach— as children of God, as members of their age-group, and as individuals.

3

REACHING OUT TO THE ONE

A teacher improvement coordinator reported the following experience:

"I had been asked to serve as instructor of a course for all the teachers in the Sunday School. I knew I would be teaching people with personalities, backgrounds, and needs very different from one another. One was an experienced teacher who had often worked with youth. Another seemed to have no confidence as a teacher, and she keenly felt her inadequacies. One brother was embarrassed to come because he did not know much about the scriptures.

"I decided that I needed to find a way to reach out to each one of them. Before the first lesson, I assigned the brother who was uneasy about teaching with the scriptures to talk briefly about making a personal plan for studying the gospel. This gave me a chance to meet him outside of class and express my confidence in him. During the lesson I encouraged the experienced teacher to share some of her insights about teaching. And I found an opportunity to thank the underconfident sister for the humble testimony she had borne in another class a few weeks earlier. All three responded very well.

"During that lesson I noticed another teacher sitting apart from the rest. I decided to pay her a visit after class, and I showed my interest in her and asked if I could help her with an assignment I had given. Each week I kept looking for opportunities to reach out to every person in the class.

"As we got into the course, it became clear to me that this was an unusual group.

They all participated in lively discussions and sharing of experiences. They seemed united in love. I could see that the more I tried to reach out to and serve them individually, the more they were willing to listen to and share with one another. As I look back, I realize how much the simple effort to extend myself to each of them may have been the most important thing I did as a teacher of that course. It seemed to inspire them to do the same for one another."

Part of your work as a gospel teacher is to help learners understand and feel Heavenly Father's love for them. This cannot be done with words alone. It requires reaching out to individuals—those you see often, those you see occasionally, and those you would not see without making special effort. It requires reaching out to them whether they are cooperative, disinterested, or defiant. The Lord has exhorted us to remember that "the worth of souls is great in the sight of God" (D&C 18:10).

Reaching Out to Individuals When You Meet Together

Even when you teach many people at the same time, you can reach out to individuals. For example, you reach out to individuals when you greet each person warmly at the beginning of class. Small acts such as this can make an important difference.

You also reach out when you make participation inviting and safe. In family home evening and in Church classes, you can help learners prepare a part of the lesson. You can plan special reports, musical numbers, or discussion questions that will recognize and draw on the talents of particular individuals. For example, one less-active brother with a good singing voice gradually returned to activity in the Church because he was occasionally invited to sing in classes and other ward functions.

Individuals are touched when their contributions are acknowledged. You might make a special effort to acknowledge each person's comments and, if possible, make the comments part of class discussions. At times it is helpful to restate someone's questions or comments so everyone can hear and understand.

Reaching Out at Other Times

You should search for ways to reach out to those you teach. The things you do for people outside the teaching setting can make a profound difference in their attitude toward studying the gospel. You can spend time with family members individually. You can go out of your way to talk with class members when you see them. You can encourage and help them in times of trial, remember important events in their lives, visit their homes, and attend activities in which they participate.

President Thomas S. Monson related the following story:

"Louis Jacobsen . . . was the son of a poor Danish widow. He was small in stature, not comely in appearance—easily the object of his classmates' thoughtless jokes. In Sunday School one Sabbath morning, the children made

light of his patched trousers and his worn shirt. Too proud to cry, tiny Louis fled from the chapel, stopping at last, out of breath, to sit and rest on the curb. . . . Clear water flowed along the gutter next to the curb where Louis sat. From his pocket he took a piece of paper which contained the outlined Sunday School lesson and skillfully shaped a paper boat, which he launched on the flowing water. From his hurt boyish heart came the determined words, 'I'll never go back.'

"Suddenly, through his tears Louis saw reflected in the water the image of a large and well-dressed man. Louis turned his face upward and recognized George Burbidge, the Sunday School superintendent.

" 'May I sit down with you?' asked the kind leader.

"Louis nodded affirmatively. . . . Several boats were formed and launched while the conversation continued. At last the leader stood and, with a boy's hand tightly clutching his, they returned to Sunday School" (in Conference Report, Apr. 1977, 106; or *Ensign,* May 1977, 72).

4

HELPING NEW MEMBERS AND LESS-ACTIVE MEMBERS

President Gordon B. Hinckley counseled:

"It is not an easy thing to become a member of this Church. In most cases it involves setting aside old habits, leaving old friends and associations, and stepping into a new society which is different and somewhat demanding.

"With the ever increasing number of converts, we must make an increasingly substantial effort to assist them as they find their way. Every one of them needs three things: a friend, a responsibility, and nurturing with 'the good word of God' (Moroni 6:4). It is our duty and opportunity to provide these things. . . .

"This is a work for everyone. . . .

"I ask each of you to please help in this undertaking. Your friendly ways are needed. Your sense of responsibility is needed" (in Conference Report, Apr. 1997, 66, 68; or *Ensign,* May 1997, 47–48).

As a gospel teacher, you may serve people who have recently joined the Church or who are returning to activity in the Church. You can follow President Hinckley's counsel by befriending them, giving them opportunities to participate in lessons, and ensuring that they are nurtured with the word of God. Following are some suggestions to help you do this.

"A Friend"

The First Presidency has counseled us to "extend the hand of fellowship to investigators and new members, providing loving relationships that help them make the social transition to new friends and new patterns of life" ("Helping New Members," attachment to First Presidency letter, 15 May 1997).

You can help others make this transition by inviting them to class, welcoming them by name when they come, and introducing them to other class members.

"A Responsibility"

In Church classes, all class members are responsible to contribute to the learning atmosphere (see pages 77–78).

However, new members and less-active members may need special encouragement to accept this responsibility. A few ideas for helping them participate in lessons are listed below:

- In class discussions, ask them questions that you know they will be able to answer.

- Encourage them to share their testimonies and their personal experiences in learning gospel truths.

- Invite them to read aloud. To give them time to prepare, talk to them in advance about the scripture passages or other material that you would like them to read.

- Invite them to pray. To avoid making them feel uncomfortable, extend this invitation in advance.

- If you are giving assignments, do so in advance so they will have sufficient time to prepare. Offer to help if they have questions.

As new members and less-active members participate in class discussions and other learning activities, they will grow stronger in their understanding of the gospel and commitment to the Lord and His Church. They will also strengthen you and other class members.

"Nurturing with 'the Good Word of God'"

New converts and members who are returning to activity are generally eager to learn about the gospel. You can help them maintain this enthusiasm and increase in their knowledge of the gospel. Consider the following suggestions:

- Express your enthusiasm about the gospel.

- Bear your testimony.

- Share your love for the scriptures.

- Take time to speak with them outside of class—to befriend them and to ensure that they are understanding the principles you teach.

- Tell them about experiences you have had as you have lived the gospel.

- Encourage them to study the scriptures on their own.

5

TEACHING THOSE WITH DISABILITIES

Elder Boyd K. Packer shared the following experience from his first year as a seminary teacher:

"In my class was a teenage girl who disturbed me a great deal by a seemingly insolent attitude. She wouldn't participate and she disturbed the class continually. On one occasion I asked her to respond in class with something that took no previous preparation. She said, with some impudence, 'I won't.'

"With some pressing I insisted, but with increased impudence she refused. I said something very foolish to the effect that 'students who are not willing to respond are not to be given grades or credit.' And under my breath I said, 'We'll see. You'll either conform or else.'

"A few weeks later in a parent-teacher visiting session her mother described her as being shy and retiring and hesitant to participate. Shy and retiring conduct would not have disturbed me; it was the impudence and insolence that had concerned me.

"Fortunately, before I could describe her impudence to her mother, her mother added, 'That's because of her speech impediment.'

"In surprise I asked what that was. The mother said, 'Oh, haven't you noticed?' I hadn't noticed! 'She will do almost anything to keep from participating in groups,' her mother informed me. 'Her speech impediment is such an embarrassment to her.'

"After the conference with her mother I felt about two inches tall! I should have

sensed that there was some *reason* for her to react the way she had. I spent that year making my repentance complete. I counseled with the girl and drew her out. 'We will work together on this,' I told her.

"Before the end of the year she was responding in class and participating often, with the help and cooperation of the other students" (*Teach Ye Diligently*, rev. ed. [1991], 92–93).

During His mortal ministry, the Savior showed great compassion to people who had imperfections of body and mind. He offered them hope, understanding, and love. As you teach such people, you should follow His example. Try not to feel uncomfortable about their disabilities. Recognize that all people are different in one way or another.

With love and sensitivity, you can help class members with disabilities participate in lessons. You may need to work with others you teach to help them understand and accept those with disabilities.

Below are descriptions of different kinds of disabilities and ways you might help class members who have these disabilities.

Hearing Loss

Hearing loss can vary in degree from slight loss to complete deafness. Some people hear well enough to understand the spoken word with hearing aids, while others must use sign language or lip reading to understand.

When you discover that a class member has a hearing problem, be especially attentive and sensitive to him or her. As needed, meet with the individual to determine the best place for him or her to sit in class in order to follow discussions and activities. It may be important for the person to sit where he or she can easily see you as you speak. He or she may prefer sitting on one side of the room rather than the other. Explore these options in a spirit of helpfulness and friendship and in a way that shows your desire for the person to participate in class.

Language and Speech Disorders

Language and speech disorders affect a person's ability to interact and communicate with others. The disorders may be mild or severe, and they may be present at any age. Individuals with language disorders may not understand spoken and written words well. They may have difficulty forming words and sentences to express ideas. Some people with language disorders try to hide them, while others, particularly children, are unaware of them.

If you believe that a class member might have such a disorder, be careful about inviting that person to participate in front of the class. Show the person extra attention, and learn more about his or her learning capacity. You might prepare learning activities that will help the person contribute without embarrassment, such as discussion groups in which he or she works with class members who are particularly kind and patient. As you become better acquainted with the person and as his or her confidence grows, look for additional opportunities for the person to contribute in class. Help the person identify the steps he or she is willing to take to feel better about participating.

Mental Disabilities

A person with a mental disability may have a slower rate of development in the ability to communicate, interact, study, work, or establish independence. Some individuals who are mentally disabled require support in most aspects of life, while others need help in only a few specific areas.

Be sensitive and friendly to a class member who is mentally disabled. Talk to him or her in a normal way about normal things. Invite the person to participate in class in ways that will be comfortable for him or her. You may want to help the person prepare in advance. Occasionally, you might also divide the class into small groups or pairs in which the person can associate with patient and helpful class members.

Difficulties with Reading

Some individuals have difficulty reading. They may have dyslexia or another reading disorder. They may be struggling to read in a language that is not native to them. They may have poor eyesight for reading. Or they may simply lack experience with reading.

When you discover that a class member has difficulty reading, be particularly careful about how you ask him or her to participate in a lesson. Do not cause embarrassment by asking the person to read aloud if he or she has not volunteered. Seek to become better acquainted with the person. Learn more about his or her ability and willingness to read. If a person is willing to read but needs time to prepare, you can help him or her prepare to read certain passages in upcoming lessons. In other cases, you may need to look for ways to include the person without asking him or her to read. Discuss these possibilities with the person. Work together to find the best way for him or her to participate in class.

Visual Impairment

Visual impairment can vary from slight loss of sight to complete blindness. Some visually impaired individuals can see well enough if they sit close to the front of the class or if they wear glasses. Others rely on hearing and braille for their learning. Help those with visual impairments sit where they can learn most effectively and participate in class. In a spirit of friendship, speak with them about their needs and what you can do to help.

Additional Information

The preceding information is a brief summary only. If you become aware that a class member has a disability, counsel with the person and his or her family members and friends about how you can help. Befriend the class member. You may also want to counsel with leaders. Seek the Spirit's guidance to help you know how to help the person succeed and find joy in your class.

For further information about ministering to members who have disabilities, see pages 310–14 in the "Gospel Teaching and Leadership" section of the *Church Handbook of Instructions*.

Resources for Members Who Have Disabilities

Materials for members who have disabilities are listed in the annual *Church Materials Catalog*.

Questions about materials for members who have disabilities may be addressed to:

Members with Disabilities
Floor 24
50 East North Temple Street
Salt Lake City, UT 84150-3200
Telephone: 1-801-240-2477

TEACH BY THE SPIRIT

If we have the Spirit of the Lord to guide us, we can teach any person,
no matter how well educated, any place in the world. The Lord knows
more than any of us, and if we are his servants, acting under his Spirit,
he can deliver his message of salvation to each and every soul.

Elder Dallin H. Oaks

6

THE SPIRIT IS THE TRUE TEACHER

The impression of the Holy Ghost on a soul who hears the word of God is "the power of God unto the convincing of men" (D&C 11:21). President Joseph Fielding Smith taught:

"The Spirit of God speaking to the spirit of man has power to impart truth with greater effect and understanding than the truth can be imparted by personal contact even with heavenly beings. Through the Holy Ghost the truth is woven into the very fibre and sinews of the body so that it cannot be forgotten" (Doctrines of Salvation, *comp. Bruce R. McConkie, 3 vols. [1954–56], 1:47–48).*

"When a man speaketh by the power of the Holy Ghost the power of the Holy Ghost carrieth it unto the hearts of the children of men" (2 Nephi 33:1). No mortal teacher, no matter how expert or experienced, can bring the blessings of testimony and conversion to another person. That is the office of the Holy Ghost, or the Spirit. People come to know that the gospel is true by the power of the Holy Ghost (see Moroni 10:5; D&C 50:13–14).

The Spirit's Role in Gospel Teaching

As we teach the gospel, we should humbly recognize that the Holy Ghost is the true teacher. Our privilege is to serve as instruments through whom the Holy Ghost can teach, testify, comfort, and inspire. We should therefore become worthy to receive the Spirit (see "Seeking the Spirit," page 13). We should pray for the Spirit's guidance as we prepare lessons and as we teach (see "Recognizing and Following the Spirit in Your Teaching," pages 47–48). We should do all we can to create an atmosphere in which those we teach can feel the influence of the Spirit (see "Inviting the Spirit As You Teach," pages 45–46).

Elder Gene R. Cook of the Seventy counseled: "Who will do the teaching? The Comforter. Be sure you don't believe you are the 'true teacher.' That is a serious mistake. . . . Be careful you do not get in the way. The major role of a teacher is to prepare the way such that the people will have a spiritual experience with the Lord.

You are an instrument, not the teacher. The Lord is the One who knows the needs of those being taught. He is the One who can impress someone's heart and cause them to change" (address delivered to religious educators, 1 Sept. 1989).

Humbly Serving as Instruments in the Lord's Hands

We may at times be tempted to think that people will draw closer to Heavenly Father because of our efforts alone. We may suppose that it is our persuasiveness that convinces them of the truth. Or we may imagine that our eloquence and our knowledge of a particular gospel principle will inspire and edify them. If we begin to believe such things, we "get in the way" of the convincing power of the Holy Ghost. We should always remember the Lord's command to "declare glad tidings . . . with all humility, trusting in [Him]" (D&C 19:29–30).

As you prepare yourself spiritually and acknowledge the Lord in your teaching, you will become an instrument in His hands. The Holy Ghost will magnify your words with power.

Elder Richard G. Scott of the Quorum of the Twelve taught of the difference between a humble person who allows the Holy Ghost to teach and a proud person who relies on his or her own strength:

"Some years ago I had an assignment in Mexico and Central America similar to that of an Area President. . . .

"One Sunday, . . . I visited [a] branch priesthood meeting where a humble, unschooled Mexican priesthood leader struggled to communicate truths of the gospel. It was obvious how deeply they had touched his life. I noted his intense desire to communicate those principles. He recognized they were of great worth to the brethren he loved. He read from the lesson manual, yet his manner was of pure love of the Savior and those he taught. That love, sincerity, and purity of intent allowed the influence of the Holy Ghost to envelop the room. . . .

"Subsequently, I visited the Sunday School class in the ward where my family attended. A well-educated university professor presented the lesson. That experience was in striking contrast to the one enjoyed in the branch priesthood meeting. It seemed to me that the instructor had purposely chosen obscure references and unusual examples to develop his assigned topic—the life of Joseph Smith. I had the distinct impression that he used the teaching opportunity to impress the class with his great knowledge. . . . He did not seem as intent on communicating principles as had the humble priesthood leader. . . .

" . . . The humility of the Mexican priesthood leader was requisite to his being used as an instrument for spiritual communication of truth" (*Helping Others to Be Spiritually Led* [address to religious educators, 11 Aug. 1998], 10–12).

Additional Information

For more on teaching by the Spirit, see lesson 3 in the Teaching the Gospel course (pages 198–202).

7

TEACHING WITH TESTIMONY

"The crowning, convincing, converting power of gospel teaching is manifest," said Elder Bruce R. McConkie, "when an inspired teacher says, 'I know by the power of the Holy Ghost, by the revelations of the Holy Spirit to my soul, that the doctrines I have taught are true'" (*The Promised Messiah* [1978], 516–17).

President Brigham Young learned this truth before he was baptized a member of the Church. The testimony of a humble missionary helped him feel the converting power of the Holy Ghost. He later recalled, "When I saw a man without eloquence, or talents for public speaking, who could only say, 'I know, by the power of the Holy Ghost, that the Book of Mormon is true, that Joseph Smith is a Prophet of the Lord,' the Holy Ghost proceeding from that individual illuminated my understanding, and light, glory, and immortality were before me" (in *Journal of Discourses,* 1:88).

President Young was reminded of the power of testimony in his early days as a missionary. He observed: "I had only traveled a short time to testify to the people, before I learned this one fact, that you might prove doctrine from the Bible till doomsday, and it would merely convince a people, but would not convert them. You might read the Bible from Genesis to Revelations, and prove every iota that you advance, and that alone would have no converting influence upon the people. Nothing short of a testimony by the power of the Holy Ghost would

bring light and knowledge to them— bring them in their hearts to repentance. Nothing short of that would ever do" (in *Journal of Discourses,* 5:327).

What Is a Testimony?

It is important to understand what a testimony is and what a testimony is not. First, it is not an exhortation, a call to repentance, a travelogue, a sermon, or an instruction. It is a simple, direct declaration of belief—a feeling, an assurance, a conviction. It is usually stated in the first person, *I,* followed by a strong verb expressing belief, such as "I know that . . . ," "I testify that . . . ," "I bear testimony that . . . ," or "I have a strong assurance that . . ." You probably have heard special witnesses of Jesus Christ use the words "I give you my witness that . . ." or "I witness that . . ." Testimonies are often most powerful when they are short, concise, and direct.

Consider the following examples from the scriptures. Note that these testimonies appear in the context of other messages—at the beginning, in the middle, or at the end.

"*This is the testimony,* last of all, which we give of him: That he lives! For we saw him, even on the right hand of God; and we heard the voice bearing record that he is the Only Begotten of the Father—that by him, and through him, and of him, the worlds are and were created, and the inhabitants thereof are begotten sons and daughters unto God" (D&C 76:22–24; italics added).

"*I know of myself that* whatsoever I shall say unto you, concerning that which is to come, is true; and I say unto you, that *I know that* Jesus Christ shall come, yea, the Son, the Only Begotten of the Father, full of grace, and mercy, and truth" (Alma 5:48; italics added).

"And now, behold, *I will testify unto you of myself that* these things are true. Behold, I say unto you, that *I do know that* Christ shall come among the children of men, to take upon him the transgressions of his people, and that he shall atone for the sins of the world; for the Lord God hath spoken it" (Alma 34:8; italics added).

"For *I do know that* whosoever shall put their trust in God shall be supported in their trials, and their troubles, and their afflictions, and shall be lifted up at the last day" (Alma 36:3; italics added).

Other examples are found in Jacob 7:12, Alma 7:8 and 36:30, and Joseph Smith—History 1:25.

Making Testimony a Part of Your Teaching

To be able to teach by the convincing, converting power of the Holy Ghost, you must have a testimony of what you are teaching. President David O. McKay said: "It is your duty to teach that Jesus Christ is the Redeemer of the world, that Joseph Smith was a Prophet of God, and that to him in this last dispensation there appeared God the Father and his Son in person. Do you believe it? Do you feel it? Does that testimony radiate from your being? . . . If so, that radiation will give life to the people whom you go to teach. If not, there will be a dearth, a drought, a lack of that spiritual environment in which the Saints grow. . . . You can teach effectively only that which you yourselves feel" (*Gospel Ideals* [1953], 190).

You can obtain a testimony and continue to strengthen it by (1) studying the scriptures and the teachings of latter-day prophets, (2) praying, (3) fasting, and (4) obeying God's commandments. You will also see that your testimony becomes stronger as you continue to share it.

As you prepare to teach each lesson, pray for the Spirit to help you know when to share your most sacred feelings. You may be prompted to bear testimony several times during a lesson, not just at the conclusion.

Testimony Inspires Testimony

In bearing testimony by what you say and do, you help motivate others to strengthen their own testimonies. A full-time missionary wrote the following letter to a man who had been his teacher the year before he began his missionary service:

"I know you are a person who doesn't seek any praise, honor, or recognition. But I hope you will allow me to express heartfelt thanks for our class in which we studied the Book of Mormon. I recall time and time again your testifying that although many discard the Book of Mormon because they suppose it to be poorly written or inferior in its ideas, the Book of Mormon has inherent beauty and unequaled depth. In the class and in my personal study I came to love this book. I remember sitting in your class, just waiting for you to bear testimony of some plain and simple truth. I remember when we studied Alma 32 and you bore your testimony of how the seed of truth can grow in all of us. When you bore your testimony, you allowed the Spirit to witness to me the truth of the principle.

"Now here I am, one month into my mission, and I have a burning testimony of the Book of Mormon. What I have received is not merely spiritual reserve which will waste away. You led me to the tree of life. Like Lehi, you wanted nothing more than to help others partake of it. That's what touched me so much—I could see the blessings of the fruit in your life."

8

INVITING THE SPIRIT AS YOU TEACH

As a teacher, you can prepare an environment that invites the Spirit to attend your teaching. Then the Spirit can bear witness of the truthfulness of the principles you teach. The following suggestions will help you invite the Spirit as you teach.

Pray

The Lord has said, "Pray always, and I will pour out my Spirit upon you, and great shall be your blessing—yea, even more than if you should obtain treasures of earth and corruptibleness to the extent thereof" (D&C 19:39). Prayer encourages reverence and helps us prepare to learn the gospel. Those you teach should take turns offering prayers before and after each lesson. In their prayers, they may ask for the guidance of the Spirit during the lesson and as they apply the truths they have learned.

As you teach, pray in your heart for the Spirit to guide you, to open the hearts of the learners, and to testify and inspire. Occasionally you might invite learners to pray in their hearts for you as the teacher and for themselves and others who are striving to learn (see 3 Nephi 20:1).

If you teach small children, you can do much to help them feel reverent as they prepare for prayer. You can remind them to sit quietly. You can fold your arms to set an example. You can teach the language of prayer, helping them use the words *Thee, Thou, Thy,* and *Thine* in place of *you* and *your.* Until they learn to use their own words, you can prompt them as they pray. You can thank children for the prayers they

have offered and comment briefly and thoughtfully about what they have said.

Teach from the Scriptures and the Words of Latter-day Prophets

The teachings in the scriptures and the words of latter-day prophets have great power to help us feel the influence of the Spirit (see "The Power of the Word," pages 50–51). The Lord said:

"These words are not of men nor of man, but of me; wherefore, you shall testify they are of me and not of man;

"For it is my voice which speaketh them unto you; for they are given by my Spirit unto you, and by my power you can read them one to another; and save it were by my power you could not have them;

"Wherefore, you can testify that you have heard my voice, and know my words" (D&C 18:34–36).

Bear Testimony

As you bear testimony of the principles you teach, the Holy Ghost can witness to each person of the truth of what you say (see "Teaching with Testimony," pages 43–44). Testify whenever the Spirit prompts you to do so, not just at the end of each lesson. Provide opportunities for those you teach to bear their testimonies.

Share Experiences

Our testimonies are often strengthened because of experiences we have. Perhaps you have had an experience that has strengthened your testimony that Heavenly Father answers prayers. Or you may have been blessed for obeying a certain commandment. When you share such experiences, you are a living witness of gospel truths, and the Spirit can bear witness to others that what you say is true. In addition to sharing your own experiences, you should encourage learners to share their experiences as they feel comfortable doing so (see "Stories," pages 179–82).

Use Music

Music enables us to express spiritual feelings that we may have difficulty expressing

through the spoken word. Elder Boyd K. Packer said that "we are able to feel and learn very quickly through music . . . some spiritual things that we would otherwise learn very slowly" ("The Arts and the Spirit of the Lord," *Ensign,* Aug. 1976, 61).

Church hymns and Primary songs teach gospel principles. You can use them in almost any lesson to introduce or summarize an idea. Primary songs allow children to bear their testimonies simply and beautifully. (See "Music," pages 172–74.)

For ideas on how to use sacred music in Church meetings, in the home, and in your personal life, read the preface to the hymnbook (see *Hymns,* pages ix–x).

Express Love for the Lord and for Others

You can express love for those you teach by listening attentively to them and being sincerely interested in their lives. Christlike love has the power to soften hearts and help people be receptive to the whisperings of the Spirit (see "Love Softens Hearts," pages 31–32).

Additional Information

For more on teaching by the Spirit, see lesson 3 in the Teaching the Gospel course (pages 198–202).

9

RECOGNIZING AND FOLLOWING THE SPIRIT IN YOUR TEACHING

If you have properly prepared yourself, the Holy Ghost will enlighten and guide you as you teach. You may receive impressions about those you teach, what you should emphasize in teaching them, and how you can teach them most effectively. Your diligent efforts will be magnified as you humbly obey the whisperings of the Spirit. You will also be able to help those you teach recognize the influence of the Spirit. You will be prepared to experience the fulfillment of the Lord's words: "Wherefore, he that preacheth and he that receiveth, understand one another, and both are edified and rejoice together" (D&C 50:22).

Recognizing the Spirit

Elder Dallin H. Oaks taught:

"We should recognize that the Lord will speak to us through the Spirit in his own time and in his own way. . . . We cannot force spiritual things.

"In most cases, 'his own way' is not the thunderous interruption or the blinding light, but what the scriptures call 'the still small voice' (1 Kgs. 19:12; 1 Ne. 17:45; D&C 85:6). . . . We need to know that the Lord rarely speaks loudly. His messages almost always come in a whisper" ("Teaching and Learning by the Spirit," *Ensign,* Mar. 1997, 10–12).

When the Lord speaks to us through the Spirit, He may occasionally "cause that [our] bosom shall burn within [us]" (D&C 9:8). This burning, Elder Oaks explained, surely "signifies a feeling of comfort and serenity" (*Ensign,* Mar. 1997, 13). Most often we will feel enlightenment, joy, and peace (see Romans 15:13; Galatians 5:22–23; D&C 6:23; 11:13).

President Howard W. Hunter explained how we can discern different manifestations of the Spirit:

"I get concerned when it appears that strong emotion or free-flowing tears are equated with the presence of the Spirit. Certainly the Spirit of the Lord can bring strong emotional feelings, including tears, but that outward manifestation ought not to be confused with the presence of the Spirit itself.

"I have watched a great many of my brethren over the years and we have shared some rare and unspeakable spiritual experiences together. Those experiences have all been different, each special in its own way, and such sacred moments may or may not be accompanied by tears. Very often they are, but sometimes they are accompanied by total silence. Other times they are accompanied by joy. Always they are accompanied by a great manifestation of the truth, of revelation to the heart. . . .

"Listen for the truth, hearken to the doctrine, and let the manifestation of the Spirit come as it may in all of its many and varied forms. Stay with solid principles; teach from a pure heart. Then the Spirit will penetrate your mind and heart and every mind and heart of your students" (*Eternal Investments* [address to religious educators, 10 Feb. 1989], 3).

The Spirit Can Guide You As You Prepare to Teach

As you prayerfully prepare to teach, as you study the scriptures, and even as you perform your daily tasks, open your mind and heart to the Lord's guidance. You may receive "sudden strokes of ideas" from the Spirit (*Teachings of the Prophet Joseph Smith,* sel. Joseph Fielding Smith [1976], 151). You may be led to emphasize certain principles. You may gain an understanding of how best to present certain ideas. You may discover examples, object lessons, and inspiring stories in the simple activities of life (see "Looking for Lessons Everywhere," pages 22–23). You may feel impressed to invite a particular person to assist with the lesson. You may be reminded of a personal experience that you can share. Write these ideas down, and prayerfully follow them.

Elder C. Max Caldwell shared the following experience: "Some years ago I prepared to teach a class on a subject I felt would be particularly difficult. The night before the scheduled class, I prayed for guidance and then retired, still troubled in my mind. When I awoke, a certain thought was introduced to my mind that I shared with the class later that morning. After the class, a young man spoke with me privately and said, 'The lesson was for me. I now know what I have to do.' Later I learned that he had come to that class as his first contact with the Church in many years. He then proceeded to get his life in order and eventually served a faithful mission. Presently he is experiencing the happiness associated with keeping eternal family covenants" (in Conference Report, Oct. 1992, 40; or *Ensign,* Nov. 1992, 29–30).

The Spirit Can Guide You While You Teach

Generally, you will teach by the Spirit when you follow what you have prayerfully and thoughtfully prepared. In addition, the Spirit may from time to time prompt you while you teach. As the Lord has promised, you will be given "in the very hour, yea, in the very moment, what ye shall say" (D&C 100:6). You may occasionally feel a prompting to leave something out of a lesson or to add something that you have not prepared. You may feel impressed to bear your testimony or to invite others to share their testimonies. When learners ask questions, you may feel prompted to lay aside your preparations and thoughtfully discuss those questions. Make certain that these promptings come from the Spirit and not just from students' questions. Humbly follow these feelings. Allow the Spirit to work through you to touch the hearts of those you teach.

You Can Help Others Recognize the Spirit

As you become more familiar with the voice of the Spirit, you will be able to help those you teach recognize the Spirit's influence. Elder Richard G. Scott said, "If you accomplish nothing else in your relationship with your students than to help them recognize and follow the promptings of the Spirit, you will bless their lives immeasurably and eternally" (*Helping Others to Be Spiritually Led* [address to religious educators, 11 Aug. 1998], 3).

Kristi, who was eight years old, attended a special missionary meeting with her father. As part of the meeting, her father showed pictures of Jesus Christ and bore his testimony of the Savior. After the meeting was over, Kristi turned to her father and said, "I feel like crying." Her father recognized that she was feeling the influence of the Spirit. He knelt down, gave her a hug, and told her that those feelings of tenderness were the promptings of the Holy Ghost, helping her know that the things she had heard that night were true. He bore testimony to her that she could always know when something was true by recognizing the same sweet feeling she was now experiencing.

Take advantage of every opportunity to help others recognize and be grateful for the peace and joy that come when they obey the whisperings of the Spirit.

TEACH THE DOCTRINE

I cannot save you; you cannot save me; we cannot save
each other, only so far as we can persuade each other to
receive the truth, by teaching it. When a man receives the truth
he will be saved by it. He will be saved not merely because someone
taught it to him, but because he received and acted upon it.

President Joseph F. Smith

10

THE POWER OF THE WORD

At the close of his 14-year mission to the Lamanites, Ammon exclaimed, "Behold, how many thousands of our brethren has [God] loosed from the pains of hell; and they are brought to sing redeeming love, and this because of the power of his word which is in us" (Alma 26:13).

When Alma, high priest of the Nephites, learned that the people called the Zoramites had separated themselves from the Nephites and were engaging in wicked practices, "his heart . . . began to sicken because of the iniquity of the people. For it was the cause of great sorrow to Alma to know of iniquity among his people." In addition, the Zoramites presented a great military danger to the Nephites. The Nephites "greatly feared that the Zoramites would enter into a correspondence with the Lamanites, and that it would be the means of great loss on the part of the Nephites." (See Alma 31:1–4.)

In similar situations, many leaders would want to take up arms and go to war. But in his concern for his Zoramite brethren, Alma proposed a better way: "And now, as the preaching of the word had a great tendency to lead the people to do that which was just—yea, it had had more powerful effect upon the minds of the people than the sword, or anything else, which had happened unto them—therefore Alma thought it was expedient that they should try the virtue of the word of God" (Alma 31:5).

The word of God can have a powerful influence. Sometimes we may be tempted to think that those we teach would rather talk about something else or be entertained. But effective parents, leaders, home teachers, visiting teachers, and classroom teachers in the Church know that when they teach the doctrine by the Spirit, those they teach are often awakened to a desire for the things of God.

Why We Should Teach the Word of God

When Alma was preaching to the Zoramites, he spoke to a group of people whose afflictions had prepared them to receive the word of God. He taught them about the power of the word. By studying what he said, we can better understand why we should use the word of God as the source of all our gospel teaching.

He compared the word to a seed that can be planted in our hearts. If you have tended a garden, you have seen that the seeds you plant, though very small, can burst with life not long after they receive a little moisture. The energy in a seed is so powerful that it may even push aside hardened ground in order to send up its first sprout. That is what happens when we "give place" for the word of God to be planted in our hearts. If we do not cast out the seed—or, in other words, if we do not resist the Spirit of the Lord—the seed will begin to swell and grow. Alma said, "It will begin to swell within your breasts; and when you feel these swelling motions, ye will begin to say within yourselves—It must needs be that this is a good seed, or that the word is good, for it beginneth to enlarge my soul; yea, it beginneth to enlighten my understanding, yea, it beginneth to be delicious to me" (Alma 32:28).

When this happens within us, we know that the seed, or the word of God, is good: "Behold, as the seed swelleth, and sprouteth, and beginneth to grow, then you must needs say that the seed is good. . . . And now, behold, because ye have tried the experiment, and planted the seed, and it swelleth and sprouteth, and beginneth to grow, ye must needs know that the seed is good" (Alma 32:30, 33). Alma continued, "If ye will nourish the word, yea, nourish the tree as it beginneth to grow, by your faith with great diligence, and with patience, looking forward to the fruit thereof, it shall take root; and behold it shall be a tree springing up unto everlasting life" and bearing fruit that is "most precious" (Alma 32:41–42).

Elder Boyd K. Packer said: "True doctrine, understood, changes attitudes and behavior. The study of the doctrines of the gospel will improve behavior quicker than a study of behavior will improve behavior" (in Conference Report, Oct. 1986, 20; or *Ensign*, Nov. 1986, 17). No worldly ideas or principles have this power. No spellbinding lectures or entertaining presentations can touch individuals so profoundly that they turn their hearts to Christ. Centering our teaching on the truths of the gospel is the only way we can become instruments in God's hands to help instill the faith that will lead others to repent and come unto Him.

The teaching of doctrine protects us against spiritual waywardness. It can call us back when we go astray. Elder Russell M. Nelson explained:

"Years ago as a young medical student I saw many patients afflicted with diseases that are now preventable. Today it is possible to immunize individuals against conditions that once were disabling—even deadly. One medical method by which acquired immunity is conferred is inoculation. The term *inoculate* is fascinating. It comes from two Latin roots: *in,* meaning 'within'; and *oculus,* meaning 'an eye.' The verb *to inoculate,* therefore, literally means 'to put an eye within'—to monitor against harm.

"An affliction like polio can cripple or destroy the body. An affliction like sin can cripple or destroy the spirit. The ravages of polio can now be prevented by immunization, but the ravages of sin require other means of prevention. Doctors cannot immunize against iniquity. Spiritual protection comes only from the Lord—and in his own way. Jesus chooses not to inoculate, but to indoctrinate. His method employs no vaccine; it utilizes the teaching of divine doctrine—a governing 'eye within'—to protect the eternal spirits of his children" (in Conference Report, Apr. 1995, 41–42; or *Ensign,* May 1995, 32).

Teaching from the Scriptures and the Words of Latter-day Prophets

When we use the scriptures and the words of latter-day prophets as the source of all our teaching, we invite the Spirit to bear witness. This brings to our teaching "the power of God unto the convincing of men" (D&C 11:21).

A bishop related the following experience at a stake leadership meeting:

"Almost 30 years ago I served as priests quorum adviser in our ward. In our quorum lessons, we made sure to read the scriptures and words of the living prophets and to emphasize the doctrines. Because the Spirit was there, our meetings were memorable and sweet.

"Included in the quorum was a young priest, Paolo, who seldom came home; his parents usually did not know

where to find him. Occasionally I was able to contact him, and from time to time he would show up at quorum meeting. We were striving in the quorum to gain a better understanding of the principles of the gospel, and we concentrated on learning our lessons from the scriptures. When Paolo came, I was spiritually aware that these truths were touching his heart even though he would then disappear from town for weeks.

"One Sunday morning Paolo appeared at church, cleanshaven and dressed in a suit, white shirt, and tie. We were all happily surprised. We learned later that he had had an experience the night before, far away from home. He had fallen into deep discouragement. About midnight his mind opened up to a realization or spiritual experience that God and Satan were fighting for his soul, and that Satan was winning. Right then, in the middle of the night, he got up from where he was and walked many miles until he reached his home, woke his parents and told them what had happened, and then, as dawn broke, cleaned himself up and came to church.

"He never looked back. He repented of the wrongs he had done and later fell in love and married one of the noblest young women in our ward. Today he is an upstanding father, priesthood holder, and citizen.

"I have often reflected that what Paolo heard in those quorum meetings had a lot to do with the turnaround he made in his life. I knew at the time that he was being touched when we talked of gospel truths in the quorum. I think those truths kept reminding him of who he really was and what God expected of him. I think they worked upon his mind and heart and made him more and more uncomfortable with the lifestyle he was choosing. Through that slim wedge in his hardened heart, the Spirit could speak to him and warn him. How grateful I am that we did not waste our quorum time talking about cars or sports or my idea of how the boys were supposed to be living! I think Paolo heard the Lord call to him through the gospel truths that we studied together."

We can show those we teach how to find the power in the scriptures. Elder Boyd K. Packer declared: "You are to teach the scriptures. . . . If your students are acquainted with the revelations, there is no question—personal or social or political or occupational—that need go unanswered. Therein is contained the fulness of the everlasting gospel. Therein we find principles of truth that will resolve every confusion and every problem and every dilemma that will face the human family or any individual in it" (*Teach the Scriptures* [address to religious educators, 14 Oct. 1977], 5).

11

KEEPING THE DOCTRINE PURE

Moroni chapter 8 contains a letter written by Mormon to his son Moroni. The topic of the letter is infant baptism, which was being practiced by some in the Church. To help his son correct this false teaching, Mormon restated the correct doctrine of account-ability and instructed Moroni to teach it throughout the land. Read Moroni 8 as an example of the need to keep the doctrine and principles of the Church pure and undistorted.

It is humbling and inspiring to ponder the price people have paid for the truth. Many have been baptized despite being rejected by their families for their decision. Prophets and many others have died rather than deny their testimonies. Referring to the martyrdom of Joseph and Hyrum Smith, Elder John Taylor declared that the Book of Mormon and the Doctrine and Covenants "cost the best blood of the nineteenth century to bring them forth" (D&C 135:6).

Each person who teaches the gospel is required to pass on to others, in pure and undistorted form, the truths for which such great sacrifices have been made. President Gordon B. Hinckley stated: "I have spoken before about the importance of keeping the doctrine of the Church pure, and see-ing that it is taught in all of our meetings. I worry about this. Small aberrations in doctrinal teaching can lead to large and evil falsehoods" (*Teachings of Gordon B. Hinckley* [1997], 620).

Your Responsibilities as a Teacher

As you prepare and present lessons, you should take the following precautions to ensure that you teach the truth as the Lord has revealed it.

Teach by the Spirit from the Scriptures and the Words of Latter-day Prophets

President Ezra Taft Benson taught: "What should be the source for teaching the great plan of the Eternal God? The scriptures, of course—particularly the Book of Mormon. This should also include the other modern-day revelations. These should be coupled with the words of the Apostles and prophets and the promptings of the Spirit" (in Conference Report, Apr. 1987, 107; or *Ensign*, May 1987, 85).

Use Church-Produced Lesson Materials

To help us teach from the scriptures and the words of latter-day prophets, the Church has produced lesson manuals and other materials. There is little need for commentaries or other reference material. We should study the scriptures, teachings of latter-day prophets, and lesson materials thoroughly to be sure we correctly under-stand the doctrine before we teach it.

Teach the Truths of the Gospel and Not Other Things

When Alma ordained priests to teach those he had baptized in the waters of Mormon, "he commanded them that they should teach nothing save it were the things which he had taught, and which had been spoken by the mouth of the holy prophets" (Mosiah 18:19). When the Savior's twelve Nephite disciples taught the people, they "ministered those same words which Jesus had spoken—nothing varying from the words which Jesus had spoken" (3 Nephi 19:8). As you teach the gospel of Jesus Christ, you should follow these examples.

Teach Gospel Truths Clearly So That No One Will Misunderstand Them

President Harold B. Lee stated, "You're to teach the old doctrines, not so plain that they can just understand, *but you must teach the doctrines of the Church so plainly that no one can misunderstand*" ("Loyalty," in *Charge to Religious Educators,* 2nd ed. [1982], 64).

Cautions for Gospel Teachers

As you strive to keep the doctrine pure, you should avoid the following problems.

Speculation

"In presenting a lesson there are many ways for the undisciplined teacher to stray from the path that leads to his objective.

One of the most common temptations is to speculate on matters about which the Lord has said very little. The disciplined teacher has the courage to say, 'I don't know,' and leave it at that. As President Joseph F. Smith said, 'It is no discredit to our intelligence or to our integrity to say frankly in the face of a hundred speculative questions, "I don't know"' [*Gospel Doctrine,* 5th ed. (1939), 9]" (Joseph F. McConkie, "The Disciplined Teacher," *Instructor,* Sept. 1969, 334–35).

Misquoting

"The disciplined teacher will be sure of his sources and will also make every effort to determine whether a statement properly represents the doctrine of the Church or is merely the opinion of the author" (*Instructor,* Sept. 1969, 334–35).

We should not attribute statements to Church leaders without confirming the source of the statements. When we quote scriptures, we should ensure that our use of them is consistent with their context (see "Teaching from the Scriptures," pages 54–55).

Gospel Hobbies

"Gospel hobbies—the special or exclusive emphasis of one principle of the gospel—should also be avoided by teachers" (*Instructor,* Sept. 1969, 334–35).

President Joseph F. Smith said: "Hobbies give to those who encourage them a false aspect of the gospel of the Redeemer; they distort and place out of harmony its principles and teachings. The point of view is unnatural. Every principle and practice revealed from God is essential to man's salvation, and to place any one of them unduly in front, hiding and dimming all others, is unwise and dangerous; it jeopardizes our salvation, for it darkens our minds and beclouds our understandings" (*Gospel Doctrine,* 116–17).

Sensational Stories

"Perhaps the greatest temptation of the teacher struggling to maintain the attention of [a] class is the use of the sensational story. There are a number of these, of very questionable origin, continually being circulated throughout the Church. . . . These are not teaching tools: stability and testimony are not built on sensational stories. Direction

for us from the Prophet is dispensed through proper priesthood channels. Careful attention should be paid to the messages of the General Authorities in stake and general conferences, and Church publications should be read regularly. Meaningful attention will be accorded the teacher who establishes the reputation of being orthodox and sound in doctrine" (*Instructor,* Sept. 1969, 334–35).

Reshaping Church History

President Ezra Taft Benson cautioned: "There have been and continue to be attempts made to bring [a humanistic] philosophy into our own Church history. . . . The emphasis is to underplay revelation and God's intervention in significant events and to inordinately humanize the prophets of God so that their human frailties become more apparent than their spiritual qualities" ("God's Hand in Our Nation's History," in *1976 Devotional Speeches of the Year* [1977], 310).

Speaking of these attempts, President Benson later said, "We would warn you teachers of this trend, which seems to be an effort to reinterpret the history of the Church so that it is more rationally appealing to the world" (*The Gospel Teacher and His Message* [address to religious educators, 17 Sept. 1976], 11).

Private Interpretations and Unorthodox Views

President J. Reuben Clark Jr. said, "Only the President of the Church, the Presiding High Priest, is sustained as Prophet, Seer, and Revelator for the Church, and he alone has the right to receive revelations for the Church, either new or amendatory, or to give authoritative interpretations of scriptures that shall be binding on the Church, or change in any way the existing doctrines of the Church" (in *Church News,* 31 July 1954, 10). We should not teach our private interpretation of gospel principles or the scriptures.

Elder Spencer W. Kimball stated: "There are those today who seem to take pride in disagreeing with the orthodox teachings of the Church and who present their own opinions which are at variance with the revealed truth. Some may be partially innocent in the matter; others are feeding their own egotism; and some seem to be deliberate. Men may think as they please, but they have no right to impose upon others their unorthodox views. Such persons should realize that their own souls are in jeopardy" (in Conference Report, Apr. 1948, 109).

12

TEACHING FROM THE SCRIPTURES

Latter-day prophets have instructed us to use the scriptures to teach the doctrines of the gospel. President Ezra Taft Benson said: "Always remember, there is no satisfactory substitute for the scriptures and the words of the living prophets. These should be your original sources. Read and ponder more what the Lord has said, and less about what others have written concerning what the Lord has said" (*The Gospel Teacher and His Message* [address to religious educators, 17 Sept. 1976], 6).

President Gordon B. Hinckley said: "The truest source of divine wisdom is the word of the Lord in these sacred volumes, the standard works of the Church. Here is found the doctrine to which we must hold fast if this work is to roll forth to its divinely charted destiny" (in Conference Report, Apr. 1982, 67–68; or *Ensign,* May 1982, 45).

The following suggestions can help you teach from the scriptures.

"Seek to Obtain [the] Word"

Before we can teach from the scriptures, we must study the scriptures on our own (see "Seeking to Obtain the Word," pages 14–15; "Developing a Personal Plan for Studying the Gospel," pages 16–17).

Conduct Discussions and Use Questions

As you teach from the scriptures, it is particularly important to conduct discussions and use questions, because these methods encourage those you teach to think about the scriptures and share insights. When learners discuss principles from the scriptures, they develop skills they need for their personal scripture study. (For help with conducting discussions and using questions, see pages 63–65 and 68–70.)

Provide Context

The setting or background of a scripture passage is called the context. Learners will better understand what is happening or being said in a scripture passage when they know its context.

To begin looking for context, ask the following questions:

- Who is speaking?
- Whom is that person speaking to?
- What is he or she speaking about?
- What is he or she responding to?
- Why is he or she saying this?

For example, Luke 15:11–32 contains the Savior's parable of the prodigal son. The Prophet Joseph Smith said that he gained an understanding of this parable by looking to its context:

"I have a key by which I understand the scriptures. I enquire, what was the question which drew out the answer, or caused Jesus to utter the parable? . . . While Jesus was teaching the people, all the publicans and sinners drew near to hear Him; 'and the Pharisees and scribes murmured, saying: This man receiveth sinners, and eateth with them.' This is the keyword which unlocks the parable of the prodigal son. It was given to answer the murmurings and questions of the Sadducees and Pharisees, who were querying, finding fault, and saying, 'How is it that this man as great as He pretends to be, eats with publicans and sinners?' " (*Teachings of the Prophet Joseph Smith,* sel. Joseph Fielding Smith [1976], 276–77).

As the Prophet Joseph pointed out, the context of the parable of the prodigal son starts in Luke 15:1–2, several verses before the parable begins. One way to find the context is to read the verses before and after the passage you are studying.

This approach is helpful even when the speaker in a scripture passage is responding not just to people but to the important events of the day. An example of this is summarized at the beginning of "The Power of the Word" (page 50). When we understand who the Zoramites were, the awful spiritual state they were in, and the threat they presented to the Nephites, we can better understand the importance of Alma's statement that he and his brethren should "try the virtue of the word of God" in their effort to turn the Zoramites from their ways (Alma 31:5).

Sometimes it is also helpful to study the political, social, or economic history of the times in which a scripture was given. For example, to gain an understanding of the Lord's comfort and promises in Doctrine and Covenants 121 and 122, it is helpful to know about the afflictions the Saints were suffering in Missouri at that time and the conditions the Prophet Joseph and his companions endured in Liberty Jail. To increase our understanding of the epistles of Paul, we can benefit from a basic knowledge of the area in which he traveled and the condition of the branches of the Church to which he wrote. The Bible Dictionary can be an excellent source for this and other background information on passages in the Bible.

In providing context, it is essential to not lose sight of its purpose, which is to contribute to a better understanding of a particular scripture passage. Be careful not to turn context—such as the history, politics, economics, or language of the people in the scriptures—into the main focus of a lesson.

Share Scriptural Stories

It is often easier to understand a gospel principle when it is expressed as part of a scriptural story. Stories engage people's interest and show how gospel principles apply in everyday life. In addition, stories are often easier to remember than abstract statements of principles. (For suggestions on sharing stories, see "Stories," pages 179–82.)

A scriptural story may contain many principles and applications (one example is the book of Enos, which contains only 27 verses but illustrates many gospel principles). You will need to decide which of these you will highlight in the stories you use.

It is often helpful for learners to read a story aloud together, taking turns reading (see "Read Aloud," page 56). If the story is long, it is usually best to summarize it, having learners read a few key verses at important points in the story. Chapter or section headings can be helpful when you prepare and present summaries.

Share Biographical Information

When we study the lives of individuals in the scriptures, we often see gospel principles at work over a period of time. For example, the complete story of Zeezrom in the Book of Mormon shows that a person can repent and go on to serve the Lord in righteousness. If you read the verses cited in the index of your scriptures under "Zeezrom," you can follow the story of Zeezrom's attack against the Church, his conversion, and finally, his valiant service as a missionary and gospel teacher. Other instructive biographies include those of Ruth, King David, Samuel, Esther, the Apostle Paul, Alma the Elder, King Benjamin, Alma the Younger, Corianton, Mormon, and Moroni.

Use "Look for" and "Listen for" Approaches

When you teach from the scriptures, it is often helpful to have learners look or listen for something specific. Following are some examples of things you might ask them to "look for" or "listen for."

Gospel principles illustrated in people's lives. Example: "As we read Moses 5:4–9, look for statements that illustrate Adam's obedience, even before he fully understood the principles involved."

Questions. Example: "As we read Alma 5:14–32, listen for questions Alma asked."

Lists. Example: "As we study Doctrine and Covenants 25, look for the qualities of an 'elect lady.'"

Definitions of words or concepts. Example: "Look for definitions of *Zion* in Doctrine and Covenants 97:21 and Moses 7:18."

Imagery and symbols. Example: "In John 15:1–6, look for the Savior's comparison of Himself to a vine and His disciples to the branches."

Prophetic commentary on a principle or event. Example: "As I read Alma 30:60, listen for Mormon's commentary on the fate of Korihor."

"If, then" relationships. Example: "Listen for Isaiah's promises to us if we keep the Sabbath day holy." (See Isaiah 58:13–14.)

Conduct that pleases or displeases God. Example: "As we read Alma 39:1–9, look for the specific counsel that Alma gave to his son Corianton."

Patterns of events, characteristics, or actions. Example: "As we study these passages, look for patterns that show the need for righteous desires as we seek for truth." (See 1 Nephi 10:17–22; 11:1–23; D&C 11.)

As you look and listen for these things in your personal study and preparation, you will be better able to conduct "look for" and "listen for" activities with those you teach.

"Liken All Scriptures unto Us"

See "Likening," pages 170–71.

Read Aloud

Reading the scriptures aloud engages learners' interest, sharpens their focus on particular passages, and helps them be receptive to the influence of the Spirit. When one person reads aloud, you should encourage others to follow along in their scriptures. Invite them to listen and look for specific principles or ideas. Allow time for them to turn to each scripture passage before it is read. If a passage contains unusual or difficult words or phrases, explain these before the passage is read. If anyone in the group might have difficulty reading, ask for volunteers instead of having them take turns. Work individually with those who have trouble reading so they can eventually come prepared to read a passage successfully.

Use the Study Helps in the Scriptures

President Howard W. Hunter said: "We ought to have a Church full of women and men who know the scriptures thoroughly, who cross-reference and mark them, who develop lessons and talks from the Topical Guide, and who have mastered the maps, the Bible Dictionary, and the other helps that are contained in this wonderful set of standard works. There is obviously more there than we can master quickly. Certainly the scriptural field is 'white already to harvest'" (*Eternal Investments* [address to religious educators, 10 Feb. 1989], 2–3).

Bible Dictionary

The Bible Dictionary is located in the appendix of the Latter-day Saint edition of the King James Bible, immediately following the Topical Guide. It is a teaching and study resource that provides explanations of names and places mentioned in the Bible. It also provides short articles on cultural items and a few key doctrines such as the Atonement, baptism, the Holy Ghost, and resurrection. It includes a chronology of important dates.

You can use the material in the Bible Dictionary to enrich lessons. You might ask learners to prepare reports, give definitions, or even teach a segment of a lesson from the Bible Dictionary.

To appreciate the enrichment that the Bible Dictionary provides, look up the word *grace* (page 697). Study the definition carefully. Then read the scripture references provided. Note how these verses of scripture have greater significance when you ponder the definition of *grace*.

Footnotes and Cross-References

Pages of scriptural text usually contain footnotes. In Latter-day Saint editions of the scriptures, the footnotes contain several kinds of information. For example, they contain alternate Greek (GR) or Hebrew (HEB) translations for selected words. They contain references to the Topical Guide (TG). They also contain explanations of idioms and difficult constructions (IE). Footnotes with the notation "JST" are excerpts from Joseph Smith's inspired translation of the Bible. Short Joseph Smith Translation entries appear in the footnotes. Longer entries appear in a special section in the appendix, immediately after the Bible Dictionary.

The most common type of footnote is a cross-reference to other scripture passages in the standard works. These additional passages often clarify or add insight to the passage you are reading. For example, look up Doctrine and Covenants 11:21. Read the verse, and then read the passages listed in footnote *b*. How do these passages increase your understanding of the verse?

When teaching a passage of scripture, you can use the footnotes and cross-references to help learners better understand the passage.

Headings of Chapters and Sections

A heading provides an overview of the chapter or section that follows. It may include information about doctrine, historical context, or people. The heading to 2 Nephi 27, for example, explains that the chapter is similar to Isaiah 29 and that it contains a prophecy about the coming forth of the Book of Mormon.

You may want to invite learners to mark scripture passages according to the highlights contained in the chapter or section heading. For example, the major principles in the Word of Wisdom are described in the heading for Doctrine and Covenants 89. You could have learners read these principles in the heading and then highlight them in the scripture text.

You may want to ask learners to silently read chapter or section headings before they comment on selected scriptures. This can help them properly understand the context of the scriptures.

Introductory Pages

Each one of the standard works has introductory pages, which contain useful background information about the purpose and origin of the book. For example, the introductory pages to the Book of Mormon contain testimonies from Joseph Smith and others and information about the origin of the book. The introductory pages to the Doctrine

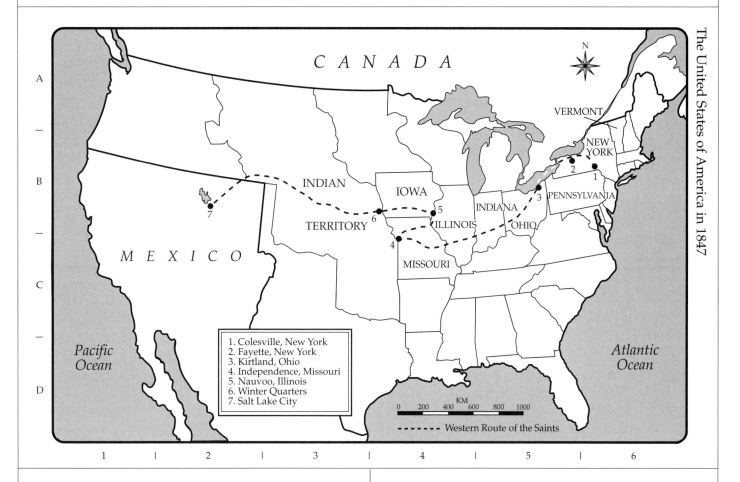

1. Colesville, New York
2. Fayette, New York
3. Kirtland, Ohio
4. Independence, Missouri
5. Nauvoo, Illinois
6. Winter Quarters
7. Salt Lake City

KM
0   200   400   600   800   1000

- - - - - Western Route of the Saints

and Covenants explain how the revelations in the book were received and compiled.

This material can be used to teach the background, history, chronology, and organization of the scriptures. Entire lessons may be organized using material from these pages. For example, the explanatory introduction to the Doctrine and Covenants contains a brief review of the Restoration of the gospel and lists scripture references pertaining to the subject.

Maps

Latter-day Saint editions of the scriptures contain maps of scriptural sites and areas that are important in Church history. By knowing the geography of the lands discussed, learners can better understand events described in the scriptures.

Topical Guide

The introduction to the Topical Guide states that it is "intended to help the reader find scriptures most often used in gospel classes and study. Because of space limitations, the guide is not intended to be comprehensive. It is also recommended that the reader look up each scripture and examine it in its context, in order to gain a better understanding of it."

Turn to the Topical Guide in your scriptures and look up the word *abide*. Note that the names of books of scripture appear in bold. Scripture passages from each book follow. Each scripture passage in the list contains the word *abide,* shown by the abbreviation *a.* The entry also contains cross-references to other words in the Topical Guide that provide information on the subject.

You may want to study the Topical Guide to learn more about a lesson topic and to find scripture passages to use in a lesson. As part of a lesson, you could ask learners a question and invite them to use the Topical Guide to find answers.

Scripture Marking and Margin Notes

It is helpful to mark scriptures, highlighting story lines, themes, and principles so they will be easy to find. This can be likened to a personal filing system. As you teach, you can encourage learners to mark their scriptures by saying something like, "This verse contains an important principle. You may want to mark it."

There is no single way to mark scriptures. A person's marking system should reflect his or her personal approach to scripture study. If you teach adults or youth, you might consider asking some learners to share the methods they use.

Methods for marking scriptures include, but are not restricted to, the following:

- Shading, underlining, bracketing, or outlining an entire verse or block of verses with a pencil or colored marker.

- Underlining only a few key words in each verse of scripture. This creates a highlighted version of the chapter or section that you can scan quickly to pick out the main concepts.

- Circling or underlining key words and, with straight lines, linking together those that relate closely to one another.

- Marking an entire verse or block of verses and linking the key words within that passage.

- Noticing when a series of related points is mentioned and numbering the points within the text or in the margin.

Scripture Linking

Most gospel principles are expressed in many different passages of scripture, with each passage providing its own insight. You can gain a more complete understanding of a principle when you study various passages about it. One way to do this is to compile a list of passages on a subject and then write that list in your scriptures. Depending on the topic, a list may be long or as short as two or three key verses. This method, sometimes called scripture linking, can be a valuable tool in studying the scriptures and teaching from them. You can link a list of scripture passages in the following way:

In the margin beside each scripture passage, write the reference of the next passage in the list. Continue doing this until you reach the last passage. Beside the last passage, write the reference to the first one. Then you can start at any point on the list and continue through the chain until you have read all the passages.

You may develop some lists that need to be put in a certain sequence to provide a more complete understanding of their subjects. To always know where to start such a sequence, you can write the reference to the first passage in parentheses under each of the other references. Or you can write only the reference to the first passage by each of the other passages, and on the page where the first passage appears, you can write the entire list.

Margin Notes

Making notes in the margins of your scriptures can be a valuable way to personalize the scriptures. Such notes provide a way to record insights, identify cross-references that are important to you, and record ways that you can apply scripture passages in your daily life.

You may want to encourage learners to make margin notes. You might say something like, "I want to share a thought about this chapter. I have written it in the margin" or "Here is an excellent passage on repentance. You may want to write the word *repentance* in the margin next to it."

Suggestions for Using the Scriptures to Teach Children

You can bless the lives of children by helping them become comfortable with the language of the scriptures. When you teach children, you should use the scriptures frequently and find ways to have the children become comfortable using the scriptures. Following are examples of what you might do:

- Help children become familiar with the names and order of the books in the scriptures. Use the songs "The Books in the Old Testament," "The Books in the New Testament," and "The Books in the Book of Mormon" from the *Children's Songbook,* pages 114–17 and 119.

- Help children understand the language of the scriptures. When you read scriptures together, explain the meaning of important words. Help children pronounce difficult words and names. Have them listen for certain words, phrases, or ideas.

- When you want children to find a certain scripture passage, give them the page number of the passage as well as the reference.

- Share a scripture account in your own words. Help learners visualize the events and the people as you describe what happened (see "Stories," pages 179–82). Then read key scripture passages aloud.

- Have children read aloud from the scriptures. Be aware of each child's abilities, and help each participate successfully.

- If children are too young to read, invite them to watch as you read a scripture and point to the words. You could also have older children assist younger children in finding and reading scriptures.

- Have children read scripture accounts from the illustrated books of scripture stories published by the Church, such as *Book of Mormon Stories.*

- Help the children discuss scripture accounts. Teach them to ask questions when they read, such as, "What is happening? Why is this happening? Who is speaking? How does this apply to me?"

- Use the methods described in part F of this book (pages 157–84). For example, in presenting a story from the scriptures, you could use a flannel board, simple chalkboard illustrations, or pictures drawn by the children. You could have children retell a scripture story or sing songs that relate to specific scriptures.

- At the end of some Primary lessons, there is a section called "Suggested Home Reading." Invite the children to read with their families the scriptures mentioned there.

INVITE DILIGENT LEARNING

Each of us is responsible to learn the gospel through diligent effort. We are also privileged at various times to serve as teachers—to inspire and help others in their responsibility to learn the gospel.

We render this important service by doing all we can to:
1. Awaken and hold the interest of those we teach.
2. Encourage their active participation in lessons.
3. Show them how to live according to the truths they learn.

We are to do these things with love and by the power of the Spirit. This means that we should focus not so much on our performance as on how well we help others learn the gospel diligently and live it faithfully.

13

HELPING INDIVIDUALS TAKE RESPONSIBILITY FOR LEARNING THE GOSPEL

Each Individual's Responsibility to Learn the Gospel

In a letter about studying the gospel, Elder Bruce R. McConkie wrote: "Now let us come to . . . a conclusion that will have an important bearing on our eternal salvation. It is that each person must learn the doctrines of the gospel for himself. No one else can do it for him. Each person stands alone where gospel scholarship is concerned; each has access to the same scriptures and is entitled to the guidance of the same Holy Spirit; each must pay the price set by a Divine Providence if he is to gain the pearl of great price.

"The same principle governs both learning truth and living in harmony with its standards. No one can repent for and on behalf of another; no one can keep the commandments in the place and stead of another; no one can be saved in someone else's name. And no one can gain a testimony or press forward in light and truth to eternal glory for anyone but himself. Both the knowledge of the truth and the blessings that come to those who conform to true principles are personal matters. And as a just God offers the same salvation to every soul who lives the same laws, so he offers the same understanding of his eternal truths to all who will pay the truth seeker's price.

"The Church system for gaining gospel knowledge is as follows:

"a. The responsibility rests upon each person to gain a knowledge of the truth through his own efforts.

"b. Next, families should teach their own family members. Parents are commanded to bring up their children in light and truth. The home should be the chief teaching center in the life of a Latter-day Saint.

"c. To help families and individuals, the Church, as a service agency, provides many opportunities to teach and to learn. We are commanded to 'teach one another the doctrine of the kingdom' (D&C 88:77). This is done in sacrament meetings, in conferences and other meetings, by home teachers, in priesthood and auxiliary classes, through seminaries and institutes, and through the Church educational system" ("Finding Answers to Gospel Questions," in *Charge to Religious Educators*, 3rd ed. [1994], 80).

The Teacher's Role in Helping Individuals Learn the Gospel

Knowing that individuals are responsible to learn the gospel, we may ask, What is the role of teachers? It is to help individuals take responsibility for learning the gospel—to awaken in them the desire to study, understand, and live the gospel and to show them how to do so.

Sister Virginia H. Pearce, who served as first counselor in the Young Women general presidency, said:

"A teacher's goal is greater than just delivering a lecture about truth. It is to invite the Spirit and use techniques that will enhance the possibility that the learner will discover the truth [and] be motivated to apply it. . . .

" . . . Imagine hundreds of thousands of classrooms every Sunday, each with a teacher who understands that 'the learning has to be done by the pupil. Therefore it is the pupil who has to be put into action. When a teacher takes the spotlight, becomes the star of the show, does all the talking, and otherwise takes over all of the activity, it is almost certain that he is interfering with the learning of the class members' [Asahel D. Woodruff, *Teaching the Gospel* (1962), 37].

"A skilled teacher doesn't think, 'What shall I do in class today?' but asks, 'What will my students do in class today?'; not, 'What will I teach today?' but rather, 'How will I help my students discover what they need to know?' [*Teaching the Gospel: A Handbook for CES Teachers and Leaders* (1994), 13]. The skilled teacher does not want students who leave the class talking about how magnificent and unusual the teacher is. This teacher wants students who leave talking about how magnificent the gospel is!" (in Conference Report, Oct. 1996, 13–14; or *Ensign*, Nov. 1996, 12).

Teachers who understand their true responsibility respect the agency of each person they teach. They rejoice when those they teach study the scriptures on their own, discover gospel principles for themselves, and make insightful contributions to discussions. Teachers are most successful when learners diligently study and grow in the gospel and draw strength from God.

Excellent teachers do not take the credit for the learning and growth of those they teach. Like gardeners who plant and tend crops, they strive to create the best possible conditions for learning. Then they give thanks to God when they see the progress of those they teach. Paul wrote, "Neither is he that planteth any thing, neither he that watereth; but God that giveth the increase" (1 Corinthians 3:7).

Encouraging Self-Reliance in Gospel Learning

The following suggestions can help you encourage others to take responsibility for learning the gospel:

- Nurture your own enthusiasm for studying the scriptures and the teachings of latter-day prophets. Your enthusiasm may inspire those you teach to follow your example.

- As you teach, always draw attention to the scriptures and the teachings of latter-day prophets. This will help members appreciate how rich and meaningful the word of God is.

- Ask questions that require learners to find answers in the scriptures and the teachings of latter-day prophets. While it is sometimes good to ask learners what they think about certain subjects, it is often a better idea to ask them what the scriptures and the latter-day prophets teach.

- Show learners how to use the study helps in the scriptures. The scriptures can seem overwhelming to some, especially those who are relatively inexperienced in the Church. You can help by teaching them how to use the footnotes, the Topical Guide, the Bible Dictionary, the excerpts from the Joseph Smith Translation, and the maps (see "Teaching from the Scriptures," pages 54–59, for specific ideas). Individuals who learn how to use these study helps become more confident in their ability to study the scriptures.

- Give assignments that require study of the scriptures and the teachings of latter-day prophets. Consider ending a lesson by asking a question or giving an assignment that requires those present to search the scriptures and the teachings of latter-day prophets. Even little children can be given this kind of assignment. For example, after a lesson about prayer, you could ask children to read with their parents a scripture account or general conference talk about prayer.

- Help learners understand that the people in the scriptures were real people who experienced trials and joy in their efforts to serve the Lord. The scriptures come alive as we remember that the prophets and other people in the scriptures experienced many of the same things we experience.

- Show learners how to find answers to life's challenges in the scriptures and the teachings of latter-day prophets. For example, you could help them use the Topical Guide in the scriptures or the index in conference issues of the Church magazine to search for counsel on topics such as comfort, repentance, forgiveness, revelation, or prayer.

- Openly encourage those you teach to study the scriptures and the teachings of latter-day prophets. Some have never understood their responsibility to learn the gospel. Some have forgotten. A bishop remarked that he had once attended a Primary training meeting where the challenge was given to study the scriptures every day. As a direct result of that experience, he missed only one day of study during the next 13 years. He said that this study changed his life.

- Bear testimony of the Savior as the center of all that the scriptures and the latter-day prophets teach. Be especially bold in bearing your testimony of the Savior. As those you teach see the Savior in the scriptures and the teachings of latter-day prophets, their hunger to study will increase and their testimonies will be strengthened.

Additional Information

For more on helping individuals take responsibility for learning the gospel, see lesson 5 in the Teaching the Gospel course (pages 208–12).

14

CONDUCTING DISCUSSIONS

Meaningful discussions are fundamental to most gospel teaching. We invite the influence of the Spirit when we teach the gospel to one another and give respectful attention to one another.

Discussions can bring results that seldom occur without them. For example, they can:

- Promote diligent learning. Through well-conducted discussions, learners' interest and attentiveness are increased. Each person present can be encouraged to become actively engaged in the learning process. As you and those you teach ask questions, search the scriptures together, and listen to one another, all who are present will be able to gain skills and motivation that can help in individual gospel study.

- Encourage unity among those you teach. As they share their own insights and experiences and listen and respond to one another respectfully, they become more unified and create a positive atmosphere for learning.

- Increase understanding. Good discussions are more than friendly conversations in which opinions are shared. They broaden and deepen each participant's understanding of gospel principles.

- Reduce misunderstanding. Learners' comments reveal how well they are understanding the principles being taught. This can help you know when to further develop, emphasize, or review particular principles.

Suggestions for Conducting Discussions

Use Questions

Questions can encourage those present to participate in discussions. They can help learners understand a principle, think about it more deeply, and relate it to their lives. They can lead learners to turn to the scriptures for answers.

Most lesson manuals provide questions for getting discussions started and keeping them going. You may use these questions and prepare your own. Ask questions that encourage thoughtful comments and help individuals truly ponder the gospel. (For additional help, see "Teaching with Questions," pages 68–70.)

Select Teaching Methods That Relate the Discussions to the Lessons

After you have planned questions, ask yourself, "What else can I do? What methods can I use to enrich the discussion?" You can use many different teaching methods to begin discussions and keep them going. For example, you could begin a lesson by relating a story, using an object lesson, or singing a hymn together and having those present look in the hymn for the answer to a question.

Be Sensitive to the Spirit's Influence on Those Present

The Holy Ghost may prompt one or more of those you teach to contribute insights that others need to hear. Be open to promptings you receive to call on specific people. You may even feel impressed to ask a person who has not volunteered to express his or her views.

Find Ways for All to Participate

Those you teach will benefit from each other's participation. However, you may find yourself asking for comments only from those who raise their hands. Occasionally people choose not to participate because they have no opinion about the topic or prefer to give others the chance to speak. Or they may fear being wrong or think that they cannot express themselves as well as others. They may feel that they are not accepted by the group.

Be sensitive and prayerful as you consider each individual. You may decide to ask for a person's opinion about a topic rather than ask a factual question that he or she may not be able to answer. For example, rather than asking, "What gifts of the Spirit does Paul list in 1 Corinthians?" you could ask, "Why do you think charity is the greatest of all the gifts of the Spirit?" You may ask someone to prepare a brief presentation for a lesson; you may even help him or her prepare it. You may want to first befriend some individuals, letting them know that you value what they have to say.

Maintain the Focus of the Lessons

Occasionally learners share ideas that do not relate to the lesson. If you feel that a comment detracts from a lesson, you can guide the discussion back to the main points of the lesson by saying something such as, "That is an interesting observation, but I believe we are straying into another area. Could we leave that discussion for another time and get back to the original question?" Or you could say, "I don't think I am prepared to talk about that today. Perhaps we could discuss that idea another time."

There may also be times when you do not know the answer to a question. If this happens, simply say that you do not know. You may want to say that you will try to find the answer. Or you may want to invite learners to find the answer, giving them time in another lesson to report on what they have learned.

Maintain Order

Sometimes several learners may be anxious to comment on an idea. Encourage them to raise their hands when they wish to comment and to wait until you can call on them. Point out how much they can learn from one another, and invite them to listen respectfully to each other's ideas.

Occasionally an individual may disrupt a lesson by arguing with you and others, speaking irreverently, or raising controversial issues. Such a person introduces a spirit of contention, which makes it difficult to teach and can weaken the faith of some. For suggestions on how to work with such individuals, see "Helping Those Who Become Disruptive," pages 84–87.

Do Not Talk Too Much

Teachers who lecture most of the time or answer every question themselves tend to discourage learners from participating. You should be careful not to talk more than

necessary or to express your opinion too often. These actions can cause learners to lose interest. Think of yourself as a guide on a journey of learning who inserts appropriate comments to keep those you teach on the correct path.

Your main concern should be helping others learn the gospel, not making an impressive presentation. This includes providing opportunities for learners to teach one another. When an individual asks a question, consider inviting others to answer it instead of answering it yourself. For example, you could say, "That's an interesting question. What do the rest of you think?" or "Can anyone help with this question?"

Do Not End Discussions Too Soon

Be careful not to end good discussions too soon in an attempt to present all the material you have prepared. Although it is important to cover the material, it is more important to help learners feel the influence of the Spirit, resolve their questions, increase their understanding of the gospel, and deepen their commitment to keep the commandments.

Listen

Make every effort to listen sincerely to learners' comments. Your example will encourage them to listen carefully to one another. If you do not understand someone's comment, ask a question. You might say, "I'm not sure I understand. Could you explain that again?" or "Could you give me an example of what you mean?" (For additional help, see "Listening," pages 66–67.)

Acknowledge All Contributions

You can help those you teach feel more confident about their ability to participate in a discussion if you respond positively to every sincere comment. For example, you might say, "Thank you for your answer. That was very thoughtful" or "What a good idea! I had never thought of that before" or "That is a good example" or "I appreciate all that you have said today."

Never ridicule or criticize any question or comment, but show courtesy and love as you do your best to respond. When people feel that their comments are valued, they will share their experiences, feelings, and testimonies more freely (see "Teaching Others to Contribute to a Learning Atmosphere," pages 77–78; "How Teachers Can Contribute to a Learning Atmosphere," pages 79–81).

Rescue Learners Who Give Incorrect Answers

Occasionally someone might say something that is incorrect. You can rescue the learner with a response like

"I had not thought of it that way before." Or you might say, "Perhaps you are thinking of something else" or "I'm glad you brought that up." In some cases, you might take responsibility for an incorrect answer. For example, you could say, "I didn't make myself very clear, did I? I'm sorry."

Bringing Discussions to a Close

It is important to end discussions at the right time. Much of the spirit of an uplifting discussion is lost when it lasts too long. The following suggestions may help you:

- Manage the time. Know when the lesson should end. Give yourself enough time to summarize what has been said and to bear your testimony.

- Give learners a time limit. You could say something like, "We have time for only two more comments." Or you could say, "We'll listen to one more comment, and then I'll conclude with a final thought."

In addition to bringing discussions to a close at the right time, it is important to end discussions in the right way. When you end a discussion, thank the learners for participating. Then summarize the main points you have covered during the discussion or invite someone else to do so. Emphasize the gospel principles discussed. Review any new insights gained from the discussion, and encourage those you teach to use their deepened understanding in applying the principles to their lives. As prompted by the Spirit, bear your testimony or invite someone else to do so.

15

LISTENING

Listening is an expression of love. It often requires sacrifice. When we truly listen to others, we often give up what we want to say so they can express themselves.

How Careful Listening Can Help Those You Teach

As a teacher, you can do much good by listening. When you listen, you focus your teaching on the needs and interests of individuals. You demonstrate your respect for their ideas, opinions, and experiences. You show that you care about them individually. When they know that their insights are important to you, they are more likely to:

- Be receptive and enthusiastic.

- Share thoughts and experiences.

- Learn diligently.

- Live what they learn.

Some may suppose that listening attentively to one member of a group means ignoring the others and doing them a disservice. This is not so. Listening carefully to one person helps the others know that you care about individuals. And as you listen to family members or class members one at a time, you set an example for others to do the same.

How Careful Listening Can Help You as a Teacher

Your careful listening will help you as a teacher. As you listen with love and respect to learners' comments, you will be able to:

- Determine how actively learners are engaged in the learning process.

- Determine how much they are learning.

- Better understand their needs.

- Perceive and remove obstacles that may limit their learning, such as discouragement or preoccupation with other things.

- Better understand the questions that trouble them so you can guide them to answers.

- Know when to continue with a point that is important to them.

- Know when they need an opportunity to speak.

- Decide when to repeat specific principles or give more explanation.

- Know when to adapt a lesson presentation.

Listening will also bring great benefits to you personally. As you listen to those you teach, you will see that they have much to teach you.

Suggestions for More Effective Listening

How will those you teach know that you are listening? You can demonstrate that you are listening by displaying an expression of interest. You can look at the speaker rather than at your lesson materials or other things in the room. You can encourage the speaker to complete his or her thoughts without interruption. You can avoid jumping into conversations prematurely with advice or judgments. When you understand what is being said, you can make comments that show your understanding. When you do not understand, you can ask questions.

Consider the following ideas as you strive to increase your ability to listen.

Ask Questions

Questions such as the following can show that you care about each individual's ideas and feelings.

- Can you tell me more about that?

- How did you feel when that happened?

- I'm not sure I understand. Are you saying that . . . ?

- Would you explain that to me?

Pause

Do not be afraid of silence. People often need time to think about and reply to questions or to express what they are feeling. You might pause after you have asked a question, after a spiritual experience has been shared, or when a person is having difficulty expressing himself or herself. Be sure to give the speaker time to complete his or her thought before you respond. Of course, you should not pause for too long, especially when someone feels uncomfortable or pressured to speak.

Attend to What the Speaker Is Saying

Sometimes people have the tendency to think of what they are going to say rather than listen to what others are saying. Make sure you are really concentrating on the speaker rather than planning your response.

Attend to the Speaker's Unspoken Messages

People often communicate their feelings by the way they sit, their facial expressions, what they do with their hands, their tone of voice, and the movements of their eyes. These unspoken messages can help you understand the feelings of those you teach.

Restate What the Speaker Says

After listening for spoken and unspoken messages, you may want to restate what you have understood.

Summarize the messages in your own words to see if you have understood correctly. After doing this, you may check with the person by asking, "Is that what you were saying?" or "Do we need to talk more about that?" When you do this, be sure that you do not speak in a condescending manner.

Teach Learners to Listen to One Another

Remind learners that listening is one way we show love. The following suggestions may help you encourage learners to listen to one another:

- After one person has responded to a question or offered an insight, invite the others to either add to the comment or express a different opinion.

- When someone asks a question, redirect it to others rather than answer it yourself. For example, you could ask, "Would anyone care to answer that question?"

- In advance, ask one or more people to prepare to summarize the ideas that are shared during a discussion.

The Savior constantly watched and listened to those He taught, adjusting His teaching to the needs He perceived. For example, after teaching the Nephite people, He said, "Go ye unto your homes, and ponder upon the things which I have said" (3 Nephi 17:3). However, just as He was to leave, "he cast his eyes round about again on the multitude, and beheld they were in tears, and did look steadfastly upon him as if they would ask him to tarry a little longer with them" (3 Nephi 17:5). He perceived their needs and stayed longer to minister to them and teach them. As you listen carefully and respond appropriately to those you teach, you can help meet their needs for gospel learning.

16

TEACHING WITH QUESTIONS

Jesus Christ, the Master Teacher, often asked questions to encourage people to ponder and apply the principles He taught (see, for example, Matthew 16:13–15; Luke 7:41–42; 3 Nephi 27:27). His questions prompted thought, soul-searching, and commitment.

General Guidelines for Preparing Questions

Church-produced lesson manuals suggest many questions that you can use in lessons. Read them carefully to decide which will be most helpful for those you teach. You may also prepare your own questions. As you consider questions to use in a lesson, ask yourself, "Will they help those I teach understand the main ideas of the lesson? Will these questions help those I teach apply the gospel principles being taught?"

The following ideas may help you prepare your own questions.

Questions That Can Be Answered Yes or No

Questions that can be answered *yes* or *no* have limited use in gospel instruction. You should use them primarily to obtain commitments or to determine if someone agrees or disagrees.

Factual Questions

Factual questions are used to establish the basic facts of a scripture passage, event, or gospel principle. They have specific answers. They can help learners begin to study scripture passages, understand major points, review ideas, and overcome misconceptions. For example:

- When Nephi's brothers asked to be forgiven for binding him with cords, what was his immediate response?

- When and where was the Church organized?

Make sure that you do not ask only factual questions. They do not require much thought, and they may discourage those who do not know the answers. When you do use them, you should generally make sure that the information necessary to answer them is available to those you teach.

With factual questions, you can help everyone begin a discussion at the same point. You can then move to questions that prompt deeper thinking and help learners see how gospel principles apply in their lives.

Questions That Prompt Deeper Thinking

Some questions encourage learners to think deeply about the meaning of scripture passages and gospel principles. These questions often begin with the words *what, how,* or *why*. They cannot be answered with *yes* or *no,* and they usually have more than one right answer. For example:

- Why do you think this revelation came at this time in the history of the Church?

- What can this story teach about how the Lord helps those in need?

- How would you define faith?

- What does it mean to be meek?

- How is this object like the gospel principle we are discussing? (This is a good question to ask with an object lesson.)

- How was the reaction of Laman and Lemuel different from Nephi's reaction?

When asking such questions, be open to all answers (see "Listening," pages 66–67). Encourage learners to ponder the scriptures and gospel principles being discussed and to express their ideas. Do not try to get them to give specific answers to questions; they will quickly become aware of what you are doing and either stop participating or start guessing instead of thinking. When you need a specific answer, it is best to ask a factual question or present the information in some other way.

Questions That Help Learners Apply Gospel Principles

It is important to ask questions that help learners apply gospel principles in their lives. For example:

- How has this promise from the Lord been fulfilled in your life?

- How do we sometimes make the same error as the people in this story?

- How can God's chastening be a blessing to us?

- What are some circumstances today that are similar to the events in this scripture account?

- If you were this person, what would you do?

Ask learners to share examples of how they or others have applied the gospel principles being discussed. As prompted by the Spirit, encourage them to bear testimony of the principles they discuss.

General Guidelines for Asking Questions

Ask Questions That Learners Can Answer

Do not use questions to show your own knowledge. Ask questions that will prompt thoughtful answers from those you teach.

Respond to Incorrect Answers with Respect and Courtesy

Occasionally someone will give an incorrect answer or an answer that shows little understanding. Others in the group might laugh at such an answer. This might embarrass the individual and make him or her hesitant to participate in the future. It can interfere with his or her learning.

Respond to incorrect answers with respect and courtesy. Ensure that the individual still feels comfortable participating. You may choose to take responsibility yourself by saying something like, "I'm sorry. I don't think I asked that question very clearly. Let me try again." Or you could rescue the individual by saying, "Perhaps you were thinking of something else" or "Thank you for bringing that up, but I'm not sure my question was clear." Such responses will help those you teach feel more and more comfortable participating, even when they think they might be risking a wrong answer.

Wait for Responses

Do not be concerned if learners are silent for a few seconds after you have asked a question. Do not answer your own question; allow time for learners to think of responses.

However, prolonged silence may indicate that they do not understand the question and that you need to rephrase it.

Use Follow-Up Questions

Follow-up questions can help learners think more deeply about a principle they are discussing. For example, if learners suggest one way that a scripture account can be likened to themselves, you might ask, "What else can we learn from this story?"

Give Everyone an Opportunity to Speak

To encourage more learners to participate, you may want to direct some follow-up questions to those who have not yet made comments during the lesson.

If several people have comments about a subject, you may want to say something like, "We'll hear your comments first and then yours." Then those you teach will remain orderly because they know that they will have an opportunity to speak.

Help Learners Prepare to Answer Questions

To help learners prepare to answer questions, you may want to tell them before something is read or presented that you will be asking for their responses (see the "look for" and "listen for" approaches in "Teaching from the Scriptures," page 55). For example, you could say, "Listen as I read this passage so that you can share what most interests you about it" or "As this scripture is read, see if you can understand what the Lord is telling us about faith."

Avoid Questions That Create Controversy or Encourage Argument

The Savior said, "He that hath the spirit of contention is not of me" (3 Nephi 11:29; see also verses 28 and 30). Be careful not to ask questions that promote argument or highlight sensational issues. Do not ask questions that create doubt or that lead to discussions that fail to edify. Make sure that your questions move learners toward a unity of faith and love (see Mosiah 18:21). When there is disagreement, strive to emphasize points of agreement and correct doctrine.

Occasionally Ask Questions That Prompt Silent Reflection

You may occasionally choose to ask questions that learners should ponder silently rather than answer in an open discussion. For example:

- What have you done today that is moving you toward eternal life?

- Have you failed to do something today that would have moved you toward eternal life?

Creative Uses of Questions

You may want to use questions in some of the following ways:

- Write questions on wordstrips, and tape the wordstrips to the bottoms of chairs. At appropriate times during the discussion, ask each person to remove the question from his or her chair. Then have him or her read the question and respond to it.

- Ask each learner to write one question based on a gospel principle or verse of scripture. Gather the questions and discuss them.

- Ask individuals to role-play characters of their choice in the lesson, and let the others ask them questions (see "Role Playing," page 178). This works particularly well with children.

- During the week before the lesson, give questions to a few learners. Ask them to prepare to respond to those questions as part of the coming lesson.

- Use the following questions to discuss a gospel principle: "What do we already know about this principle?"

"What do we want to know?" "What have we learned today?" You can form the basis of the lesson by having learners answer these questions and then writing their answers in three columns on the chalkboard.

- Write a question on the chalkboard before class begins so that learners can begin pondering it as soon as they arrive.

- Have learners answer questions by finding and reading appropriate scriptures or hymns. Ask learners to respond to questions by sharing examples from their own lives.

- Divide the class into small groups. Give each group a few questions to consider. Then have each group report their answers to the class.

Additional Information

For additional help, see "Plan and Conduct Meaningful Discussions," pages 303–4 in the "Gospel Teaching and Leadership" section of the *Church Handbook of Instructions*.

17

HELPING LEARNERS BE ATTENTIVE

A Sunday School teacher shared the following insight about a lesson he had taught:

"I felt like I had taken the class on a hike through the forest. As we started to walk down the trail together, I pointed out interesting scriptural insights as we passed them along the way. I carefully explained the ideas of the lesson, like a guide would explain the different kinds of foliage found along a forest trail.

"At one point, I turned around, as it seemed, to look for my class members. I discovered they were quite a ways back on the scriptural trail. None of them had kept up with me. Some were lingering; some were stuck; others had wandered off the trail and were lost. It was as if I had to go back down the trail, gather the class up, and try to move forward again."

As this experience illustrates, a teacher can sometimes get "separated" from learners during lessons. Learners sometimes lose interest or become distracted.

How can teachers help learners remain attentive? There is no single answer to this question, but there are things you can do that will make a difference.

Observe and Listen to Those You Teach

You can often tell if those you teach are getting "separated" from you. You may notice that they are more restless than usual, that they are not reading along when others read scripture passages aloud, or that they are talking to each other about things that do not relate to the lesson. You may

sense a lack of thought or enthusiasm in their responses to questions that you ask.

Be careful when interpreting clues to learners' attentiveness. Some who appear to be "separated" may actually be following a lesson closely. For example, a class member who is not looking at you may be thinking about something that has been said in class or pondering a prompting he or she has received from the Holy Ghost.

When you are teaching by the Spirit, you will often be blessed to discern the attentiveness of those you teach. At times you may be prompted to make changes in a lesson to help redirect learners' attention.

How to Help Learners Be Attentive

The following suggestions can assist you as you help learners be attentive:

- Make the material relevant. Help those you teach see how the lesson material applies in their lives. If they cannot see how the material applies to them, they most likely will not be interested or attentive.

- Vary your teaching voice. Do you talk too slowly, too fast, too softly, too loudly? Do you use the same tone of voice, with little inflection? Is your speech clear? Are you enthusiastic about what you teach? How you use your voice can influence the attention level of those you teach.

- Maintain eye contact. Use eye contact as a way to draw learners into lessons. When you teach eye to eye, your attention is focused on those you are teaching, not on lesson materials. Making eye contact as you listen to their comments and questions helps them know that you are interested in what they have to say. Be careful not to let your eyes wander around the room as you speak. Arrange the chairs in the room so you can see each person's face and so each person can see your face. Young children will be more attentive if you sit close to them and talk to them at eye level.

- Use movement. Try moving about the room as you teach, but do not pace back and forth. Moving closer to learners when asking a question demonstrates your interest and invites a response. Appropriate hand and arm movements can help emphasize a lesson point. Move about in a natural way, consistent with your personality. If your movements are staged, unnatural, or overused, they might distract learners and cause them to lose interest in the lesson.

- Vary the pace of lessons. The pace at which you cover lesson material can influence learners' attentiveness. If the lesson moves too quickly, learners can become confused. If you cover the material too slowly, they can lose interest. Some parts of a lesson presentation can seem to drag on or become bogged down in discussions or stories. Some material may be important but less relevant than other material for those you teach. You should treat such material quickly so you can move to the main points of the lesson.

- Use a variety of teaching methods. Different teaching methods can help you vary the pace of a lesson, focus learners' attention at the beginning of the lesson, recapture their attention during the lesson, or make a transition from one part of the lesson to another. For example, discussions in small groups can instantly involve those who seem to be losing interest and concentration. (See "Teaching with Variety," pages 89–90.)

Individuals' Responsibility to Participate

As you seek to help learners be more attentive, remember that they are ultimately responsible for their own participation. If someone does not participate, do not pressure that person to participate. Instead, continue to be interested, respectful, and helpful, remembering this counsel from the Lord to priesthood bearers: "No power or influence can or ought to be maintained . . . , only by persuasion, by long-suffering, by gentleness and meekness, and by love unfeigned" (D&C 121:41).

18

HOW TO TELL
IF THEY ARE LEARNING

A Primary teacher was presenting a lesson to a class of nine-year-olds. The main principles of the lesson were that the President of the Church receives revelation for the entire Church and that individuals can receive personal revelation to guide them in their own lives. The lesson was well planned. It included scripture marking, chalkboard discussions, activities suggested in the lesson manual, and a review.

Toward the end of the lesson, the teacher asked a review question: "Who has the authority to receive revelation for the Church?" All the children raised their hands. They all knew the answer: the President of the Church.

Then the teacher asked, "What kinds of things can you receive revelation about?" There was no response. Because they had discussed this topic during the lesson, the teacher was surprised that no one answered the second question. The teacher reworded the question slightly, but again there was no response. Then Sarah, one of the class members, raised her hand and asked, "What does *revelation* mean, anyway?"

Because the class members had recited correct answers, the teacher had not realized that they did not understand the basic principles of the lesson. If Sarah had not asked a question, the lesson would have been incomplete for her and possibly for other class members. They would have learned very little that was meaningful to them. How could the teacher have made sure earlier in the lesson that everyone was understanding?

How to Determine If Learners Understand

Elder Boyd K. Packer taught: "The eyes of the alert teacher move constantly back and forth across the class, taking in each movement, recording each expression, responding quickly to disinterest or confusion. They read immediately a puzzled expression or sense at once when learning has taken place" (*Teach Ye Diligently,* rev. ed. [1991], 164–65).

By observing the progress of those you teach, you can sensitively make adjustments in the lesson presentation. For example, you can repeat or reemphasize ideas, stop for a discussion, share a story, or bear testimony. You can also know when to reach out to an individual. To be attentive and able to focus on learners, you must prepare well so you will not be overly dependent on notes or the lesson manual.

Some teaching methods can help you determine if learners understand the principles you are teaching. Consider the following suggestions:

- Ask learners to restate principles in their own words. This will help you know early in the lesson whether they understand certain words or ideas. If they do not understand, you can offer explanations that will make the rest of the lesson more meaningful for them.

- Use several short case studies. Plan the case studies so that some of them correctly illustrate the principles you are teaching and others do not. Ask those you teach to identify the case studies that apply the principles correctly. (See "Case Studies," pages 161–62.)

- Ask questions that require learners to express their understanding of the principles being taught. Learners' responses may indicate the need to review certain lesson points and adjust the lesson plan.

- Conduct a discussion. As you listen carefully to learners' comments, you will know whether they have a correct understanding of the principles you are teaching. Turn to the scriptures, teachings of latter-day prophets, or the lesson manual to correct, clarify, or reinforce important points. (See "Conducting Discussions," pages 63–65.)

19

HELPING OTHERS LIVE WHAT THEY LEARN

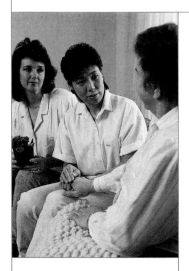

Jesus taught, "Not every one that saith unto me, Lord, Lord, shall enter into the kingdom of heaven; but he that doeth the will of my Father which is in heaven" (Matthew 7:21). It is not enough to know the gospel; we must live it.

One teacher shared the following analogy: "I have learned a great lesson from the letters of the alphabet. . . . We can repeat them frontwards or backwards, but when we do they have little meaning because they have not been put together with purpose and direction. When we put them together with real purpose and direction the result is sacred hymns, the scriptures, great poetry and prose, wonderful songs, and so on. As it is in the letters of the alphabet, so it is in our lives. . . . Action is important, but we need to have the right kind of action—purposeful action" (William H. Bennett, in Conference Report, Tonga Area Conference 1976, 15).

As a teacher, you can help others be "doers of the word, and not hearers only" (James 1:22). To accomplish this, you must teach in a way that will help learners apply gospel principles in their lives.

Ensure That Learners Understand the Principles You Teach

You can help learners understand gospel principles in a way that will enable them to apply them in their lives. For example, when a child earns or is given money, a father can explain what the scriptures and the latter-day prophets teach about tithing and how it is used. He can then help the child take 10 percent of the money, complete a donation receipt, place the money and the receipt in a tithing envelope, and give the envelope to the bishop.

Help Others Learn by the Spirit

It is not enough to simply understand gospel principles. For people to truly live what they learn, they must receive a witness that it is true. This will happen only when you teach by the Spirit and they learn by the Spirit (see "Inviting the Spirit As You Teach," pages 45–46).

Many different methods can be used to help others learn by the Spirit. For example, when you or those you teach share true stories about overcoming challenges, the Spirit can help learners gain courage to live the gospel. In one Aaronic Priesthood class, the teacher told vividly of his brother, who had quit smoking and had received great blessings for doing so. This story touched a young man in the class and inspired him to quit his own smoking habit.

Encourage Learners to "Go, and Do . . . Likewise"

After the Savior shared the parable of the good Samaritan, He commanded His listeners, "Go, and do thou likewise" (Luke 10:37). You should frequently invite learners to apply the principles they learn. Such assignments should be realistic and attainable. For example, in a lesson about prayer, you could encourage family members or class members to pray every morning and night. In a lesson about service, you could encourage them to help a neighbor in need.

You should normally follow up on the invitations you extend; this will help learners appreciate the importance of what is asked of them.

CREATE A LEARNING ATMOSPHERE

Order and self-discipline are essential for learning.
These qualities are best established when we love one another
and want to help each other grow. When we are considerate,
courteous, and reverent, we focus better on gospel learning.
The Spirit is with us more abundantly. Disruptions are less likely.

As teachers, we can do much to create an atmosphere of mutual
consideration. We should also teach others to help create a learning
atmosphere. In this way, we teach them to be better disciples of the
Savior, and we become better disciples ourselves.

20

PREPARING THE CLASSROOM

A comfortable and inviting environment for learning can contribute to learners' self-discipline, willingness to concentrate on lessons, and receptiveness to the Spirit. Whether you are a classroom teacher or a parent preparing for family home evening, you should do all you can to improve the physical surroundings in which you teach.

Suggestions for Preparing the Classroom

Cleanliness

Ensure that the area is clean. You may need to sweep, pick up papers, or erase the chalkboard. Also ensure that you are clean and modest in appearance.

Temperature

If possible, make sure the room is not too hot or too cold. If you teach in a Church classroom, you may need to work with your leaders to make the temperature comfortable.

Lighting

Ensure that the room has adequate lighting. Arrange the chairs so that the sun will not shine in anyone's eyes.

Personal Touches

Create warmth and interest by occasionally bringing something to improve the appearance of the room. For example, you could bring flowers or display pictures or objects that relate to the lesson.

Lesson Materials

Be sure you have all the lesson materials you need, such as chalk, an eraser, crayons, tape, or visual resources. If you are using any equipment, test it before you use it in a lesson. This will give you enough time to change your plans if the equipment is not working properly.

Seating

Arrange seating so that learners can see and hear you and each other. Try to make it possible for you to look each individual in the eye. Also ensure that the seating arrangement will allow everyone to see the chalkboard and other visual materials.

If possible, see that the chairs are comfortable. Children are more comfortable in chairs or benches that allow their feet to touch the floor. They may occasionally enjoy sitting on the floor. Chairs for adults and youth should be an appropriate size and should be arranged for easy access, with enough legroom.

When necessary, designate seating in a way that will separate children who disturb each other. Consider writing the children's names on pieces of paper and placing the pieces of paper on the backs of the chairs or on the floor in front of the chairs before class begins.

If more than one class must meet in the same room, arrange chairs so that the classes face away from each other on opposite ends of the room. If dividers are available, use them.

Space

Allow adequate space for the activities you plan. For example, if you are planning a dramatization, make sure there is enough room for the participants to stand and move about. For such activities in your home, you may need to rearrange furniture.

Asking Learners to Help You

As the teacher, you are responsible for the physical surroundings of the area in which you teach. But you do not need to make all the preparations yourself. Allow those you teach to participate in improving the learning environment. You may want to give them specific responsibilities, either regularly or occasionally.

21

TEACHING OTHERS TO CONTRIBUTE TO A LEARNING ATMOSPHERE

"Appoint among yourselves a teacher, and let not all be spokesmen at once; but let one speak at a time and let all listen unto his sayings, that when all have spoken that all may be edified of all" (D&C 88:122).

Characteristics of a Learning Atmosphere

When we meet to learn the gospel, we do not come together merely as teachers, students, and friends. We come together as brothers and sisters—children of Heavenly Father. Our baptismal covenant further unites us, for we share the responsibilities that Alma described to the Saints who had recently been baptized in the waters of Mormon: we should "look forward with one eye, having one faith and one baptism, having [our] hearts knit together in unity and in love one towards another" (Mosiah 18:21).

This understanding of our baptismal covenant should inspire us to help each other learn and live the gospel so we can return to live with our Father in Heaven. One way in which both learners and teachers can do this is to create a learning atmosphere.

In a learning atmosphere, we (1) edify each other through our participation, (2) love and help each other, and (3) desire to search for truth together.

Teachers and learners edify each other through their participation. We edify each other when we listen carefully to each other's comments, participate in discussions and other learning activities, ask thoughtful questions, pray together, offer personal experiences and insights, and bear testimony (see D&C 88:122).

Teachers and learners love and help one another. People learn more effectively when they feel that they are among friends who care about them. If they feel that they might be ridiculed or embarrassed, they will be less likely to contribute to lessons and grow in the gospel. We can show by our words and actions that we care about them and that we want them to progress. The following counsel from Elder Henry B. Eyring relates to the love we should feel when we meet to learn the gospel: "Our Heavenly Father wants our hearts to be knit together. That union in love is not simply an ideal. It is a necessity" (in Conference Report, Apr. 1998, 85; or *Ensign*, May 1998, 66).

Teachers and learners all desire to search for truth. As we join with one another in the grand purpose of learning to understand and live the gospel, our opportunities for learning increase. When we become more unified in our search for truth, we invite the Spirit of the Lord to be with us in abundance.

Teaching Others about a Learning Atmosphere

Part of your responsibility as a teacher is to help learners understand what they can do to create an atmosphere conducive to learning. Each learner is responsible for helping the others have a good learning experience. As you strive to establish a learning atmosphere in your class, you are not merely correcting behavior or making sure that your presentation is not interrupted. You are fulfilling your divine commission to help others become better disciples of the Savior.

To teach family members or class members to contribute to a learning atmosphere, consider conducting a discussion using the following suggestions:

- Express your feelings about the gospel, and explain that you want to help others learn gospel truths.

- Discuss the responsibility we have to help one another learn the gospel (see page 77).

- Talk about the importance of participating in lessons.

- Ask those present to suggest things they can do to help create a learning atmosphere.

A teacher who had been called to teach the seven- and eight-year-olds in Primary conducted such a discussion the first time she met with the class. "My dear friends," she said that Sunday morning, "the bishop has called me to be your teacher. He laid his hands on my head and blessed me that I will be able to understand you, love you, and teach you true things. This makes me so happy. In our class I will try to prepare lessons that are interesting and true. I will be sure to give you many opportunities to ask and answer questions, to sing, to listen to stories, and to tell me things that you know are true."

The teacher continued: "Before we were born, all of us lived with our Heavenly Father. We are His children, and so we are brothers and sisters. In our class we want to help each other learn so that we can return to live with Heavenly Father again. What are some things that each of us can do to help others in the class learn the important things we will be talking about? Let's each think of something we can do."

The teacher listed the class members' ideas on the chalkboard. The list included such things as treating each other kindly, participating in the lessons, sharing experiences and testimonies, listening, and trying hard to understand the gospel principles.

Then the teacher asked, "Can you think of anything that would interfere with our learning?" She made another list on the chalkboard. This list included such things as making fun of someone and talking while someone else is talking.

From these two lists the teacher and class members made a few class rules describing what they should expect from one another.

This was not the only time the teacher talked about these principles. She discussed them privately with class members from time to time and, as needed, with the class as a whole.

As you prepare to teach, consider how you can adapt this teacher's approach or use other ideas to help others contribute to a learning environment. If you are observant and prayerful, you will find many opportunities to teach that learning occurs best when we (1) edify each other through our participation, (2) love and help each other, and (3) desire to search for truth together.

Additional Information

For more on creating a learning atmosphere, see lessons 6 and 7 in the Teaching the Gospel course (pages 213–21).

22

HOW TEACHERS CAN CONTRIBUTE TO A LEARNING ATMOSPHERE

"The preacher was no better than the hearer, neither was the teacher any better than the learner; and thus they were all equal, and they did all labor, every man according to his strength" (Alma 1:26).

In addition to helping learners understand how they can contribute to a learning atmosphere (see pages 77–78), there are a number of things that you as a teacher can do to contribute to such an atmosphere.

Prepare Yourself Spiritually

Your own spiritual preparation contributes much to the learning atmosphere in the home or classroom. When you are prepared spiritually, you bring a spirit of peace, love, and reverence. Those you teach feel more secure in pondering and discussing things of eternal worth. When you are upset, preoccupied, angry, or critical and have not prepared spiritually, they may be less able to learn by the Spirit. (For suggestions on preparing yourself spiritually, see pages 11–20.)

Love and Reach Out to Each Individual

Jesus said, "A new commandment I give unto you, That ye love one another; as I have loved you, that ye also love one another" (John 13:34). You should seek to love those you teach—not only when they are easy to love, but also when they try your patience (see "Seeking the Gift of Charity," page 12).

Each person you teach is precious in the sight of the Lord, and each person should be precious in your sight as well. Find ways to reach out to each person you teach (see "Reaching Out to the One," pages 35–36). As those you teach realize that you love them and are concerned about them, they

will learn to trust you. They will become more teachable and less likely to cause disruptions (see "Love Softens Hearts," pages 31–32).

Dress Appropriately

Your dress and appearance should not detract from the lesson. If you teach youth, you do not need to dress like them to gain their confidence.

Greet Learners Warmly

If you are a classroom teacher, smile as class members enter the room. Greet individuals with a handshake. Tell them that you are glad to see them. Express appreciation for them. Just one or two sentences of warm greeting can put them at ease and help them prepare to learn.

You can also make family home evening and family scripture study special occasions by extending a warm welcome to each family member as you begin.

Begin in a Manner That Invites Attention

There will often be informal conversation and activity before you teach a lesson. One of your responsibilities is to bring that activity to a close and help everyone focus their attention on learning. This may include leading class members to their places or playing a recording of a hymn. It may require simply looking into the eyes of each person before asking someone to offer the opening prayer. Occasionally you may choose to offer the opening prayer yourself. (See "Beginning the Lesson," page 93.)

Children usually live up to what they feel others expect from them. When you express positive feelings to them, you help them maintain a good learning atmosphere. Some examples of positive comments you might make are listed below:

- *Each of you is special. Each of you is truly a child of God. There is no one else just like you anywhere in the world.*

- *You have helped make our lesson interesting by telling about your experiences.*

- *It makes me happy when we work together so well.*

- *I know Heavenly Father is pleased with each one of us today.*

- *I appreciate the good things you do. We are all trying to do what is right.*

- *We should take turns talking. Every person has good ideas, and we need to listen to each other.*

Encourage Mutual Respect

Invite learners to think of things they can do to help each other feel loved and appreciated. By the things you do and say, those you teach can learn to show respect for one another. Your responses to questions can show them how to respond respectfully to each other's comments and questions (see "Listening," pages 66–67). Reassure them that all sincere questions will be welcome. One person's questions may help you clarify principles that others also do not understand.

Encourage Enthusiasm for Learning the Gospel

Learners may come to class for a variety of reasons. However, when they arrive you should help them focus with enthusiasm on one purpose: learning the gospel. You can do this by helping them see that the gospel will help them solve their problems, enrich their lives, and increase their happiness.

Encourage those you teach to come to class prepared to learn and participate. When they are striving individually to learn the gospel, they are more likely to contribute to the learning atmosphere during lessons (see "Helping Individuals Take Responsibility for Learning the Gospel," pages 61–62).

Simple out-of-class assignments sometimes help, especially when they encourage learners to apply gospel principles in everyday life (see "Helping Others Live What They Learn," page 74). When you give out-of-class assignments, you should usually give class members an opportunity to report later. This will help them understand the value you place on what they have learned and accomplished.

Teach of Christ

Everything we teach should point family members and class members to Christ— to His redemptive mission, His perfect example, His ordinances and covenants, and His commandments. Remember this as you prepare and present your lessons.

It will bring a spirit of unity and hope to the learning atmosphere.

Use a Variety of Teaching Methods That Invite Participation

The learning atmosphere is enhanced when all present are interested in the lesson and participate in discussions and other activities. To help maintain a high level of interest and participation, use a variety of teaching methods (see "Teaching with Variety," pages 89–90).

Share Your Feelings, Experiences, and Testimony

As you share your feelings, experiences, and testimony, others may be inspired to do the same. This will strengthen those who share as well as those who listen. New converts especially may need to see that in the Church we all teach and learn from one another, regardless of our level of experience. Each person has something to contribute. We listen to each other's contributions so that "all may be edified of all" (D&C 88:122).

Additional Suggestions for Those Who Teach Children

Express Positive Feelings to the Children

When children are criticized or spoken to in a negative way, they often feel inadequate or rejected. They may try to gain attention by disturbing other children or otherwise misbehaving. On the other hand, positive comments will help them understand that you expect the best from them. Recognize and thank them for the good things they do, and ignore minor problems. As you do so, they will begin to feel that they are accepted, loved, and understood. (For more suggestions, see the videocassettes *Primary Leader Training* and *Teach the Child.*)

Set and Maintain Standards

Children need and appreciate rules and limits. Work with the children you teach to establish a few simple, clear rules (no more than three or four). This will help

Scolding	Understanding
You always cause a disturbance in the class. I'm tired of it.	I know it's sometimes hard to sit still, but you'll have to do your very best for a little longer. Would it help if you sat here by me?
Why can't you keep your hands off the other children?	It is tempting to tease other people, but we don't tease. It keeps all of us from learning.
How can you be so thoughtless of others?	Sometimes you may feel like saying unkind things to others, but in our class we try very hard to be kind and thoughtful. Let's try to help others feel the way we like to feel.
You're not paying a bit of attention to me. Turn around immediately!	It's hard for me to teach when I can't see your eyes, so I need you to help me by paying close attention.
Stop this rowdiness! I won't put up with it another minute!	Everyone seems tired and restless. Let's stand up for a minute and stretch.

them govern themselves. Explain that following the rules helps everyone enjoy learning together. Also discuss what will happen when rules are broken. You may want to decide together on a signal for restoring order, such as the teacher standing with folded arms.

After you and the children have established a few rules, make a chart listing the rules. If the children cannot read, use drawings to show how they should act. Whenever a child breaks one of the rules, stop the lesson and calmly ask, "What is the rule?" Patiently wait until the child repeats the rule. Ask him or her to suggest how to follow the rule. Then continue with the lesson.

Help the Children Participate

Keep the children busy and interested by presenting lessons that include a variety of activities. This is probably the best way to prevent disruptive conduct. When you teach, look the children in the eye; if you read out of the lesson manual, you may lose their attention. If children become restless, say things like "We need your best thinking to answer this question" or "Will you hold the picture for the whole class to see?" Ignore most minor

disturbances, and try to shift the children's attention to something else. For example, you could say, "You're going to be interested in what comes next" or "Please raise your hand when you think you know the answer."

Be Understanding

Make sure the children know that you understand and love them, even in difficult times. Remember that they need understanding more than scolding, so be patient and courteous with them. As you do these things, you can help turn difficult situations into opportunities for them to learn. The chart on this page illustrates the difference between scolding and understanding.

Do not expect perfection from yourself or the children. Have a happy, positive attitude that helps the children know that you love them. Help the children see that problems can be solved harmoniously.

Additional Information

For more information on creating a learning atmosphere, see lessons 6 and 7 in the Teaching the Gospel course (pages 213–21).

23

REVERENCE

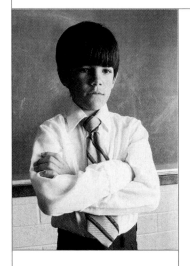

Elder Boyd K. Packer taught:

"When we meet to learn the doctrines of the gospel, it should be in a spirit of reverence. . . .

"The world grows increasingly noisy. . . .

"This trend to more noise, more excitement, more contention, less restraint, less dignity, less formality is not coincidental nor innocent nor harmless.

"The first order issued by a commander mounting a military invasion is the jamming of the channels of communication of those he intends to conquer.

"Irreverence suits the purposes of the adversary by obstructing the delicate channels of revelation in both mind and spirit. . . .

" . . . Reverence invites revelation" (in Conference Report, Oct. 1991, 27–28; or *Ensign*, Nov. 1991, 21–22).

President David O. McKay said that "reverence is profound respect mingled with love" (in Conference Report, Apr. 1967, 86; or *Improvement Era*, June 1967, 82).

Elder L. Tom Perry observed, "Reverence flows from our admiration and respect for Deity" (in Conference Report, Oct. 1990, 90; or *Ensign*, Nov. 1990, 70).

President Spencer W. Kimball counseled: "True reverence is a vital quality, but one that is fast disappearing in the world as the forces of evil broaden their influences. We cannot fully comprehend the power for good we can wield if the millions of members of Christ's true church will serve as models of reverent behavior. We cannot imagine the additional numbers of lives we could touch. Perhaps even more impor-

tant, we cannot foresee the great spiritual impact on our own families if we become the reverent people we know we should be" (*The Teachings of Spencer W. Kimball*, ed. Edward L. Kimball [1982], 224–25).

These statements by latter-day prophets, seers, and revelators show that reverence is much more than being quiet and sitting still during a lesson. It is an attitude that permeates all righteous behavior. It is manifest in our respect and love toward God and each other. A Primary song teaches:

Rev'rence is more than just quietly
  sitting:
It's thinking of Father above,
A feeling I get when I think of his
  blessings.
I'm rev'rent, for rev'rence is love.
[*Children's Songbook*, 31]

Setting an Example of Reverence

To be able to teach others to be reverent, we must be reverent ourselves. We must reflect President McKay's definition of reverence: "profound respect mingled with love." The following suggestions may help you consider your efforts to be reverent.

- Keep the sacramental covenants to remember the Lord always and take His name upon yourself (see D&C 20:77, 79). Strive to always think of Him and His goodness and to "stand as [a witness] of God at all times and in all things, and in all places" (Mosiah 18:9).

- Use the names of Deity appropriately and reverently. Elder Dallin H. Oaks taught: "When the names of God the Father and his Son, Jesus Christ, are used with reverence and authority, they invoke a power beyond what mortal man can comprehend. It should be obvious to every believer that these mighty names—by which miracles are wrought, by which the world was formed, through which man was created, and by which we can be saved—are holy and must be treated with the utmost reverence" (in Conference Report, Apr. 1986, 67; or *Ensign*, May 1986, 51).

- Show proper respect for General Authorities, Area Authority Seventies, members of general auxiliary presidencies, and local priesthood and auxiliary leaders. Always use their titles, such as "President," "Elder," "Bishop," or "Sister," when addressing them and talking about them. Address and refer to other adults in the Church as "Brother" and "Sister."

- Avoid using coarse language or words that demean, belittle, or criticize others. Use courteous language, such as "please," "thank you," and "excuse me," with family members as well as others.

- Show proper respect when handling the scriptures and using the Lord's property (such as buildings and surrounding grounds, furnishings, and books).

Specific Ways to Teach Reverent Conduct

Although your example is often all that is needed to help others be more reverent, at times you may need to specifically teach reverent conduct. This may be especially necessary with children and youth.

A teacher of 10- and 11-year-old girls learned the necessity of giving specific instructions about reverence. During a lesson about the mission and martyrdom of the Prophet Joseph Smith, the girls became silly and disrespectful. The teacher listened in unhappy disbelief to the irreverent comments and took a silent moment to decide what to do. Then, with emotion in her voice, she announced firmly that their talk and laughter were inappropriate and that their words offended the deep reverence she felt for Joseph Smith and his experiences. They immediately became quiet. She told them that she loved them and enjoyed teaching their class but that she could not allow such behavior. It was a sobering experience for both the teacher and the class members.

The following suggestions may help you encourage others to be reverent.

- Set limits. Define behavior that is acceptable and behavior that is unacceptable. For example, do not allow language that makes light of sacred things or that is vulgar, profane, or unkind. Discourage impolite behavior, such as eating or going in and out of the room during the lesson. As those you teach interact with one another and with you, encourage them to listen to one another without interrupting. Also encourage them to use courteous language, such as "please," "thank you," and "excuse me."

- Organize and prepare so that there will be as little confusion as possible. If you are a classroom teacher, arrive early to the classroom.

- Begin and end on time. This will show respect for those you teach.

- Speak in a pleasant, courteous manner. Always greet those you teach with a smile.

- Be considerate of learners' contributions to discussions.

- If you teach children, anticipate simple things you can do to remind them to be reverent. You may be able to restore a reverent atmosphere by quietly singing or humming a reverent song, displaying a picture, or using a hand signal that the children recognize as a reminder to be reverent.

- Remember that it is especially difficult for children to sit still for long periods of time. Help children listen and participate actively. Give them breaks periodically.

- Take time to explain the importance of reverence, especially to children. Explain the purpose of prelude music. Talk about why it is important to listen, participate in the singing, and talk quietly. Help children understand that reverent behavior pleases Heavenly Father. Explain that as they are reverent, they will feel good inside and their testimonies will grow.

- Do not reward reverent behavior with prizes or food. Do not have contests to see who can be the most reverent. These tend to focus on the wrong things. Teach about the real rewards of reverence, such as increased understanding and the influence of the Spirit.

- Use music. Elder Boyd K. Packer said: "Music can set an atmosphere of worship which invites [the] spirit of revelation, of testimony" (in Conference Report, Oct. 1991, 28; or *Ensign*, Nov. 1991, 22). Use prelude music to set a reverent tone. Use music in the lessons you teach.

- Help learners recognize the influence of the Spirit. Bear your testimony as prompted.

- Center all your teaching on the Savior. Display a picture of the Savior in the classroom.

24

HELPING THOSE WHO BECOME DISRUPTIVE

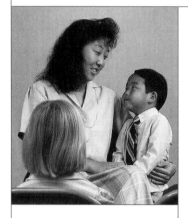

Elder Boyd K. Packer taught:

"It is essential for a teacher to understand that people are basically good. It is essential to know that their tendency is to do the thing that is right. Such an exalted thought is productive of faith. It makes all the difference when we stand before our own children or go before a class of young people to teach them.

" . . . If we are to teach, we must constantly remind ourselves that we are dealing with the sons and daughters of God and that each, being His offspring, has the possibility of becoming as He is" (Teach Ye Diligently, *rev. ed. [1991], 89).*

Speaking about the environment in the home, President Gordon B. Hinckley said: "When little problems occur, as they inevitably will, restrain yourself. Call to mind the wisdom of the ancient proverb: 'A soft answer turneth away wrath.' (Prov. 15:1.) There is no discipline in all the world like the discipline of love. It has a magic all its own" ("The Environment of Our Homes," *Ensign,* June 1985, 6).

As President Hinckley observed, little problems will inevitably occur. Whether you are teaching in the home or at church, your lessons may at times be disrupted by the behavior of those you teach. In your efforts to help those who become disruptive, remember that you should not simply try to correct inappropriate behavior or make sure everyone is quiet; you should help learners become better disciples of the Savior. The following information will help you handle disruptions in a Christlike way.

Remember the Worth of Souls

The Lord counseled, "Remember that the worth of souls is great in the sight of God" (D&C 18:10). Those you teach have divine characteristics and divine destinies. Your responses to their actions can help them remember their infinite worth as sons and daughters of God. Through your example, you can help them increase in their desire to help each other learn the gospel and live according to its principles.

Seek to Understand Those You Teach

As you think about ways to help those who become disruptive, consider all pos-

sible reasons for their behavior, including the classroom environment. Pray for the guidance of the Spirit. Sometimes people act disruptively because of something you do or something another person does. Sometimes they speak and act improperly because they are troubled, angry, tired, or frustrated. You should carefully review these possibilities as you think about the causes of problems. When you understand those you teach, you will be able to help them contribute to lessons in positive ways. (See "Understanding Those You Teach," pages 33–34. To review the needs of learners in different age-groups, see "Teaching Children," pages 108–9; "Age Characteristics of Children," pages 110–16; "Understanding and Teaching Youth," pages 118–20; "Understanding and Teaching Adults," pages 123–24.)

Evaluate Your Own Efforts

When those you teach behave disruptively, it is easy to focus on their conduct and fail to review your own. But the Savior said: "How wilt thou say to thy brother: Let me pull the mote out of thine eye—and behold, a beam is in thine own eye? . . . First cast the beam out of thine own eye; and then shalt thou see clearly to cast the mote out of thy brother's eye" (3 Nephi 14:4–5).

In your efforts to solve problems with disruptions, first consider whether the real source of the problem is something that you are doing. Ask yourself, "Am I keeping the Savior and His doctrine at the center of my teaching? Am I doing all I can to teach by the Spirit? Have I helped those I teach take responsibility for their learning? Have I helped them contribute to a learning atmosphere? Do I give them the opportunity to learn from one another? Could I improve my lesson preparation? Am I continually seeking to improve as a teacher?"

Examine the teaching methods you are using. Ask yourself, "Do they help those I teach understand and apply gospel truths? Am I using a variety of methods in order to help those I teach stay interested and participate actively?"

Evaluate Your Motives

The Lord taught that those who have desires to assist in His work must "be humble and full of love, having faith, hope, and charity" (D&C 12:8). Only those who are motivated by love will have a positive, powerful influence on those they teach. Pray to be filled with Christlike love toward every person you teach, especially those who sometimes behave inappropriately. (See "Seeking the Gift of Charity," page 12; "Love Softens Hearts," pages 31–32.)

Ask yourself, "Am I more concerned about helping others learn the gospel or about presenting my lesson material without interference?" Think about the experience class members are having rather than the experience you are having. As you continually reach beyond your own needs to the hearts of those you teach, they will feel more comfortable participating in edifying ways.

Help All Class Members Contribute to a Learning Atmosphere

From time to time, you may want to review with learners the principles that will help them contribute to a learning atmosphere (see "Teaching Others to Contribute to a Learning Atmosphere," pages 77–78). Remind them of their responsibility to participate in discussions, allow each other to contribute, listen to one another, and bring their scriptures. Also tell them what you will do as the teacher to contribute to this learning environment.

Assure them that you will prepare well to teach them and that you will conduct discussions and other activities that will give them all the opportunity to participate.

Respond in Simple Ways to Occasional Disturbances

Sometimes it is best to simply ignore small disturbances and focus on good behavior. When you need to respond to an occasional disruption, consider the following suggestions:

- Be silent. Wait quietly until the person stops talking or being disruptive.

- Move closer to the person being disruptive. This small action can serve as a quiet reminder to be more attentive.

- Use light humor. With a lighthearted touch, you may be able to turn the person back to the lesson. However, you should never be sarcastic or use humor to embarrass or control.

- Help the person participate in positive ways. Consider asking him or her to read, paraphrase something, give an example, or respond in some other way. The point of this idea is not to humiliate the person but to invite him or her to participate.

- Help everyone participate. If one person dominates a discussion, make an effort to call on those who have not yet contributed. Give them the first opportunity to answer questions. If this does not work, gently turn the focus away from the individual and back to the class by saying, "Let's hear from someone else" or "You have made several interesting comments. Would someone else like to add to what has been said?" (For specific suggestions about conducting discussions, see "Conducting Discussions," pages 63–65; "Teaching with Questions," pages 68–70.)

- Redirect discussions that do not invite the Spirit. If someone argues with you or others, speaks irreverently, or raises controversial issues, use love and meekness when deciding how to respond. You may simply say something like, "That is an interesting observation, but it will probably take us away from today's lesson."

- Introduce a different activity. Provide an immediate break by changing to an activity that requires different participation.

Make Special Efforts to Help Those Who Persistently Cause Disruptions

In spite of your efforts to create a learning atmosphere, someone may persistently disrupt the lessons you teach. If someone is seriously disrupting the learning of others, you should neither ignore the problem nor act in an unkind way. In such a situation, remember the Lord's instruction to maintain influence only "by persuasion, by long-suffering, by gentleness and meekness, and by love unfeigned;

"By kindness, and pure knowledge, which shall greatly enlarge the soul without hypocrisy, and without guile—

"Reproving betimes with sharpness, when moved upon by the Holy Ghost; and then showing forth afterwards an increase of love toward him whom thou hast reproved, lest he esteem thee to be his enemy;

"That he may know that thy faithfulness is stronger than the cords of death" (D&C 121:41–44).

In applying this counsel, it is helpful to understand the words *betimes* and *sharpness*. *Betimes* means promptly or in good time. In this passage, *sharpness* refers to the need to give clear, well-defined instructions.

You should be gentle and meek when giving correction. Note that reproving should be done only "when moved upon by the Holy Ghost" and should be followed by an increase of love.

The following suggestions may help you if someone you teach becomes persistently disruptive. You can find ways to adapt some of these suggestions for use at home.

Speak Privately with the Person

It is sometimes helpful to speak privately with a person who persistently causes disruptions. You should do so tactfully and with love. Describe the conduct that is disruptive while at the same time making clear that you love and respect the person. Ask for the person's support, and try to find solutions together. Then do all you can to show increased love. As Brigham Young counseled, "Never chasten beyond the balm you have within you to bind up" (in *Discourses of Brigham Young,* sel. John A. Widtsoe [1941], 278).

Seek Help from Others

Your leaders want to help you with your teaching challenges. You can benefit from their ideas and assistance. For example, they might ask someone to help with certain activities or sit next to a child who is misbehaving. In your regular contact with a leader in your organization, you can discuss ways to help individuals in your class (see "Obtaining Support from Your Leaders," page 28).

You may want to ask one of your leaders to attend your class and give special attention to the learning atmosphere during the lesson. After class, discuss the problem with the leader and work out solutions together. Continue to counsel with your leaders as you implement solutions.

If a child or youth has a pattern of disruptive behavior, seek the help of his or her parents. Parents want to know about their children's behavior, and they are willing to help. If possible, include the young person in these conversations; this will show your respect for his or her maturity and agency. Together you can make specific plans and later review your progress.

If the person causing disruptions has special needs, learn what you can do to help him or her learn more effectively and behave more appropriately (see "Teaching Those with Disabilities," pages 38–39; see also "Ministering to Members Who Have Disabilities," pages 310–14 in the "Gospel Teaching and Leadership" section of the *Church Handbook of Instructions*).

Be Patient

Remember that change takes time. Keep working patiently, and never give up on someone who is having problems. Be consistently positive in your approach to the person. Do not be discouraged if he or she has a negative attitude in class. Even if the person seems to be getting little out of the lessons you teach, he or she still has the

opportunity to learn about the gospel of Jesus Christ and feel the influence of the Spirit. He or she also has the opportunity to be with a loving teacher and caring leaders and friends.

Specific Suggestions for Primary Teachers

If a child is causing a disruption, kindly ask him or her to stop. For example, if a class member named Linda is disturbing another class member, you could say, "Linda, please do not do that." Thank her if she obeys. If she does not, state your request more firmly, but still with kindness: "Linda, you need to stop doing that now." Thank her if she obeys.

If she still does not comply, arrange to talk privately with her about what is expected in class. Tell her what bothers you and why. For example, you could say, "Linda, I was disturbed about what happened in class today. We cannot learn when the class is not reverent." Then you could ask her how she feels about the situation. After listening attentively to her response, you could let her know that you understand her feelings. Perhaps you could say, "I understand that you feel restless and that it's hard to sit still." Then ask, "How can we solve this together?

What can I do to help? What will you do?" Discuss a solution together.

After speaking with Linda, you would need to develop your own plan to help her and the class if her disruptions continue. The plan might include any of the following actions:

- Move a chair away from the other children. Have Linda sit there quietly for a short period of time, such as two minutes. During this time, do not interact with the child. Invite her into the group when she has been quiet for the assigned time.

- Ask a member of the Primary presidency or another leader to take the child to a vacant room or quiet place in the meetinghouse where the parents can help. You might say, "I am sorry you have not kept the class rules, Linda. Sister Davis will take you to talk with your parents. I hope you will be back soon. When you have decided to keep the rules, you may come back to class." The leader should stay with the child. When the child is in control again, she can be invited back into the group. Let her know that she is loved and that she is an important part of the class.

USE EFFECTIVE METHODS

To help others want to learn, our teaching must be interesting.
To help them understand, our teaching must be clear.
To help them retain and ponder what they learn, our teaching must be memorable.
These are the reasons for selecting teaching methods carefully and
using them effectively: to make lessons interesting, clear, and memorable.

25

TEACHING WITH VARIETY

President David O. McKay said, "Every teacher has the responsibility of determining how best to approach the members of the class in order to make appeals that will be lasting" (Gospel Ideals [1953], 439).

Using a Variety of Methods from Lesson to Lesson

When a homemaker plans a week of dinner menus, she is not likely to decide to prepare identical meals on seven consecutive nights. Even when her budget is so limited that she has to prepare potatoes every night, she soon learns that there are many ways to serve potatoes.

The gospel can likewise be presented in a number of different ways. No teacher should fall into a monotonous pattern of presenting the same kind of lesson week after week. When you use a variety of learning activities, learners tend to understand gospel principles better and retain more. A carefully selected method can make a principle clearer, more interesting, and more memorable.

As you prepare to teach, ensure that you use a variety of teaching methods from lesson to lesson. This may mean using something as simple as a colorful poster or wall chart in one lesson and a list of questions on the chalkboard in another.

Using a Variety of Methods in Each Lesson

In addition to using a variety of methods from lesson to lesson, you should teach each lesson with variety. Children, with their natural curiosity, respond especially well to a variety of learning activities—usually between five and seven per lesson. Youth also respond well to a variety of methods. Even if you teach adults, you should consider using at least three methods in each lesson.

Selecting and Preparing a Variety of Teaching Methods

There are many resources available to help you choose methods when preparing your lessons. Keep in mind the following ideas as you plan which methods to use in a particular lesson:

- Consider first the suggestions given in the lesson manual. When necessary, adapt them to the needs of those you teach.

- Have a definite purpose for using a method. Choose methods that support and reinforce the main purpose of the lesson. They should be true to fact and life and emphasize truth, goodness, and beauty. Do not choose methods merely to amuse or take up time.

- Select methods that are appropriate and effective. Some methods, such as stories and using the chalkboard, will be used far more frequently than others, such as panel discussions and games. (See "Choosing Appropriate Methods," page 91; "Choosing Effective Methods," page 92.)

- When appropriate, choose methods that actively engage the learners. This is important for all learners, but especially for children.

- Practice using the methods before you teach the lesson. This is especially important if you have not used a particular method before.

Keeping Variety in Your Lessons

The chart on page 90 can help you determine if there is enough variety in your lessons. You may want to make a similar chart in your journal or in a notebook. At the top of the blank columns, write the title of each of your next five lessons. As you prepare the lessons, put a check in the "lesson" column opposite each method you use.

The methods listed at the top of the chart are those most commonly used in gospel teaching. You may find yourself using some of these methods in almost all of your lessons. The other methods listed can also be effective depending on what you are teaching and the needs of those you teach.

As you use this chart, you may begin to see patterns in your teaching. There may be some methods that you use in every lesson and others that you never use.

METHODS I CAN USE	Lesson	Lesson	Lesson	Lesson	Lesson
Commonly Used Methods					
Chalkboard					
Comparisons and Object Lessons					
Discussions					
Examples					
Lectures					
Likening					
Music					
Questions					
Scriptures					
Stories					
Visuals					
Other Methods					
Activity Verses					
Application Techniques					
Attention Activities					
Audiovisual Materials					
Brainstorming					
Buzz Sessions					
Case Studies					
Demonstrations					
Dioramas					
Dramatizations					
Drawing Activities					
Flannel Boards					
Games					
Guest Speakers					
Maps					
Memorization					
Overhead Projectors					
Panel Discussions					
Paper Stand-Up Figures					
Pictures					
Readers' Theaters					
Role Playing					
Roller Boxes					
Special Reports					
Stations					
Work Sheets					

26

CHOOSING APPROPRIATE METHODS

As a gospel teacher, you stand as the Lord's representative before those you teach. You should ensure that all you do is in accordance with His will and that in each lesson you show reverence for gospel truths.

The Lord has said, "Remember that that which cometh from above is sacred, and must be spoken with care, and by constraint of the Spirit" (D&C 63:64). The methods you use to teach gospel truths will help develop learners' sensitivity toward sacred things. Therefore, you should ensure that the methods are appropriate for the principles being taught and that they are in keeping with Church standards. While there may be several methods that could help you communicate a certain message, some of these methods may be inappropriate for a particular lesson because of the subject matter or the ages or experiences of those you teach.

Whenever you consider using a particular method, ask yourself the following questions to ensure that the method is appropriate.

Will the method invite the Spirit?

The Spirit must be present for a gospel message to be carried to the hearts of those you teach (see 2 Nephi 33:1; D&C 42:14). Therefore, you should use methods that will set the proper tone for the lesson and invite the Spirit. For example, one Gospel Doctrine teacher used music to discuss the martyrdom of the Prophet Joseph Smith. In preparation for the lesson, the teacher invited a ward member to prepare to sing "A Poor Wayfaring Man of Grief" (*Hymns*, no. 29). In class, the hymn directed class members' thoughts and feelings to the moment shortly before the mob attacked, when John Taylor sang this hymn to his brethren in Carthage Jail. The Spirit carried the sweetness and the gravity of that moment into the class members' hearts.

Does the method match the sacredness of the principles I am teaching?

Some teaching methods are more lighthearted and informal than others and are therefore appropriate only in certain lessons. For example, it would be inappropriate to use a role play to discuss the Resurrection. However, a role play might be an appropriate way to teach how to be a good neighbor.

Will the method edify and strengthen those I teach?

Gospel learning should be a positive, joyful experience that helps learners realize their divine nature. Those you teach should feel that you love and respect them.

Material that is controversial or sensational does not build faith and testimony and should not be used. Do not use any method that could embarrass or belittle anyone.

Is the material Church-approved?

Use the current editions of the standard works and the lesson materials published by the Church. Consider the methods suggested in the lesson manual before consulting other resources for ideas. Any materials or ideas you use that are not found in the manual should emphasize truth and goodness. To supplement lesson materials and the scriptures, you may use general conference addresses, Church magazines, and Church-produced audiovisual materials and pictures.

Have I followed correct procedures in preparation to use the method?

Some methods require special preparation. For example, you must obtain the bishop's approval to invite guest speakers, and the stake president's approval is required for inviting guest speakers to stake meetings (see *Church Handbook of Instructions, Book 2: Priesthood and Auxiliary Leaders* [1998], 325).

Additional Information

For more information on choosing methods, see lessons 8 and 9 in the Teaching the Gospel course (pages 222–29).

27

CHOOSING EFFECTIVE METHODS

Elder Boyd K. Packer taught: "When we teach moral and spiritual values, we are teaching things that are intangible. Perhaps no teaching is so difficult to accomplish, nor so rewarding when successfully done. There are techniques to employ and tools to use. There are things that teachers can do to prepare themselves and their lessons so that their students . . . can be taught, and their testimonies can be conveyed from one to another" (Teach Ye Diligently, *rev. ed. [1991], 62).*

Effective teaching methods make lessons clear, interesting, and memorable. Whenever you consider using a particular method, ask yourself the following questions to ensure that it will be effective.

Will the method help learners better understand the principles I am teaching?

Effective methods can be used to explain principles and reinforce lessons. For example, a young missionary was teaching an investigator about the need for the gospel to be restored to the earth. The investigator responded that his church had taught him many valuable truths and that it had always been good enough for his family. To help the investigator better understand the meaning of the Apostasy and the need for the Restoration, the missionary brought a yardstick to the next discussion. She explained that the stick was exactly one yard in length. If only a few inches were taken away, the remainder of the stick would still be useful for measuring certain distances, but it no longer would measure a complete yard. After the death of the Apostles, pieces of the truth were lost here and there. Changes crept into the doctrine when there was no prophet to speak for the Lord. Parts of the truth remained, and they were good, but they did not represent the fulness of the truth. For a church to be the Church of Jesus Christ, it must have all the truth He taught. Otherwise, it teaches only a small measure of what it should.

Will the method make wise use of time?

Many teachers feel that they have plenty of time at the beginning of a lesson. Consequently, they may use the first minutes unwisely by spending too much time on an enjoyable teaching method. Then, halfway into the lesson time, they realize that they still need to teach the majority of the lesson. To make up the lost time, they tend to rush along, skipping important parts of the lesson. They often rush the conclusion rather than take the opportunity to bring together ideas and help learners see how to apply the principles that have been taught.

Carefully plan the methods you will use in the lesson and the time you will spend on them. This will help you use a good variety of methods without letting them become the focus of the lesson.

Make sure that the methods you use are not too lengthy for the principles you are teaching. For example, working in small groups may be an effective method to teach a complex principle, but since it takes quite a bit of time it might not be the best way to teach a simple principle.

Will the method meet the needs of those I teach?

The methods you use should help learners understand the principle you are teaching and increase their desire to live it. Learn about learners' backgrounds, achievements, goals, and so forth so you can choose methods that will be instructive, memorable, and inspiring for them. When you understand those you teach, you can avoid methods that may offend or confuse them.

Do I use the same method too often?

Even a persuasive teaching technique can become tiresome if overused. Make sure you use a variety of teaching methods.

Additional Information

For more information on choosing methods, see lessons 8 and 9 in the Teaching the Gospel course (pages 222–29).

28

BEGINNING THE LESSON

Before a symphony begins, concertgoers often hear a confusing combination of sounds. All the musicians prepare for the concert at the same time by tuning their instruments and practicing music individually. However, when the conductor walks onto the stage and lifts a baton, they all become silent, attentive, and ready to work together to play beautiful music.

Like a conductor who brings musicians together at the beginning of a concert, you should bring family members or class members together at the beginning of a lesson. Before you begin a lesson, some people may be reading, others may be sitting quietly, and others may be talking to one another. You may hear several conversations at the same time. Even after an opening prayer, those present may not be completely focused on contributing to the lesson. And although it takes more than lifting a baton, there are several simple ways to focus everyone's attention on a lesson.

Guidelines for Beginning a Lesson

Introductions to lessons should do more than get learners' attention. If an introduction does not relate to the lesson, it will probably detract more than help. For example, if a Sunday School teacher tells a joke at the beginning of a lesson, the class members may become attentive, but they also may be led to think about things that will keep them from focusing on the principles to be taught. You should avoid apologies (such as "I feel unprepared")

and other expressions that do not lead directly to the lesson.

As you teach different lessons, do not begin with the same method every time. Variety will add interest and an element of surprise. You may want to consider some of the methods described in this book on pages 159–84. For guidelines on choosing appropriate and effective methods, see pages 91–92.

Examples of Effective Lesson Beginnings

Using an Object Lesson

You can use objects to teach gospel principles (see "Comparisons and Object Lessons," pages 163–64). For example, to begin a lesson about choosing things that are of most worth to the soul, you could display a real piece of money next to a piece of play money or a plain piece of paper that is the same size as the money. Then ask those you teach which they would take as payment for the work they do. This could lead to a discussion about which teachings are genuine and which teachings are counterfeit.

Writing Questions on the Chalkboard

Questions written on the chalkboard before class will help learners begin to think about topics even before the lesson begins. For example, in a lesson about taking the name of Christ upon ourselves, you could write the following questions on the chalkboard:

- What are some things you do because you have taken the name of Christ upon yourself?
- What are some things you do *not* do because you have taken the name of Christ upon yourself?

Sharing a Story

Stories can awaken learners' interest. We can often teach a principle more effectively when we first share a story to illustrate it. This helps learners understand the principle in terms of everyday experiences.

29

CONCLUDING THE LESSON

"Oh, my time is up, but I'm not quite finished with the lesson. Just a moment. I'll hurry through this last part." Nearly everyone has heard a statement like this from a teacher. Such statements indicate that a teacher has lost an important teaching opportunity: the opportunity to bring the lesson to an effective conclusion.

Qualities of Effective Conclusions

Effective conclusions do not just happen; they must be prepared as part of the lesson. Conclusions are most effective when they have some of the following characteristics:

- They are short, concise, and focused. Generally, they should not include material that you have not taught in the lesson.

- They summarize and tie together the principles you have discussed.

- They highlight important points made by those who have participated.

- They help learners apply gospel principles in their lives.

- They are uplifting, motivating, and positive.

- They include time for testimony.

Following are some examples of ways to conclude a lesson:

- Restate the lesson objective. Ask those you teach how they will apply it in their lives during the coming week.

- Before the lesson begins, assign one or two individuals to listen carefully and

be prepared to help summarize a major point of the lesson or the entire lesson.

- Ask those you teach what they might say if someone wants to know what they have learned from the lesson.

- Use a work sheet to help those you teach summarize the main ideas of the lesson (see "Work Sheets," pages 183–84).

Allowing Time for a Conclusion

To present a good conclusion, you need to be alert and flexible in your use of time. Even well-prepared lessons do not always unfold as planned. The needs of those you teach may lead you to spend more time on a particular point than you have anticipated.

When this happens, you need to be aware of the clock. Bring the discussion to a close before the time runs out. Do all you can to make a smooth transition from the subject being discussed by including it in a quick summary of the lesson. Then conclude the lesson.

Modifying Your Prepared Conclusions

At times, you may need to alter your prepared conclusions because of a particular discussion, comment, or prompting from the Spirit. The following story is an example of a teacher who took advantage of a unique opportunity to conclude a lesson:

Toward the end of an early morning seminary class, the teacher desired to bring a discussion to a conclusion. The main idea of the lesson was that we come unto Christ as we obey the commandments. The class had talked about things some teenagers do that keep them from coming unto the Savior and fully receiving the blessings of His Atonement.

The teacher had planned to conclude by referring to a list on the chalkboard. But he had noticed a painting that a student had completed for a school art project. It was a depiction of a lamb peering through a wooden fence. The teacher asked permission to show the painting to the class, and

he explained what he saw in the painting. "As we discussed in class," he said, "the Savior is the Lamb of God, who gave His life that we all might come unto Him and through Him have eternal life. The fence in the painting is like the barriers that separate us from Him."

The teacher expressed hope that the students would remove "fences" that keep them from drawing nearer to the Savior. He testified of the Savior's invitation: "Come unto me, . . . and I will give you rest" (Matthew 11:28). The class period ended, and the teacher returned the painting. The influence of the Spirit lingered as the students left the building.

PREPARE EVERY NEEDFUL THING

As we devote ourselves to the Lord's work, we must be involved in the hard work of preparation. . . . The Lord's instruction to teach by the Spirit does not relieve us in the slightest degree from the necessity of making personal preparation. . . .

We must study the scriptures. We must study the teachings of the living prophets. We must learn all that we can to make ourselves presentable and understandable. . . . Preparation is a prerequisite to teaching by the Spirit.

Elder Dallin H. Oaks

30

TAKING TIME TO PREPARE

After the resurrected Savior had spent a day teaching the Nephites, He commanded them to take time to prepare for the teachings He would share the next day. He said, "Go ye unto your homes, and ponder upon the things which I have said, and ask of the Father, in my name, that ye may understand, and prepare your minds for the morrow" (3 Nephi 17:3). You can apply this principle in your preparation as a teacher. As you take time to prepare thoughtfully and prayerfully, you will be blessed with greater understanding. You will be more receptive to the guidance of the Spirit.

Beginning Lesson Preparation Early

You may occasionally receive teaching assignments that require last-minute preparation. But you will usually be able to begin preparation well in advance. This is an important part of teaching. The earlier you begin praying about, pondering, and preparing for your next lesson, the more time you will have to be guided by the Spirit and to look for examples, comparisons, and other ideas to enrich the lesson (see "Recognizing and Following the Spirit in Your Teaching," pages 47–48; "Looking for Lessons Everywhere," pages 22–23; "Comparisons and Object Lessons," pages 163–64). You will have time to ask those you teach to prepare special assignments, such as musical presentations (see pages 172–74). You will also have time to identify and prepare to use resources that are available in the meetinghouse library (see "Church Resources for Teaching the Gospel," page 105).

It is often helpful to begin thinking about an upcoming lesson soon after you have taught the preceding lesson. You will probably be most aware of those you teach and their needs and interests immediately after you have been with them. You will also be most aware of their response to your teaching. You can evaluate your approach and methods while they are fresh in your mind.

Finding Joy in Preparation

One teacher described the joy that comes when we take time to prepare:

"Many have discovered the joy of teaching the gospel, but there is another distinct joy to be found in connection with teaching—the joy of preparation. Often, lesson preparation is seen as a chore and is put off until the last moment. Like a hurried prayer, last-minute preparation becomes shallow and not very effective.

"I have known that kind of preparation myself. It is not pleasant, and it does not build confidence. I have also experienced great exhilaration in preparation. It can be a time of meaningful prayer and profound thoughts. I have found it to be a pleasantly productive time of worship, introspection, understanding, and inspiration. . . .

" . . . As I have tasted the joy of preparation, I have discovered great pearls of wisdom and insight. I find I learn far more through my preparation than I will ever have time to teach. . . .

"Wherever truth is taught, the need for preparation is much the same. Those who develop a path to successful preparation will find a joyful experience awaiting them" ("Random Sampler: Planning to Teach," *Ensign*, Oct. 1995, 73).

Taking Time for Personal Preparation

Remember that in your efforts to teach the gospel of Jesus Christ, it is not enough to simply prepare lessons. You also need to prepare yourself. Take time to study the counsel in this book about what you can do to prepare yourself spiritually to teach the gospel (see pages 11–20). Also, plan to attend teacher improvement meetings. In these meetings you and other teachers and leaders will come together to learn methods of teaching the gospel that will help you increase in skill and confidence.

31

PREPARING LESSONS

The short time you spend teaching a lesson at home or at church can have an eternal effect on those you teach. Each lesson can help them feel the influence of the Spirit, grow in their love for Heavenly Father and Jesus Christ, and increase their dedication to live the gospel. Keep this in mind as you prepare lessons. Your success in representing the Lord and teaching by the Spirit will be influenced by the care you give to lesson preparation.

Beginning Lesson Preparation Early

Planning a lesson takes time and attention. Soon after you finish one lesson, begin preparing for the next. You will probably be most aware of those you teach and their needs and interests immediately after you have been with them. You will also be most aware of their response to your teaching.

Three Questions to Guide Your Lesson Preparation

As you begin to prepare a lesson, prayerfully review the lesson material, considering the needs and interests of those you teach. Then ponder the three questions listed below. These questions should guide you throughout your lesson preparation.

1. What should happen in the lives of those I teach as a result of this lesson?

2. Which specific principles should be taught?

3. How should these principles be taught?

Following are some specific ways to use these questions to begin lesson preparation.

As you review a lesson in this way, write down ideas that occur to you. This will give you a structure for your continued prayerful pondering of the lesson.

1. What should happen in the lives of those I teach as a result of this lesson?

Study and ponder the lesson material and the accompanying scripture passages. Consider what those you teach should understand, feel, desire, or do as a result of the lesson. For example, in preparing a lesson about prayer, you may decide that learners should understand the importance of prayer and that they should resolve to pray each morning and night. In preparing a lesson about family responsibility, you may decide that as a result of the lesson, family members should be more diligent in completing household duties. In teaching a lesson about scripture study, you may decide that the lesson should inspire those you teach to study the scriptures daily.

Many lessons in Church-produced manuals include purpose statements. These statements can help you determine how each lesson should influence those you teach.

2. Which specific principles should be taught?

Always keep in mind the needs and backgrounds of those you teach. Ask yourself, "Which principles in the lesson will help those I teach meet the challenges they face?"

Often a lesson will contain more material than you are able to teach in the time

Examine these two illustrations. Which illustration gives the better idea of what a duck looks like? Note that the first illustration includes more details on the duck and does not include other elements that detract from the duck. As you decide to focus on one or two principles in a lesson, make sure that you do not include ideas that could detract from those principles. Prepare lessons that are like the first illustration: simple, clear, and focused.

you are given. In such cases, you should select the material that will be most helpful for those you teach.

The amount of material you cover is less important than its influence in the lives of those you teach. Because too many concepts at one time can confuse or tire learners, it is usually best to focus on one or two main principles. Then you can identify additional, supporting ideas from the manual.

Avoid trying to teach all that could be said on a particular subject. Those you teach will likely already have some understanding of the subject. Your lesson should supplement, clarify, and confirm what they know. Remember that your lesson is not the only time they will learn about the subject.

3. How should these principles be taught?

You should select teaching methods that will help learners understand and apply the principles you teach (for information about selecting appropriate and effective methods, see pages 91–92).

In selecting methods, you should first review the discussion questions, stories, and other learning activities that are suggested in the lesson manual. If you feel that these methods will help meet the needs of those you teach, familiarize yourself with the methods. If you feel that you should use other methods, begin early to determine how to teach the principles. Consider using examples, illustrations, comparisons, or personal experiences that will help teach the main principles of the lesson.

The methods you decide to use may require that you obtain materials from the meetinghouse library, such as pictures, objects, hymnbooks, or videocassettes.

Cultivating Your Ideas

After you have some initial ideas on how to teach a lesson, you can develop and refine them. If you have begun preparing early, you will be more aware of experiences, stories, and scriptures that will help

those you teach. Thoughts may come to you as you ponder the principles to be taught and the needs of those you teach. This is one way that the Spirit can guide you in your preparation. You may want to carry a notebook so you can write down ideas as they come to you.

It is helpful at this point in your planning to once again study the scripture references that will be used in the lesson. This will help you better understand them and liken them to those you are teaching.

Adjusting and Revising As Needed

As the time to teach the lesson approaches, there will likely be some final adjustments to make. This is much like the pruning a gardener does to give the right shape to a tree or shrub. During this stage you should:

- Have clearly in mind what should happen in the lives of those you teach as a result of this lesson. Ask yourself, "Will the lesson bring these results?"

- Review the specific points you want to teach from the manual: the main principles and the supporting ideas. Organize a clear outline. Be sure to plan a clear beginning and a strong, focused conclusion (see "Beginning the Lesson," page 93; "Concluding the Lesson," pages 94–95).

- Finalize the teaching methods you will use. Ensure that the methods you select will help learners apply the principles you teach.

- Finalize your choices of the materials you will use.

You may be prompted by the Spirit to make changes right up to the last minute. You may even be prompted to make changes in the very moment you are teaching. Be open to all these promptings, and recognize that it is your careful preparation that allows you to receive the ongoing guidance of the Spirit.

32

CREATING LESSONS FROM CONFERENCE TALKS AND OTHER RESOURCES

A structured lesson manual is not provided for every teaching occasion in the Church. In some settings you may teach from articles in Church magazines or from general conference addresses. In other settings you may teach from a book that includes study questions but no lesson plans.

When you prepare lessons from these resources, you should follow the suggestions in "Preparing Lessons" (pages 98–99). As you do so, the Spirit will guide you in your decisions about what to teach and how to teach it.

Example of How to Plan a Lesson from a General Conference Talk

Consider this excerpt from a general conference address by Elder Joseph B. Wirthlin:

"The last part of the thirteenth article of faith states, 'If there is anything virtuous, lovely, or of good report or praiseworthy, we seek after these things.'

"The word *seek* means to go in search of, try to discover, try to acquire. It requires an active, assertive approach to life. For example, Abraham 'sought for the blessings of the fathers . . . and to be a greater follower of righteousness' (Abraham 1:2). It is the opposite of passively waiting for something good to come to us with no effort on our part.

"We can fill our lives with good, leaving no room for anything else. We have so much good from which to choose that we need never partake of evil" (in Conference Report, Apr. 1992, 120; or *Ensign*, May 1992, 86).

The following example shows one way to prepare a lesson based on this statement.

1. Read Elder Wirthlin's statement.

Prayerfully think of those you are to teach, pondering how this passage applies to them.

2. Decide what should happen in the lives of those you teach as a result of the lesson.

For example, if you are teaching youth, you might want them to set goals that will help them seek after things that are good. This could include goals regarding scripture study, wholesome recreation, or uplifting activities with friends.

3. Decide on the main principle or principles you will teach, along with any supporting ideas.

What you choose to emphasize should depend on the needs of those you teach. As you are diligent and prayerful, you will receive guidance from the Spirit in making this decision.

For example, to teach youth the importance of seeking after that which is good, you might focus on Elder Wirthlin's statement that "we have so much good from which to choose that we need never partake of evil." Supporting ideas could include that we must actively seek after good things and that we can seek the Lord's help as we do so.

As you prepare to teach these principles, you might turn to the Topical Guide and look under the heading "Seek, Sought." There you would find scripture passages

to help you. For example, you would find Doctrine and Covenants 6:7, which says to "seek not for riches but for wisdom," and Doctrine and Covenants 46:8, which says to "seek . . . earnestly the best gifts." While studying these passages, you would identify those that would be most useful in teaching the principles in the lesson.

4. Consider how you want to teach the main ideas and the supporting ideas you have selected.

Search carefully through the teaching methods described on pages 159–84. Ideas will come to you as you consider how to teach your class.

For example, you might conduct a chalkboard activity in which learners list different ways they can spend their time. This could lead to a discussion of whether they are fulfilling Elder Wirthlin's counsel to "fill our lives with good, leaving no room for anything else."

As you consider conducting such discussions, begin thinking of questions to ask (see "Teaching with Questions," pages 68–70). For example, as you talk about the importance of living according to Elder Wirthlin's counsel, you might ask, "What changes could we make that would help us fill our lives with good?"

The more carefully you ponder the specific needs of those you teach and the more you study the various teaching methods found in this book, the more confident and creative you will be in developing ideas for teaching.

Preparing lessons from general conference talks and other resources will require added creativity. As you prepare diligently and seek the Spirit, you will be inspired in the preparation of such lessons. You and those you teach will be blessed as a result of your preparation.

33

ADAPTING LESSONS TO THOSE YOU TEACH

Church-produced lesson manuals are carefully prepared to ensure that the doctrines of the Church are kept pure. They establish guidelines for teaching in Church settings, and they ensure a consistent approach to gospel topics and principles. You should be true to the teachings and guidelines in these manuals. However, you do not need to present lessons exactly as they appear in the manuals. You may adapt the lessons according to the needs and circumstances of those you teach.

Whatever you do to adapt lessons, remember that your adaptations should help learners understand and live gospel principles. Therefore, adaptations should be made only after prayerful study of the lesson material and consideration of each individual you teach. As you seek to adapt a lesson, you should be guided by (1) the manual you have been given; (2) the three central questions discussed on pages 98–99 of this book; and (3) the standards of teaching outlined in this book, such as loving those you teach, teaching by the Spirit, and teaching the doctrine.

Examples of Lesson Adaptations

The following situations represent a few ways in which you might adapt lessons to those you teach.

Using Material from Recent Church Magazines

As you read a story in a lesson about service, you are reminded of a similar story in a recent Church magazine. You feel that the young women in your class will relate better to the story in the magazine, so you use that story instead of the one in the manual.

Developing Your Own Learning Activities

As you prepare a lesson for a group of Primary children, you read the attention activity at the beginning of the lesson. You feel that this particular activity might not help the children in your class. You ponder the needs of the children and develop an activity that will help them focus on the principles you are going to teach.

Departing from the Suggested Lesson Development

You are preparing to teach the deacons in your ward. The Aaronic Priesthood lesson manual suggests using a role play to help them apply a gospel principle. As you think about the young men you teach, you are reminded of some experiences they have had recently. You feel that a simple discussion about those experiences would be more effective than a role play.

Adapting Lessons for Different Age-Groups

For ideas on adapting lessons for different age-groups, see the part of this book titled "Teaching Different Age-Groups" (pages 107–124).

34

EVALUATING LESSON PRESENTATIONS

After teaching a lesson, a Gospel Doctrine teacher was troubled by the teaching experience. Some parts of the lesson had gone well, but other parts had been disappointing. "Why did some things go well and others not?" he asked himself. "What would I do again in presenting the lesson? What would I change?" The questions stayed with him as he pondered how to help the members of his class learn the gospel. The questions this teacher asked himself are nearly universal among teachers.

In addition to evaluating the learning of those we teach (see "How to Tell If They Are Learning," page 73), it is also important to assess our own success in presenting lessons. President Spencer W. Kimball taught of the importance of evaluating ourselves and seeking to improve: "We ascertain and establish acceptable standards of excellence . . . and measure our work accordingly. We should be less interested in excelling others but more concerned with excelling our own past records" (*The Teachings of Spencer W. Kimball,* ed. Edward L. Kimball [1982], 488).

We should take time after each lesson to follow President Kimball's counsel to "measure our work." This will help us prepare for the next lesson and continue to improve as teachers.

Whatever changes you are prompted to make, remember that evaluation of your teaching should be a positive experience, not a discouraging one. Every time you discover a way to improve your teaching, you discover a new way to help others learn the gospel and live according to its principles.

Questions to Help You Evaluate Lesson Presentations

The success of a lesson is measured by its influence on those you teach. As you evaluate each lesson you teach, try to recall the learners' responses at different points in the lesson. You may remember their responses more clearly if you review the outline you used to present the lesson.

The questions listed below may help you as you evaluate lessons. Note that the first questions help you determine what you have done well. You can usually learn more about how to improve by first focusing on successes rather than disappointments. As you humbly acknowledge your strengths, you can build on them and use them to improve your overall teaching. After considering what you have done well, you can determine what you can do better.

- At what points in the lesson did those I teach seem most willing to participate? When did they seem less willing to participate?

- At what points in the lesson did they seem to feel the influence of the Spirit most strongly? When did they seem to feel the influence of the Spirit less strongly?

- At what points in the lesson did they seem most thoughtful? When did they not seem to be thinking very deeply?

- At what points in the lesson did they seem to make the most application in their lives? When did they seem to miss the lesson's application in their lives?

As you ponder each of the questions listed above, consider these follow-up questions:

- What aspect of the lesson presentation seemed to contribute to those responses?

- What does this tell me about those I teach?

- How can this understanding help me as I prepare the next lesson?

In asking yourself these questions, consider writing your answers so you will not forget the insights and promptings you receive. You may be surprised at how much you learn.

As you prayerfully ponder ways to reach those you teach, the Spirit can help you see areas in which you can improve. You might study certain sections of this book. For example, you could review information about asking questions that generate discussion (see "Conducting Discussions," pages 63–65; "Teaching with Questions," pages 68–70). You may feel that it is important to learn how to begin lessons in a more interesting way (see "Beginning the Lesson," page 93) or develop stronger conclusions for lessons (see "Concluding the Lesson," pages 94–95).

For suggestions on developing a plan for improvement, see "Making a Plan to Improve Your Teaching" (pages 24–27).

35

CHURCH RESOURCES FOR TEACHING THE GOSPEL

The Church provides many resources to help parents, teachers, and leaders teach the gospel. The scriptures are the curriculum of the Church and the most important of these resources. Other resources include:

- *Teaching, No Greater Call*
- *Teaching Guidebook*
- The "Gospel Teaching and Leadership" section of the *Church Handbook of Instructions*
- *Family Home Evening Resource Book*
- *Gospel Principles*
- *Scripture Stories*
- Lesson manuals
- Church magazines (check these magazines regularly for stories and other ideas)
- Gospel Art Picture Kit (a collection of pictures that includes depictions of scripture stories and events, Presidents of the Church, and gospel principles in action)
- Other pictures and posters
- The Church hymnbook
- *Children's Songbook*
- Church-produced videocassettes and audiocassettes

Meetinghouse Library

If your meetinghouse has a library, it may contain most or all of these resources. To learn more about the materials available in your meetinghouse library, speak with the meetinghouse librarian.

Your meetinghouse librarian or ward clerk should have a copy of the *Church Materials Catalog* that you can use. This catalog is an annual publication that lists the items available from Church distribution centers. In addition to the items listed on this page, the catalog lists other materials that support Church members.

Your meetinghouse library may also have copies of the *Index to Periodicals of The Church of Jesus Christ of Latter-day Saints*. This is a cumulative index to the periodicals published by the Church. The periodicals indexed are the *Ensign*, *New Era*, and *Friend* magazines; conference reports; and the *Church News*.

C

TEACHING DIFFERENT AGE-GROUPS

1

TEACHING CHILDREN

When the resurrected Savior ministered to the Nephites, He showed His great love for little children:

"He took their little children, one by one, and blessed them, and prayed unto the Father for them. . . .

"And he spake unto the multitude, and said unto them: Behold your little ones.

"And as they looked to behold they cast their eyes towards heaven, and they saw the heavens open, and they saw angels descending out of heaven as it were in the midst of fire; and they came down and encircled those little ones about, and they were encircled about with fire; and the angels did minister unto them" (3 Nephi 17:21, 23–24).

Referring to this account, Elder M. Russell Ballard said, "Clearly, those of us who have been entrusted with precious children have been given a sacred, noble stewardship, for we are the ones God has appointed to encircle today's children with love and the fire of faith and an understanding of who they are" ("Great Shall Be the Peace of Thy Children," *Ensign,* Apr. 1994, 60). The Savior's example sets a pattern for us as we teach, care for, and influence children.

It is a sacred responsibility to teach children the gospel of Jesus Christ and help them learn to live it. You should teach them true doctrine, as did the prophet Nephi, who said, "We talk of Christ, we rejoice in Christ, we preach of Christ, we prophesy of Christ, and we write according

to our prophecies, that our children may know to what source they may look for a remission of their sins" (2 Nephi 25:26).

As you teach children, you will find that you receive special blessings. Children will bring joy to your soul and prompt you to be a good example. As you come to recognize the faithfulness, love, trust, and hope of children, you will grow closer to the Lord and better understand His commandment to "become as little children" (Matthew 18:3). With the Spirit to guide you, you can love and teach children in a Christlike way. You can help each child find the peace promised to those who follow the Savior: "All thy children shall be taught of the Lord; and great shall be the peace of thy children" (3 Nephi 22:13).

Guidelines for Understanding and Teaching Children

The following information can help you better understand the characteristics of the children you teach (see also "Age Characteristics of Children," pages 110–16, and, if you are teaching Primary, the introductory pages of your Primary lesson manual).

Children are believing. They believe what you say. They are receptive to the truth. You have an obligation to teach them correct doctrine simply and clearly, with language and examples that they can understand.

Children can recognize the influence of the Spirit. Teach them that the feelings of peace, love, and warmth they have when they talk or sing of Jesus Christ and His gospel come from the Holy Ghost. Help them understand that these feelings are part of a testimony.

Children take things literally. Everything is real to them. If you use complex metaphors to teach sacred gospel principles, they may become confused. Help children learn the gospel by discussing events and activities familiar to them: home, family, and the world around them. Make certain that they do not misunderstand what you teach.

Children are curious and eager to learn. They enjoy learning through varied and new experiences. They want to move about, use all their senses, explore, and try new things. Older children like the challenge of answering questions and solving problems. The children in your class will be more attentive and excited about learning when you use a variety of teaching methods and activities to teach gospel principles (see "Teaching with Variety," pages 89–90).

Children are loving and want to be loved and accepted themselves. Look for opportunities to reinforce the kind and loving behavior that comes naturally to children. Because children want to please you and enjoy helping others, give them opportunities to serve. Ask them to carry your books, hold pictures, or answer questions. Encourage them to help one another. Show your love for them. Build their confidence by expressing your appreciation for their efforts whenever possible. Listen attentively to what they say.

Children are beginning to prepare for the future. While adulthood may seem far away for children, they are preparing now for their future responsibilities in their families, the Church, and the workplace. You can help them realize how their current experiences are preparing them. For example, you might say, "Mary, I watched you help Kelly see how to find that scripture. You were so patient and kind. Someday when you're a mother, I'm sure that you will teach your children many wonderful things." Or you could say, "Matthew, what a great missionary you will be one day because you have learned to set goals and complete them. I am so proud of you!"

Children will follow your example. You are always teaching, even when you are not aware of it. You often teach more by your attitude and example than by your words. For example, children will notice whether you treat the scriptures respectfully. They will observe how you speak about Heavenly Father and Jesus Christ. They will watch how you live the principles you are teaching. Your righteous example will help them develop greater feelings of love and respect for Heavenly Father and His Son.

Little children have short attention spans, and they cannot sit still very long. Do not expect too much from them. Recognize that inattentive behavior might mean that they are tired or hungry, that they do not understand something you have said, that they need to move, or that they are bored. The best way to keep their attention and help them learn is to encourage them to participate in lessons. Because children have an abundance of energy, plan ways to allow them to move or to see, hear, smell, or touch something as part of each lesson. They enjoy learning through repetition, simple stories, songs, and activities.

Strengthening Families

If you are a teacher or leader, you can assist parents in their efforts to teach the gospel to their children. Tell parents what you are teaching in your class so they can reinforce those gospel principles in the home (see "Regular Occasions for Teaching in the Home," pages 137–39). Encourage children to share with their family what they are learning. In family home evenings, they can share songs, scriptures, games, and principles they learn in Primary classes or activities. Occasionally you might send home reports on the lessons or activities in which they have participated to help reinforce what the child has learned. You could also let parents know when their child has been particularly helpful or when their child is assigned to pray or give a talk. You can invite parents to share their experiences or their testimonies as part of a lesson.

Remember that when you help children gain a testimony and live the gospel, they can influence their families for good. As you teach children the gospel and help them learn how to live it, you help strengthen their families.

2

AGE CHARACTERISTICS OF CHILDREN

Children are continually changing physically, mentally, socially, emotionally, and spiritually. They follow a general pattern of growth and development. Parents and teachers who are aware of common characteristics of different age-groups will be able to deal with children's behavior more appropriately and teach them more effectively.

Some children may develop faster or slower than others their age. For example, a particular six-year-old may fit more closely the age characteristics of a five-year-old or a seven-year-old. Remember also that children may temporarily revert to younger behavior during emotional stress or tension.

Church lesson manuals have been prepared with children's growth characteristics in mind. As you study and prepare each lesson, be aware of how each part of the lesson can help you meet the children's needs.

Regardless of the age-group you teach, make sure you are patient, respectful, loving, and sensitive toward each child. Do not expect children to do more than they are able.

The following descriptions and suggestions can help you better understand the children you teach.

The Eighteen-Month-Old

Characteristics of the Child

- Walks, climbs, crawls, and runs. Enjoys pushing and pulling things. Is able to take things apart more easily than he or she can put them together. Is uncoordinated. Tires easily. Is usually not toilet trained.

- Makes many sounds. Has developing language skills. Uses one-word phrases, particularly "mine" and "no." Gathers knowledge through sight, sound, touch, smell, and taste. Understands more than he or she can express.

- Enjoys playing alongside other children, but often does not interact with them. Has difficulty sharing.

- Cries easily, but emotions change quickly.

Suggestions for Parents and Teachers

- Vary activities to keep the child's interest. Use activities that involve walking, pushing, and pulling. Use finger plays and musical activities.

- Provide many opportunities for talking and participation. Teach how to be reverent during prayers. Use visuals with stories. Provide toys the child can move and experiment with, such as stacking toys, balls, simple puzzles, dolls, and figures of people and animals.

- Provide toys and activities that allow the child to play alone. Help the child learn to share and get along with others.

- Hold the child when he or she is upset or feels insecure.

The Two-Year-Old

Characteristics of the Child

- Is very active. Jumps, walks, and runs. Can clap hands and kick a ball. Can handle small objects, but cannot button or zip clothing or care for himself or herself in other ways. Gets irritable and restless when tired.

- Is able to put two or three words together in a sentence. Says "no" often, even when he or she does not mean it. Has simple, direct thoughts. Cannot reason. Can make simple choices. Enjoys repetition. Has a short attention span (two or three minutes). Is curious. Moves from one activity to another. Likes simple toys, art materials, books, short stories, and music activities.

- Likes to play alone. Is developing an interest in playing with others, but is usually more interested in playing near them than with them. Often argues over toys. Has difficulty sharing and cooperating. Asks adults for things he or she wants from another child.

- Is loving and affectionate. Enjoys sitting on laps and holding hands. Likes to be close to his or her mother.

Uses emotional outbursts to express emotions, to get what he or she wants, and to show anger and frustration. Has moods that change quickly. Likes independence.

- Likes to pray. Understands that Heavenly Father and Jesus love us, but has difficulty understanding most spiritual concepts.

Suggestions for Parents and Teachers

- Use rest activities such as finger plays and those that use music. Provide activities such as beanbag tossing, marching, and jumping. Avoid activities that require skill and coordination, such as cutting and pasting.

- Keep discussions simple. Help the child participate. Use repetition. Do not leave the child alone; children this age can easily get themselves into unsafe situations. Provide opportunities for the child to make choices.

- Provide opportunities for the child to interact with others, but do not pressure the child to do so. Offer the choice to participate in activities. Provide warm, caring direction. Redirect misbehavior.

- Show love and affection. Redirect the child's attention in order to stop undesirable behavior. Encourage the child to be self-sufficient, but provide help when necessary. Allow the child to practice making choices.

- Allow the child to pray. Focus spiritual concepts on the family and the love of Heavenly Father and Jesus.

The Three-Year-Old

Characteristics of the Child

- Walks and runs, but is still uncoordinated. Likes doing things with his or her hands but does them awkwardly.

- Has more language skills. Likes to talk and learn new words. Has a short attention span. Is curious and inquisitive. Often misunderstands and makes comments that seem off the subject. Enjoys pretending. Likes finger plays, stories, and musical activities. Is unable to distinguish fantasy from reality.

- Enjoys working alone. Does not engage in much cooperative play with others, but likes to have friends around. Is self-centered. Has difficulty sharing. Prefers to be close to adults, particularly family, because they provide security.

- Wants to please adults. Needs their approval, love, and praise. Strikes out emotionally when afraid or anxious. Cries easily. Is sensitive to others' feelings. Is developing some independence. Has intense, short-lived emotions.

- Is interested in simple gospel principles such as prayer and obedience. Is more aware of Heavenly Father and Jesus Christ, and has simple faith in Them.

Suggestions for Parents and Teachers

- Use activities that include jumping, skipping, walking, and bending. Use simple art activities such as pasting, molding clay, and coloring. Avoid activities that require refined skills and coordination, such as tying or cutting. Be prepared to clean up messes.

- Teach ideas in a simple, clear way. Use summaries and visual materials to reinforce ideas. Encourage questions and responses to the lessons, but have the child take turns with other children. Use a variety of teaching methods such as stories, songs, discussions, dramatizations, finger plays, and simple games. Alternate between quiet and lively activities.

- Provide opportunities to play with others. Use activities that encourage sharing, taking turns, and cooperating. Develop a close relationship with the child, and frequently give the child opportunities to talk about his or her family.

- Show approval and confidence in the child. Avoid criticism. Emphasize the love you and the child's family have for him or her. Help the child understand others' feelings and solve conflicts. Encourage the child to be self-sufficient.

- Teach the gospel in simple, concrete ways. Teach that Heavenly Father and Jesus Christ live and are kind and loving. Share simple expressions of testimony. Help the child recognize the beauty of God's creations.

The Four-Year-Old

Characteristics of the Child

- Is very active. Moves quickly. Likes to skip, jump, race, climb, and throw.

- Enjoys talking and learning new words. Asks many questions. Is able to reason a little, but still has many misconceptions. Has trouble separating fact from fantasy. Has a short attention span. Uses artwork to express feelings. Enjoys pretending and role playing.

- Plays more cooperatively with others. Is sometimes physically aggressive, bossy, impolite, and stubborn, but can also be friendly. Is learning to share, accept rules, and take turns. Responds to sincere praise.

- Often tests people's limits. Is boastful, especially about self and family. May be agreeable one moment and quarrelsome the next. Has more self-confidence. May have fears and feelings of insecurity.

- Is becoming aware of right and wrong, and usually desires to do right. Blames others for his or her wrong-doing. Has a natural love and respect for Heavenly Father and Jesus Christ, and asks many questions about Them. Likes to pray, and wants to be good. Is becoming more interested in gospel principles.

Suggestions for Parents and Teachers

- Alternate between quiet and lively activities. Help the child learn to control and be responsible for his or her actions. Teach appropriate ways to express emotions.

- Use discussions and activities that will encourage thinking, such as simple riddles and guessing games. Clarify misunderstandings. Use pictures, objects, and actual experiences. Introduce new words. Have the child draw pictures that relate to lessons. Accept and encourage the child's creative efforts. Allow the child to explore his or her surroundings. Use role-playing activities.

- Provide opportunities for the child to play and work cooperatively with others. Teach kindness, patience, and politeness. Help the child follow simple rules such as taking turns. Help the child learn positive social behavior without punishing or scolding him or her.

- Establish and firmly follow limits. Allow the child to talk about self and family. Teach the child that he or she is special to Heavenly Father and Jesus. Express the love you and the child's parents have for him or her.

- Help the child be responsible for his or her own behavior, and teach the importance of making good choices. Teach that Heavenly Father loves His children and that we can communicate with Him through prayer. Help the child discover how to be reverent at church. Teach basic gospel principles.

The Five-Year-Old

Characteristics of the Child

- Is very active. Has a good sense of balance, and is becoming more coordinated. Can kick a ball, walk in a straight line, hop, skip, and march. Enjoys drawing, coloring, and participating in activities and games. Is learning to lace and tie shoes and button and zip clothing.

- Recognizes some letters, numbers, and words. Likes to pretend to read and write. May be learning to read. Is talkative. Asks questions, makes comments, and gives

answers that show increased understanding. Is good at problem solving. Is curious and eager for facts. Is beginning to distinguish truth from fantasy. Has a short but increasing attention span. Likes definite tasks. Enjoys jokes and tricks, but cannot laugh at himself or herself. Likes stories, singing, poetry, and dramatizations.

- Is friendly and eager to please and cooperate. Is beginning to prefer being in small groups of children, but may prefer a best friend. Creates less conflict in group play. Is beginning to want to conform, and is critical of those who do not. Is beginning to understand rules, but often tries to change them for his or her benefit.

- Centers interests on home and family. Is affectionate toward adults, and wants to please them. Gets embarrassed easily, especially by his or her own mistakes.

- Wants to be good. Is learning the difference between right and wrong. Sometimes tells untruths or blames others for his or her own wrongdoings because of an intense desire to please adults and do what is right. Is ready to be taught spiritual principles.

Suggestions for Parents and Teachers

- Engage the child in physical activities. Use simple games and other activities. Allow the child to cut and paste and to put puzzles together. Allow for independence. Express confidence in the child. Accept and encourage the child's efforts.

- Allow the child to talk and ask questions. Allow him or her to read simple words and phrases. Use wordstrips for simple words. Assign simple tasks and responsibilities. Use drawing activities, true-to-life stories, and visual materials. Vary activities, using pictures, games, songs, and discussions. Use problem-solving activities such as riddles and discussion questions. Allow the child to pretend, dramatize, and use puppets. Laugh with the child.

- Be sensitive to the child's need for your approval. Encourage friendship, and try to help the child if it seems that he or she does not have close friendships or does not belong to a group. Talk about how others feel when people are kind or unkind. Discuss the importance of loving others and expressing gratitude, and show the child how to do this. Help the child learn the value of individual differences.

- Frequently teach the value and importance of the family. Give the child an opportunity to share feelings about his or her family. Express your love, and show affection. Give specific praise for positive behavior.

Avoid activities or expressions that might embarrass the child.

- Teach appropriate behavior. Do not be shocked if the child says something that is untrue or inappropriate, but still teach the importance of accepting responsibility for one's own actions. Strengthen the child's testimony by sharing your own testimony. Share stories and ideas that will strengthen the child's love for and faith in Heavenly Father and Jesus Christ and Their teachings.

The Six-Year-Old

Characteristics of the Child

- Is very active. Is often noisy, restless, and exuberant. Likes to participate in activities and perform small tasks, though they still may be difficult to do. Dislikes being a spectator.

- Needs concepts taught in concrete ways. Has improving memory. Is talkative, and asks many questions. Is learning to make decisions, but often is indecisive. Has an increasing attention span. Likes reading, writing, singing, hearing stories, and pretending.

- Is more interested in group activities and interacting with playmates, but is still self-centered. Is sometimes bossy, aggressive, and unkind to peers. Has unstable

friendships. Is concerned with how others treat him or her. Is eager for social approval.

- Is boastful. Exaggerates and criticizes. Is easily excited, silly, and giggly. Can be generous, affectionate, and compatible, but mood can change easily.

- Is concerned with good and bad behavior, particularly as it affects family and friends. Sometimes blames others for wrongdoings. Likes scripture stories, especially those about Jesus.

Suggestions for Parents and Teachers

- Be patient with the child's abundant energy and restlessness. Use activities such as writing, coloring, cutting, pasting, and molding clay. Use games that allow the child to use his or her energy.

- Use problem-solving activities such as riddles, reviews, and open-ended stories. Use pictures, flannel cutouts, and other visual materials. Introduce new words. Ask questions. Allow the child to make decisions. Discuss the importance of choosing the right, and allow the child to practice making decisions with limited choices. Provide opportunities for reading, writing, singing, hearing stories, and role playing. Plan lessons with the child's interests in mind.

- Encourage sharing and participation with others. Give many opportunities for group activities. Give specific praise and approval. Focus lessons on showing love by helping others and being sensitive to others' needs. Encourage the child to participate in games and other activities.

- Praise the child's specific efforts so he or she feels less need to boast. Praise honesty. Do not criticize. Laugh *with* him or her, but do not laugh *at* him or her. Encourage positive moods. By your example, teach the child calm, stable behavior.

- Teach the child to be concerned with and responsible for his or her own behavior and how to improve it. Assure the child that everyone makes mistakes. Teach simple repentance. Use the scriptures to teach basic gospel principles. Help the child understand and apply the scriptures.

The Seven-Year-Old

Characteristics of the Child

- Has better muscular control. Is developing interest and skills in certain games, hobbies, and activities. Gets restless and fidgety. Has nervous habits, and sometimes assumes awkward positions. Is full of energy, but tires easily.

- Is eager to learn. Thinks seriously and more logically. Is able to solve problems that are more complex. Likes to be challenged, work hard, and take time completing a task. Has a good attention span. Enjoys hobbies and using skills. Likes to collect things and talk about personal projects and accomplishments.

- Often plays in groups, but sometimes likes to be alone and play quietly. Interacts little with the opposite sex. Is eager to be like peers and have their approval. Is less domineering and less determined to have his or her own way. Likes more responsibility and independence. Is often worried about not doing well.

- Dislikes criticism. Is more sensitive to his or her own feelings and those of other people. Is often a perfectionist, and tends to be self-critical. Is inhibited and cautious. Is less impulsive and self-centered than at earlier stages.

- Is aware of right and wrong. Enjoys learning about and practicing gospel principles such as prayer and tithe paying. Understands aspects of the gospel such as the sacrament, faith, repentance, missionary work, the Holy Ghost, and temple work. Wants to be baptized and receive the gift of the Holy Ghost.

Suggestions for Parents and Teachers

- Use activities that allow the child to use his or her energy. Allow the child to share his or her special skills. Be patient with annoyances and restlessness, and do not draw attention to awkwardness. Use varied techniques to help maintain the child's interest and prevent misbehavior. Compliment good behavior.

- Ask thought-provoking questions. Use open-ended stories, riddles, thinking games, and discussions to stimulate thinking. Allow the child to make decisions. Give him or her plenty of time to accomplish tasks. Encourage the child to pursue hobbies and interests. Provide opportunities to read scriptures, wordstrips, and stories. Use stories and situations that deal with reality rather than fiction.

- Use activities that require group play, such as games and dramatizations, but respect the child's desire to work alone occasionally. Do not force interaction with the opposite sex. Praise him or her for positive behavior such as taking turns and sharing. Give the child responsibilities and tasks that he or she can carry out, and then praise efforts and accomplishments.

- Encourage concern for others. Build confidence. Instead of criticizing, look for opportunities to show approval and affection. Accept moods and aloofness. Encourage the child to express his or her feelings.

- Provide opportunities for the child to practice making right choices. Help the child understand the consequences of his or her choices. Teach gospel principles in simple, concrete ways, and encourage the child to practice them in daily life. Teach from the scriptures. Prepare the child for baptism and confirmation by helping him or her understand the covenants that he or she will make.

The Eight-Year-Old

Characteristics of the Child

- Is becoming more coordinated. Wiggles and squirms. Has nervous habits. Plays organized games that require physical skill. Has a good attention span. Wants to be included.

- Wants to know the reasons for things. Is anxious to share his or her knowledge. Thinks he or she knows much, but is beginning to recognize that others may know even more. Is judgmental. Has heroes. Enjoys writing, reading, and pretending.

- Enjoys group play with simple rules. Prefers to be with own gender in group play. Is more cooperative and less insistent on having his or her own way. Wants to have a best friend. Has a strong need for independence, but also relies on adults for guidance and security.

- Is usually affectionate, helpful, cheerful, outgoing, and curious, but can also be rude, selfish, bossy, and demanding. Is sensitive to criticism. Criticizes self and others. Is sometimes giggly and silly. Experiences guilt and shame.

- Is receptive to gospel teachings, but may have questions about them. Is proud of Church membership. Likes living gospel principles. Learns the gospel through concrete examples and participation.

Suggestions for Parents and Teachers

- Use activities that require coordination and allow the child to use his or her energy. Be patient with clumsiness, unpleasant habits, and squirming. Alternate quiet and active periods. Praise good behavior.

- Use games, stories, pictures, and problem-solving activities to encourage learning. Use reading, writing, and role playing. Help the child set realistic goals. Encourage the child to be more concerned about his or her own behavior than that of others. Provide the child with appropriate heroes such as Church leaders and other good members of the Church.

- Provide opportunities for group interaction, cooperation, and sharing. Supervise activities closely. Recognize that his or her friendships can be intense. Help the child become part of the group if he or she does not have close friends. Praise the child for positive behavior. Let the child work with other children and with you to make class rules and other decisions. Allow him or her to work independently.

- Help the child recognize and deal constructively with negative emotions. Show interest and enthusiasm. Praise and build self-confidence; do not criticize or compare the child with other children. Recognize the child's efforts and accomplishments. Let the child enjoy humor when appropriate, and be patient with giggling. Teach him or her that others make mistakes.

- Express personal faith and testimony often. Help the child appreciate his or her Church membership and the responsibilities it brings. Challenge the child to live gospel principles. Share personal experiences, scriptures, and stories. Use activities in which the child can participate.

The Nine-Year-Old

Characteristics of the Child

- Enjoys team games. Has good body control. Is interested in developing strength, skill, and speed. Likes more complicated crafts and handwork.

- Is able to remain interested in subjects or activities for a longer period of time. Seeks facts; does not enjoy much fantasy. Likes memorization. Has definite interests and curiosity. Likes reading, writing, and keeping records. Is interested in the community and other cultures and peoples. Enjoys learning about the past and the present. Likes to collect things.

- Enjoys being with groups of people of the same gender. Likes group adventures and cooperative play, but also likes competition. Tests authority and exercises independence. Spends much time with friends.

- Has some behavior problems, especially if he or she is not accepted by others. Is becoming very independent, dependable, and trustworthy. Is concerned about being fair, and argues over fairness. Is better able to accept his or her own failures and mistakes and take responsibility for personal actions. Is sometimes silly.

- Is well aware of right and wrong. Wants to do right, but sometimes rebels. Is influenced by others' testimonies. Is ready to be taught more complex gospel principles.

Suggestions for Parents and Teachers

- Provide a variety of activities, including team games, to sustain interest and help the child develop skills.

- Give specific information and facts rather than fantasy. Do not give all the answers; allow the child time to think about and discuss answers. Encourage him or her to memorize quotations and scriptures. Respect individual differences when making assignments and giving responsibilities. Provide opportunities for reading, writing, and record keeping. Encourage him or her to keep a journal. Teach about other people and cultures and about history.

- Recognize the child's need for peer acceptance. Establish and maintain reasonable limits, but allow for independence. Teach the child how to be gracious, even when the child feels that he or she has not "won." Encourage friendships, and help the child make friends.

- Let the child know that you accept him or her, even when you do not approve of certain behavior. Provide opportunities for the child to show independence and dependability. Do not ridicule the child for wrongdoing.

- Express your love and support for the child often. Frequently share your testimony and testimonies of the prophets. Teach gospel principles that are more advanced.

The Ten- or Eleven-Year-Old

Characteristics of the Child

- May be experiencing rapid growth. Enjoys sports that require strength, speed, and skill. Has periods of playing, pushing, wrestling, poking, and giggling. Is restless, active, and impatient. May differ from peers in physical size and coordination. Does not like to be treated like a child. Is concerned about physical appearance.

- Enjoys abstract concepts and ideas. Makes conclusions based on prior learning. Likes to be challenged in mental tasks. Is decisive and reasonable. Enjoys memorization. Likes to set goals. Thinks more logically. Enjoys learning. Has a good attention span. Understands more precisely the meanings of words, and can define abstract terms. Has humor that may seem ridiculous to adults.

- Is social and competitive. Possesses strong loyalty to groups. Has much positive and negative interaction with peers. Has friendships that are more complex and intense. Relies on best friends. Values peers' opinions and standards more highly than those of adults. Is sometimes critical of adults' judgments and of others' feelings. Likes to tease or play roughly. Is sometimes rude and uncooperative, and at other times is friendly and cooperative.

- Is critical of self and resentful of others' criticism. May feel that everything he or she does is wrong, especially if criticized. Has worries and fears about school and friends. Is very sensitive, especially about self. Has doubts and insecurities. Is sometimes touchy and irritable, and is very conscious of being treated fairly. Is able to be polite, serious, honest, and sincere. Desires to be independent and have responsibilities.

- Has a strong moral sense and conscience. Is interested in self-improvement. Does not like to admit when he or she has behaved badly. Is ready to learn more about the doctrines of the gospel.

Suggestions for Parents and Teachers

- Recognize that he or she is growing and maturing. Do not force interaction with the opposite sex. Provide opportunities for him or her to participate in physical activities that provide outlets for his or her energy. Give little attention to minor misbehavior. Teach fairness and the value of participating in activities. Show interest in his or her life. Value individual differences.

- Stimulate thinking by using questions, scripture stories, scripture memorization, problem-solving activities, and discussions. Allow him or her to make decisions and set goals. Use new words, and allow him or her to define and explain their meanings. Use visuals, stories, and games.

- Respond to the need to belong to groups and be influenced by them. Provide activities that allow interaction with peers. Encourage group planning and group work. Teach him or her to be sensitive to those who are not accepted by others. Give responsibilities and assignments, and help ensure follow-through. Encourage service projects such as tending children, sharing talents, and sharing the gospel with others. Use examples and lessons to teach sensitivity and kindness. Praise courtesy, unselfishness, loyalty, and friendliness.

- Do not compare him or her to others. Encourage him or her, and praise accomplishments. Show confidence in him or her as an individual. Reinforce positive behavior, and try to ignore negative acts of small consequence. Allow for independence and expression of personal feelings. Try to understand his or her worries and what makes him or her unhappy.

- Teach specific moral concepts and values. Emphasize that true happiness and self-improvement come from keeping the commandments. Encourage him or her to commit to living gospel principles. Help him or her understand and prepare for future responsibilities and blessings. Do not ridicule him or her for wrongdoing, especially in front of friends. Teach the gospel in its fulness with scripture stories and stories from the lives of latter-day prophets. Encourage him or her to bear testimony.

3

TEACHING CHILDREN IN MIXED AGE-GROUPS

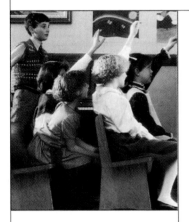

Children of widely different ages often come together to learn the gospel in the home and at church. Such group settings include family home evening and other family gatherings, Primary sharing time, achievement days, activity days, and Relief Society children's classes. These activities should be enjoyable and at the same time teach gospel principles. Elder M. Russell Ballard said: "Creative, innovative sharing times and [other] activities can be stimulating and fun, but they don't mean much if the children . . . come away having been entertained but not really enlightened, taught the gospel, or lifted spiritually. . . . Every lesson, every meeting, and every activity should be focused on bringing these little ones to Christ" ("Great Shall Be the Peace of Thy Children," *Ensign*, Apr. 1994, 61).

As you teach children in combined age-groups, you may sometimes find it challenging to make a concept simple enough for the youngest children to understand but interesting and challenging enough for the older ones. The following suggestions can help you involve all the children as they learn the gospel together.

Have Older Children Assist Younger Children

Have children work together in pairs, or have one older child assist several younger children. For example:

- An older child can sit beside a younger child and read a scripture, pointing to the words as they are read.

- An older child can help a younger child read a story, play a game, memorize a scripture, work on a project, or complete a work sheet.

- Older children can help you teach a principle or an activity. You may ask them to teach one child or several younger children. This is a good way for older children to learn gospel principles. It also helps them gain experience and confidence.

Simplify Parts of Activities for the Younger Children

If younger and older children are participating in the same activity, you may want to simplify the activity for the younger ones. For example:

- Make two sets of questions: simple questions for younger children and more difficult questions for older children. Write the questions on strips of paper. In a game or review activity, put each set of questions in a separate container. Have each child choose and answer a question from the appropriate container.

- In a dramatization, allow young children to play simple roles or be animals or part of the scenery. Older children can play more difficult roles, be narrators, and read from the scriptures. If younger children have speaking parts, older children can prompt them on what to say.

- If you are telling a story, ask younger children to hold pictures or put up flannel-board figures.

Use Stations, Dividing the Children According to Age-Groups

When younger children come to a station, the adult at the station can adapt the presentation to them. For example, if there is an activity at a station, the adult can conduct a simplified version of the activity for younger children. (See "Stations," page 179.)

4

UNDERSTANDING AND TEACHING YOUTH

When Mormon was 15 years old, he "was visited of the Lord, and tasted and knew of the goodness of Jesus" (Mormon 1:15). Joseph Smith was 14 years old when he received the First Vision. He was tutored and taught during his youth in preparation for the Restoration of the gospel. Today the Lord calls young people to serve in quorum and class presidencies, to perform sacred priesthood ordinances, and to preach the gospel as full-time missionaries. As you teach the youth of the Church, remember that the Lord knows their capacity. He has placed great trust in young people in the past, and He continues to place great trust in them today.

Understanding Young People

Young people have enthusiasm and energy that can make teaching them a delight. But to teach them the gospel, you must know how to help them channel their energy in the right direction. It is important to understand them and their concerns and challenges.

To help you understand the young people you teach, think back to your days as a youth. What experiences were most challenging or painful for you? What did you worry about? How did you feel about yourself? What were your goals and ideals? What were your social and emotional needs? Who were the people most helpful to you, and how did they help? Thinking about these questions can help you teach and guide youth more effectively.

Understanding the Challenges Young People Face

Young people face important challenges as they prepare for adulthood. If you are aware of these challenges, you can offer wise, sensitive support and encouragement. The following information can help you understand some of the challenges they face.

Adjusting to Changes in Their Bodies

Physical development during adolescence is rapid. Generally, these changes begin a year or two earlier for young women than for young men. The new feelings young men and young women experience may both excite and confuse them. They may feel awkward or inferior because they do not like their physical appearance. The physical changes they are experiencing require them to make many emotional and social adjustments.

Making Social Transitions

Because young people are in transition between childhood and adulthood, they may feel that they do not fit in with the larger society. This is especially true in societies in which their primary role is to get an education. Because of the changes they are experiencing, they recognize that they are no longer children, but they also know they are not yet able to fulfill the responsibilities of adults. Often they do not realize that the changes they are going through are normal, so they may feel self-conscious. They may think that their feelings are unique and that no one understands what they are experiencing.

Learning to Use Their Increasing Mental Abilities

Between the ages of 12 and 15, most youth increase in their ability to learn. They are better able to make good judgments, think logically, and plan for the future. You will be more likely to influence youth if you respect their mental abilities and learn from them as you would like them to learn from you.

Maintaining Emotional Connections to Their Parents and Other Adults

Youth have a strong desire to learn from their parents and other adults. They also want adults to respect, understand, and pay attention to them. Adults, however, may misjudge them because of their sometimes immature or unusual conduct. We should follow the counsel the Lord gave to Samuel: "Look not on his countenance, . . . for man looketh on the outward appearance, but the Lord looketh on the heart" (1 Samuel 16:7). An accepting and understanding adult who shows respect can make a positive difference in the life of an insecure and self-conscious youth.

You may be tempted to think that you can get closer to young people by joining them in criticizing their parents or other adults. However, this may cause them to lose respect for their parents and for you. Remember that an important part of your responsibility is to help strengthen relationships between parents and their children.

Communicate regularly with the parents of the young people you teach. Let them know about the talents, growth, and positive contributions you observe in their sons and daughters. Keep parents aware of what you are studying in class. Ask what you can do to help them as they teach their children. Direct young people to their parents, and seek to strengthen family bonds.

Establishing Their Own Identity

Some youth may try to establish an identity by wearing odd clothes or hairstyles or by expressing unusual ideas. They may do this to draw attention to themselves or to fit in with a group of peers and distinguish themselves from other groups. Generally this kind of behavior does not last long. In fact, if young people sense genuine affection from adults and are given the opportunity to express their ideas freely without being criticized, they will often feel more secure and cease acting in unusual ways.

It would be unwise to try to dress and talk like the young people you teach.

Remember that you should be one *with* them, not one *of* them.

Learning from Masculine or Feminine Role Models

It is important for young people to have masculine or feminine role models as they prepare for the future. Be aware that you and other adults serve as these role models.

Preparing to Serve in the Church and in the World

Young people spend much of their time gaining an education and preparing for a career. Encourage them to take their education seriously and to prepare well for the future. Encourage them also to think about how their schooling, their study of the gospel, and their choices between right and wrong are preparing them for future service in the Church. Help young men prepare to serve as full-time missionaries.

Preparing for Marriage and Family Life

Young people can best prepare for marriage and family life by preparing to make and keep temple covenants. Everything you do and teach should point young people to the temple. Help them understand what is required to be worthy of attending the temple, and encourage them to establish a personal goal to do so.

Internalizing the Values by Which They Will Live

The restored gospel provides the principles and standards that guide us to happiness and exaltation. Take every opportunity to help young people adopt these for themselves. Encourage them to take initiative in their own spiritual growth (see "Helping Individuals Take Responsibility for Learning the Gospel," pages 61–62).

Developing Friendships with Other People Their Age

Youth desire to find a place among people their own age and draw strength from them. Friends play important roles in a young person's preparation for adulthood. They help fill his or her need for acceptance. They enable him or her to practice social skills. They provide reassurance that others have similar needs and struggles, lessening feelings of isolation that he or she may feel. They allow him or her to learn about the feelings and ideas of others. They give support to emerging values. When young people with righteous values group together, they help insulate one another from pressures of those with differing values. The Church plays an important role in providing associations with friends and caring adults who reinforce wholesome lifestyles and values.

What Youth Need from Adults

Support

When young people feel warmth, affection, and support from a parent, teacher, or other adult, they feel encouraged to face the challenges of life optimistically. Make sure the young people you teach feel that you are available and interested in them. As you think about them and the things they must learn, ask yourself if you are doing all you can to help them progress.

Expectations of Good Conduct

When young people are expected to meet gospel standards and obey rules, they are much less likely to act in risky or deviant ways. It is wise to establish early in your teaching the expectations you have for them. Remember that being a friend to youth is not enough. You must be a good example. You must also teach true doctrine and expect good behavior so they will know how to live a faithful life. (See "The Power of the Word," pages 50–51, and the section titled "Create a Learning Atmosphere," pages 75–87.)

Respect for Individuality

When youth feel that adults respect and listen to them, they tend to feel secure and free of the need to attract attention to themselves. Work and pray to understand the young people you teach. Reach out to them individually (see "Reaching Out to the One," pages 35–36). Ask them about their interests, hobbies, and everyday experiences. Listen to them, and respect their ideas, opinions, and feelings.

A Vision of Their Future

As you teach the youth of the Church, you are helping to prepare future leaders—parents, priesthood and auxiliary leaders, missionaries, and perhaps prophets. Because young people lack experience, they sometimes have difficulty seeing beyond the present moment. As a teacher, you can give them a vision of their future and guidance in preparing for it. Encourage them to imagine themselves in the future. Teach them today the things they will need to know tomorrow.

Encouragement to Identify with the Kingdom of God

Even though youth are often concerned about themselves, they also have a great capacity to be concerned about others. They worry about the conditions of society and are naturally idealistic. They want to belong to a worthy cause. When they know they belong to a group that has a real and meaningful purpose, they are more likely to be creative, cooperative, and self-sacrificing. The cause of building the kingdom of God is more worthy of their loyalty than any other. You can encourage their unselfish desires by inspiring them to help build the kingdom of God.

5

TEACHING YOUTH THROUGH GROUP ACTIVITIES

Youth activities should be planned with gospel purposes in mind. During these activities, you should be alert for opportunities to help young people strengthen their testimonies, develop talents and leadership skills, give service, and develop friendships with others who are committed to gospel principles. The following suggestions may be helpful for leaders, teachers, and parents.

Teach by Example

During youth activities, your example is your most powerful teaching tool. You teach young people through your actions, your casual conversation about others, your solutions to problems, the language you use, and the way you extend yourself to others.

For example, a group of young women learned a lesson from their leaders when their girls' camp provided some surprising circumstances. They thought they would be attending a camp that provided cabins and electricity, and they had packed accordingly. When they arrived, however, only tents were available—with no electricity or other facilities. It would have been easy to complain, but the Young Women leaders set an example by choosing to laugh about the circumstances and do their best with what they had. Many years later, one of the young women recalled that camp as an important time for her. She said: "I will never forget sitting under a bush with some of the other girls and one of our leaders. All of us were laughing and trying to figure out how we would manage for the next three days. When I saw my leaders making the best of a difficult situation, I learned a

great lesson about cheerfully adapting and helping others."

Plan Teaching Opportunities

You should not try to make activities into formal classes. However, there are often ways to build gospel teaching into activities.

For example, when an Aaronic Priesthood adviser heard President Ezra Taft Benson encourage families to read daily from the Book of Mormon, he was impressed with the promises given. He was especially touched by the promise that families would be blessed with the Spirit of the Lord in their homes if they would follow this counsel (see Conference Report, Oct. 1988, 3–4; or *Ensign,* Nov. 1988, 4–6). The Aaronic Priesthood adviser recalled: "I thought, 'If that promise applies to families, would it also apply to my Scout troop?' I determined that we would begin having daily scripture reading time at Scout camp. Each morning before we began the day, we would gather together and read a chapter from the Book of Mormon. I testify that President Benson's blessing was realized in our troop. From the day we began to read together, we never had a serious episode of difficulty among the boys. I hope that they came to understand the power of following the counsel of the prophet."

That same leader also determined that he would never let a campfire service go by without bearing his testimony and encouraging each boy to serve a mission. Many years later, some of the young men he served thanked him for his campfire counsel and told him that it had influenced their decisions.

Take Advantage of Unplanned Teaching Moments

Often during activities, you will have unplanned opportunities to teach gospel principles (see also "Teaching Moments in Family Life," pages 140–41). For example, when a group returned from a hike one afternoon, they noticed that two young women were missing. The leader immediately called the others together. They knelt in prayer and then made a plan to search for the missing girls. What could have been a serious problem was resolved when the young women were found within a few minutes. The leader again called everyone together, and they offered a heartfelt prayer of gratitude. After the prayer, the leader expressed her love for each of the young women and bore her testimony about the reality of Heavenly Father and His willingness to answer their prayers.

Use Activities as a Basis for Teaching the Gospel

Activities can create experiences in which you and those you teach apply gospel principles. Whenever appropriate, take time after an activity to talk with the young people about the gospel principles they have applied. You can be guided by the following questions: What? So what? Now what?

What? Ask the young people to describe what happened during the activity and to talk about the people and the places involved. You might ask questions such as "What was the best part of the day?" or "What was the funniest thing that happened?" or "What was hard for you?"

So what? Ask participants to think about the activity in terms of gospel principles. You could ask questions such as "Why did we do what we did?" or "How did the activity help someone?" or "What did you learn from this activity?" or "What was difficult or easy for you?"

Now what? Ask the young people to think about how the activity might affect them in the future. This is important because it helps them feel committed to apply what they have learned. You could ask, "Will you do anything differently in the future because of what you learned today? If so, what?" Or you could ask them to finish the sentence "In the future, I will . . ."

You may want to use these questions as the basis for discussion in one or more of the following ways:

- Guide an informal conversation on the way home from an event. A group of young men and women were on their way home from a service project in which they had spent time with children at a local children's

hospital. Even though many of the young people had been nervous at first, everyone seemed to enjoy the afternoon. As they rode back to the meetinghouse, they began telling each other about the children they had worked with. They related funny things, good things, and sad things. One of the advisers was driving the car. She listened, asking questions once in a while and encouraging each person to say something about what had happened. Then she said, "Do you think our visit made a difference for any of those children?" There was a little hesitation, and then someone said, "I think so." This prompted further discussion. The adviser continued to listen as the young people talked about why they were glad they had come and what they wanted to do in the future. This brief conversation helped everyone better understand the meaning of the afternoon's experience.

- Plan a few minutes at the close of an activity to talk about what happened and the lessons that can be drawn from it. This can be done at the end of a youth conference, camping experience, or temple excursion. You can do this just before you invite the youth to bear their testimonies.

- Talk about the activity the next time you meet for a lesson. Remind the youth of what they felt and what they learned from the activity.

- Before the youth plan their next activity, invite them to talk about the most recent activity. If there is much time between the past activity and the conversation about it, you may need to spend a little more time on the "What" questions listed on this page so that everyone can remember the event clearly.

- Use activities as examples when you teach lessons. During lessons, you or assigned young people could talk about past activities that relate to the gospel principles being discussed.

- Invite young people to write about activities. You may want to invite the youth to write in their journals about an activity or to write letters to missionaries in which they tell about a service project and what they learned from it.

Guidelines and Policies for Planning Activities

Remember that activities should nurture faith and build bonds of love. Among the greatest gifts you can give young people are experiences in which they discover that the gospel applies in their lives.

For guidelines and policies for planning activities, see the "Activities" section of the *Church Handbook of Instructions.*

6

UNDERSTANDING AND TEACHING ADULTS

A counselor in a ward Relief Society often needed to ask sisters to substitute for the regularly called teachers. She was a little surprised at their hesitancy when she asked them. They said that they felt inadequate teaching so many women who, they were sure, knew more and were better prepared to teach than they.

You too may have felt inadequate in a calling to teach adults. You may have worried not only about the seemingly superior knowledge and experience of many of those you teach, but also about the wide differences between them. Often, adult class members differ greatly in their occupations, education, Church experience, family challenges, knowledge of scriptures, confidence level, and spiritual development. This can make it challenging to see how to prepare material that will be interesting and meaningful for all of them. But you can use these differing characteristics and experiences—the very attributes that may have led you to feel inadequate—to enhance the lessons you teach.

You can magnify your calling as a teacher by using the many strengths of those you teach. You can draw on their insights and experience. You can plan lessons so they will be able to learn from one another. You do not need to have all the answers or hold class members spellbound by your presentation; these are not requirements to be an effective gospel teacher. Instead, you need to be humble, diligent, prayerful, and anxious to have class members contribute to lessons. As

you go forward in this spirit, the Lord will enable you to turn your worry about your inadequacies into reliance on Him. He will magnify your efforts, give you peace, and prompt those you teach to enrich class discussions. The Lord grants us a special measure of inspiration when we gather to study the gospel.

Common Characteristics of Adult Learners

As you seek to draw on the strengths and insights of the adults you teach, be aware of the characteristics they have in common. Most adult learners share the following characteristics.

They Need to Feel That They Are Loved and Respected and Are Contributing Something of Value

The need to be loved and respected is not outgrown with age, and neither is the desire to make a meaningful contribution. An understanding of these needs will motivate you to listen to and value the ideas of those you teach. Respectfully consider all ideas offered by class members, and express gratitude for their sincere contributions. Be careful not to embarrass anyone in the class. Avoid sarcasm and demeaning humor.

They Want to Learn by the Spirit

Adults bring to class a rich resource of experiences. Many have learned in their own lives the power of true principles, and they can bear testimony of how the gospel has blessed them. Because of the trials and joys they have experienced, they feel a great need to understand the gospel and receive guidance from the Spirit.

They Want to Talk about How the Gospel Applies in Their Lives

Adults can contribute personal insights they have gained through practicing their beliefs and pondering the scriptures. They can teach and strengthen one another as they share experiences. Invite them to share their experiences during discussions. Help them understand and discuss how the principles you are studying can make a positive difference in their individual lives and in the lives of their family members.

They Desire to Be Self-Directed

Adults want to take responsibility for learning the gospel. You should use teaching methods that will help them do so (see "Helping Individuals Take Responsibility for Learning the Gospel," pages 61–62). Encourage them to complete reading assignments in preparation for lessons. Invite them to come to class prepared to ask questions and share insights and experiences.

One Gospel Doctrine teacher regularly invited class members to use the first five minutes of class to share insights or inspiration they had gained through their personal scripture study during the week. These experiences invited the Spirit and encouraged other class members to be more diligent learners. The comments often provided effective introductions to the lessons.

They Are Concerned about Their Family Responsibilities

Adults want to find solutions to the challenges they face in their families. They are anxious to learn how gospel principles apply to these challenges, and they are interested in others' insights and experiences. Discussions on such subjects are a good use of the time you spend studying the gospel together.

An elders quorum instructor was teaching a lesson based on "The Family: A Proclamation to the World." A member of the quorum had read part of the proclamation, and the instructor was about to move forward with the lesson. Then another quorum member raised his hand. "I have a question," he said. Quoting a phrase from the proclamation, he asked, "How do we teach our children 'to love and serve one another'?" This led to a valuable discussion in which quorum members shared practical ways to apply the principle.

We begin to realize the significance of the call to teach adult classes when we see how adults share what they learn—particularly when they share it with their families.

In one high priests group, the instructor taught a lesson about missionary work. As part of the lesson, he conducted a discussion about the need for older couples to serve missions. Many of the brethren had served missions as young men or later in life with their wives, and some of them testified of the responsibilities and blessings of such service.

One member of the high priests group returned home and told his wife about the discussion. The two of them had been satisfied with the contribution they were making to the lives of their family members. But the words and spirit of that lesson began to work in their hearts. Less than two months later, they spoke in sacrament meeting before leaving to serve for 18 months in another country. With emotion, the husband expressed appreciation for the high priests group instructor and the influence of that lesson on his decision. He said that he knew the decision to serve a mission would be a blessing in his life and the lives of his family members.

Working with Individual Differences

Adults vary widely in their experiences and abilities. Some know the scriptures well; some are quick with answers; some need a longer time to ponder a question; some hesitate to volunteer even though they have much to say; some have difficulty reading. By thinking about these differences carefully, you can plan learning activities that will help all class members participate.

You can teach a diverse group more effectively if you get to know them as individuals and adapt your teaching to their needs and interests (see "Understanding Those You Teach," pages 33–34). It is especially important to encourage the participation of new converts, less-active members, members who are new in the ward, and young adults just leaving their Aaronic Priesthood quorum or Young Women class. These members have experiences and insights, but they may be hesitant to share them.

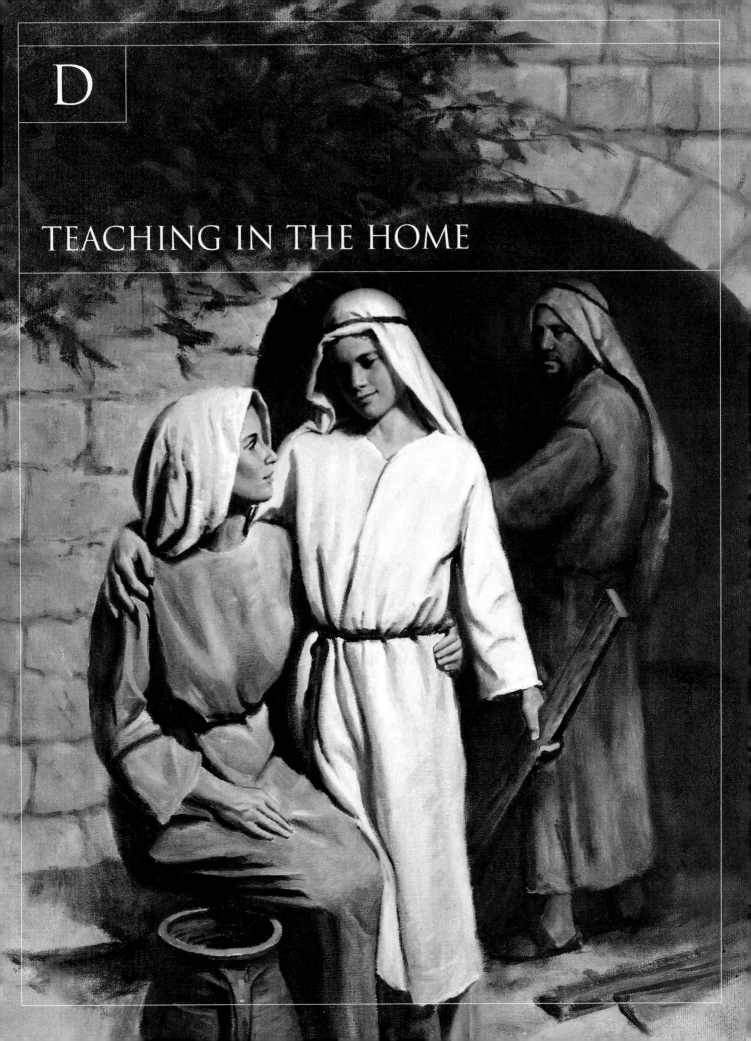

D

TEACHING IN THE HOME

TEACHING IN THE FAMILY

Teach me to walk in the light of his love;
Teach me to pray to my Father above;
Teach me to know of the things that are right;
Teach me, teach me to walk in the light.

Come, little child, and together we'll learn
Of his commandments, that we may return
Home to his presence, to live in his sight—
Always, always to walk in the light.

Hymns, no. 304

1

PARENTS' TEACHING RESPONSIBILITY

President Boyd K. Packer declared: "The ultimate purpose of all we teach is to unite parents and children in faith in the Lord Jesus Christ, that they are happy at home, sealed in an eternal marriage, linked to their generations, and assured of exaltation in the presence of our Heavenly Father" (in Conference Report, Apr. 1995, 8; or Ensign, May 1995, 8).

The family is ordained of God. It is central to His plan. He has established families to bring happiness to His children, to help them learn the gospel in a loving atmosphere, and to prepare them for eternal life. The home is the most important place to teach, learn, and apply gospel principles.

Parents have the primary responsibility for teaching their children the gospel (see D&C 68:25–28). The First Presidency and Quorum of the Twelve have declared: "Parents have a sacred duty to rear their children in love and righteousness, to provide for their physical and spiritual needs, to teach them to love and serve one another, to observe the commandments of God and to be law-abiding citizens wherever they live. Husbands and wives—mothers and fathers—will be held accountable before God for the discharge of these obligations" ("The Family: A Proclamation to the World," *Ensign,* Nov. 1995, 102).

What Parents Should Teach Their Children

The following summarizes many of the things that parents should teach their children. Resources that you can use in teaching your children include the scriptures, the words of latter-day prophets, Church magazines, and other Church-produced materials.

Basic Principles of the Gospel

The Lord has commanded parents to teach their children "to understand the doctrine of repentance, faith in Christ the Son of the living God, and of baptism and the gift of the Holy Ghost by the laying on of the hands, when eight years old" (D&C 68:25). You should teach your children of the Savior's Atonement, the nature of the priesthood and the ordinances of salvation, and the central role of families and eternal marriage in the divine plan of happiness.

Prayer

The Lord has also commanded that parents "teach their children to pray" (D&C 68:28). It is essential for children to know that they can talk to Heavenly Father and seek His guidance. You can teach them that God is always ready to help them. You can help your children learn to pray individually in the morning, at night, and whenever they need help or want to express thanks. You can also teach the importance of family prayer.

Scripture Study

You will receive great blessings as you study the gospel individually and hold daily scripture study as a family. You will be able to help your children love the scriptures and recognize the power of God's word in their lives (see "The Power of the Word," pages 50–51). You will be able to help them search the scriptures to understand true principles and to find answers to their problems. You will also be able to help them develop the study skills and habits they need to continue learning the gospel throughout their lives (see "Helping Individuals Take Responsibility for Learning the Gospel," pages 61–62).

Living the Gospel

You should teach your children to exercise their agency in righteous ways—to apply gospel teachings in all they do. As King Benjamin taught, you should teach your children "to walk in the ways of truth and soberness" and "to love one another, and to serve one another" (Mosiah 4:15).

In the home, children should learn to keep the Sabbath day holy, pay tithing, and follow latter-day prophets. They should learn to seek for all things that are "virtuous, lovely, or of good report or praiseworthy" (Articles of Faith 1:13).

Practical Skills

In addition to teaching doctrinal topics, you should teach your children practical skills such as how to manage money, maintain good health, get along with others, and take care of clothing and property. Help them learn to work hard, get a good education, and be good citizens.

How Parents Can Teach Their Children

As a parent, you should strive to establish patterns of gospel living in your home (see "Teaching through Patterns of Gospel Living," pages 135–36). Everyday patterns of gospel living can create an atmosphere of faith and obedience in the home. Following are some of the many ways you can teach your children.

Example

Example can be your most powerful teaching tool. Children learn attitudes and conduct by observing your actions (see "Living What You Teach," pages 18–19).

Regular Occasions for Teaching in the Home

Daily family prayers and scripture study, family home evening, and even family traditions can weave the gospel into every part of children's daily living (see "Regular Occasions for Teaching in the Home," pages 137–39).

Elder M. Russell Ballard taught: "Love for our Heavenly Father and His Son Jesus Christ is greatly enhanced when the gospel is taught and lived in the home. True principles of eternal life are embedded in the hearts and souls of young and old alike when scriptures are read and discussed, when prayers are offered morning and night, and when reverence for God and obedience to Him are modeled in everyday conduct" (in Conference Report, Apr. 1996, 112; or *Ensign,* May 1996, 81).

Teaching Moments

Some of your greatest teaching opportunities will be unplanned. Be alert for opportunities that arise in the course of everyday living to teach your children gospel principles (see "Teaching Moments in Family Life," pages 140–41).

It Is Never Too Late for Parents to Begin Teaching Their Children

It is important to establish patterns of gospel living when children are young. As Elder L. Tom Perry expressed, "How important it is that gospel training begin right at the start when we accept a new little spirit into our home" (in Conference Report, Oct. 1988, 87; or *Ensign,* Nov. 1988, 74). Smaller children are eager to participate in family home evening, scripture study, prayer, and service projects.

President Thomas S. Monson observed: "There are those who dismiss these responsibilities, feeling they can be deferred until the child grows up. Not so, the evidence reveals. Prime time for teaching is fleeting" (in Conference Report, Oct. 1997, 21; or *Ensign,* Nov. 1997, 17).

Still, it is never too late to begin teaching the gospel to your children—or to begin again. The teaching process will be different if you have delayed teaching your children the gospel. There may be additional challenges. But the Lord will bless you for your earnest efforts to teach true principles and establish righteous practices in your family. If you are newly awakened to your parenting responsibilities, take hope. Pray, exercise faith, and do all you can to reach your children and influence them for good.

Elder Robert D. Hales explained, "Certainly parents will make mistakes in their parenting process, but through humility, faith, prayer, and study, each person can learn a better way and in so doing bless the lives of family members now and teach correct traditions for the generations that follow" (in Conference Report, Oct. 1993, 10–11; or *Ensign,* Nov. 1993, 10).

2

FATHERS
AS TEACHERS

The First Presidency and Quorum of the Twelve stated, "By divine design, fathers are to preside over their families in love and righteousness" ("The Family: A Proclamation to the World," *Ensign,* Nov. 1995, 102). This obligation includes the responsibility to teach the gospel.

An adult member of the Church spoke fondly of the gospel lessons she had received from her father. She recalled:

"My father established a family tradition of taking his children aside each week for about two months before we turned eight years old. When it was my turn, he had a brand-new journal for me, and we sat together, just the two of us, and talked. He asked me about my feelings for Jesus, and then he discussed with me the gospel principles he had prepared.

"Over the two-month period he taught me the simple, beautiful gospel. He had me draw a visual aid as we went along. It showed the premortal existence, this earth life, and the steps I needed to take to return to live with Heavenly Father: faith in Jesus Christ, repentance, baptism, receiving the gift of the Holy Ghost, and enduring in faith to the end.

"I will never forget the love I felt from my dad as he spent that time with me. He bore his testimony about each step of the plan of salvation and was very patient with my questions. I think it was such a powerful experience because he spoke on my level and bore his testimony to me. I believe that this experience was a major reason I had a testimony of the gospel when I was baptized."

Sometimes fathers become preoccupied with the temporal welfare of their families. Some fathers leave all the responsibility for gospel teaching to the mothers. This should never be. To all fathers, President Gordon B. Hinckley said:

"Yours is the basic and inescapable responsibility to stand as the head of the family. That does not carry with it any implication of dictatorship or unrighteous dominion. It carries with it a mandate that fathers provide for the needs of their families. Those needs are more than food, clothing, and shelter. Those needs include righteous direction and the teaching, by example as well as precept, of basic principles of honesty, integrity, service, respect for the rights of others, and an understanding that we are accountable for that which we do in this life, not only to one another but also to the God of heaven, who is our Eternal Father" (in Conference Report, Oct. 1993, 78–79; or *Ensign,* Nov. 1993, 60).

President Ezra Taft Benson suggested "ten specific ways that fathers can give spiritual leadership to their children:

"1. Give father's blessings to your children. Baptize and confirm your children. Ordain your sons to the priesthood. These will become spiritual highlights in the lives of your children.

"2. Personally direct family prayers, daily scripture reading, and weekly family home evenings. Your personal involvement will show your children how important these activities really are.

"3. Whenever possible, attend Church meetings together as a family. Family worship under your leadership is vital to your children's spiritual welfare.

"4. Go on daddy-daughter dates and father-and-sons' outings with your children. As a family, go on campouts and picnics, to ball games and recitals, to school programs, and so forth. Having Dad there makes all the difference.

"5. Build traditions of family vacations and trips and outings. These memories will never be forgotten by your children.

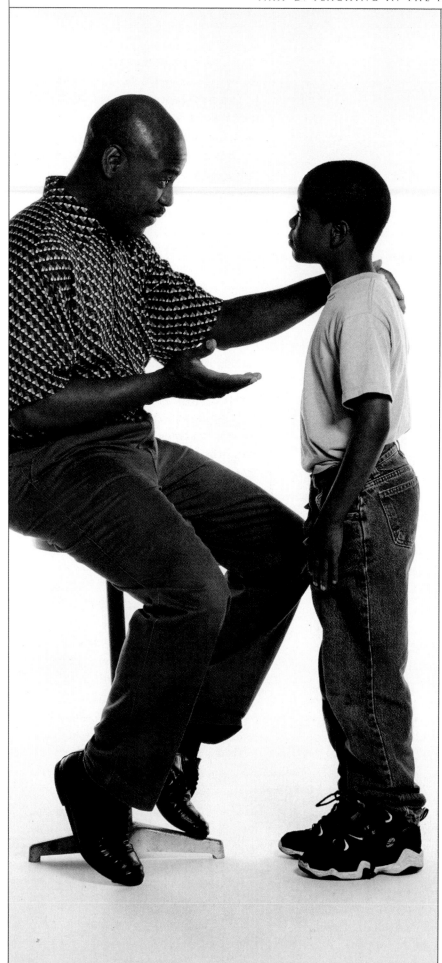

"6. Have regular one-on-one visits with your children. Let them talk about what they would like to. Teach them gospel principles. Teach them true values. Tell them you love them. Personal time with your children tells them where Dad puts his priorities.

"7. Teach your children to work, and show them the value of working toward a worthy goal. Establishing mission funds and education funds for your children shows them what Dad considers to be important.

"8. Encourage good music and art and literature in your homes. Homes that have a spirit of refinement and beauty will bless the lives of your children forever.

"9. As distances allow, regularly attend the temple with your wife. Your children will then better understand the importance of temple marriage and temple vows and the eternal family unit.

"10. Have your children see your joy and satisfaction in service to the Church. This can become contagious to them, so they, too, will want to serve in the Church and will love the kingdom."

President Benson concluded by saying, "Remember your sacred calling as a father in Israel—your most important calling in time and eternity—a calling from which you will never be released" (in Conference Report, Oct. 1987, 62–63; or *Ensign,* Nov. 1987, 50–51).

As a father, you should always remember the eternal importance of your role. Fatherhood is a divine responsibility. Elder Boyd K. Packer said, "It should have great meaning that of all the titles of respect and honor and admiration that could be given him, God himself, he who is the highest of all, chose to be addressed simply as Father" (in Conference Report, Apr. 1972, 139; or *Ensign,* July 1972, 113).

3

MOTHERS AS TEACHERS

The First Presidency and Quorum of the Twelve have said that "mothers are primarily responsible for the nurture of their children" ("The Family: A Proclamation to the World," *Ensign,* Nov. 1995, 102). Such nurture includes teaching gospel principles.

President Ezra Taft Benson remembered with love the teaching of his mother:

"I remember so well, as a little boy, coming in from the field and approaching the old farm house in Whitney, Idaho. I could hear my mother singing 'Have I Done Any Good in the World Today?' [*Hymns,* no. 223].

"I can still see her in my mind's eye bending over the ironing board with newspapers on the floor, ironing long strips of white cloth, with beads of perspiration on her forehead. When I asked her what she was doing, she said, 'These are temple robes, my son. Your father and I are going to the temple at Logan.'

"Then she put the old flatiron on the stove, drew a chair close to mine, and told me about temple work—how important it is to be able to go to the temple and participate in the sacred ordinances performed there. She also expressed her fervent hope that some day her children and grandchildren and great-grandchildren would have the opportunity to enjoy these priceless blessings" ("What I Hope You Will Teach Your Children about the Temple," *Ensign,* Aug. 1985, 8).

Regarding the importance of mothers teaching their children the gospel, President Benson said: "Mothers, you are your children's best teacher. . . . Teach your children the gospel in your own home, at your own fireside. This is the most effective teaching that your children will ever receive. This is the Lord's way of teaching. The Church cannot teach like you can. The school cannot. The day-care center cannot. But you can, and the Lord will sustain you. Your children will remember your teachings forever, and when they are old, they will not depart from them. They will call you blessed—their truly angel mother" (*To the Mothers in Zion* [pamphlet, 1987], 10–11).

As a mother, you teach in many ways. Sometimes you plan teaching opportunities, but many teaching opportunities occur spontaneously in the normal flow of family life (see "Teaching Moments in Family Life," pages 140–41). Sometimes you teach by example, sometimes by precept. Sometimes you teach by establishing patterns of gospel living in the home and sometimes by just taking time to pay attention and show love. President Benson gave 10 suggestions that can help you teach your children. Each of them emphasizes taking time:

"Take time to always be at the crossroads when your children are either coming or going . . . whether your children are six or sixteen. . . .

" . . . Take time to be a real friend to your children. . . .

" . . . Take time to read to your children. . . .

" . . . Take time to pray with your children. . . .

" . . . Take time to have a meaningful weekly home evening. . . . Make this one of your great family traditions. . . .

" . . . Take time to be together at mealtimes as often as possible. . . .

" . . . Take time daily to read the scriptures together as a family. . . .

" . . . Take time to do things together as a family. . . .

" . . . Take time to teach your children. Catch the teaching moments. . . .

" . . . Take the time to truly love your children. A mother's unqualified love approaches Christlike love" (*To the Mothers in Zion*, 8–12).

The responsibilities of motherhood can seem overwhelming. It is important to remember that the Lord does not expect mothers to be perfect or to achieve an unrealistic ideal standard of homemaking. Yet He does expect them to recognize and honor their divine role and to humbly do their best.

Elder Jeffrey R. Holland said to the mothers in the Church: "Yours is the grand tradition of Eve, the mother of all the human family. . . . Yours is the grand tradition of Sarah and Rebekah and Rachel, without whom there could not have been those magnificent patriarchal promises to Abraham, Isaac, and Jacob which bless us all. Yours is the grand tradition of Lois and Eunice and the mothers of the 2,000 stripling warriors. Yours is the grand tradition of Mary, chosen and foreordained from before this world was, to conceive, carry, and bear the Son of God Himself. We

thank all of you, including our own mothers, and tell you there is nothing more important in this world than participating so directly in the work and glory of God, in bringing to pass the mortality and earthly life of His daughters and sons, so that immortality and eternal life can come in those celestial realms on high" (in Conference Report, Apr. 1997, 48; or *Ensign,* May 1997, 36).

President Gordon B. Hinckley spoke of the great blessing of motherhood:

"Let every mother realize that she has no greater blessing than the children who have come to her as a gift from the Almighty; that she has no greater mission than to rear them in light and truth, in understanding and love. . . .

"I remind mothers everywhere of the sanctity of your calling. No other can adequately take your place. No responsibility is greater, no obligation more binding than that you rear in love and peace and integrity those whom you have brought into the world" (in Conference Report, Oct. 1993, 79; or *Ensign,* Nov. 1993, 60).

4

PARENTS' TEACHING PARTNERSHIP

In "The Family: A Proclamation to the World," the First Presidency and Quorum of the Twelve explain that fathers and mothers "are obligated to help one another as equal partners" (*Ensign,* Nov. 1995, 102). This partnership is especially necessary in parents' sacred responsibility to teach their children.

In a general conference address, President Boyd K. Packer read Doctrine and Covenants 27:15, 17: "Lift up your hearts and rejoice, and gird up your loins, and take upon you my whole armor, that ye may be able to withstand the evil day, . . . taking the shield of faith wherewith ye shall be able to quench all the fiery darts of the wicked." After reading this passage, President Packer explained the importance of mothers and fathers working together to help their children take the "shield of faith":

"That shield of faith is not produced in a factory but at home in a cottage industry. . . .

" . . . Our Father's plan requires that, like the generation of life itself, the shield of faith is to be made and fitted in the family. No two can be exactly alike. Each must be handcrafted to individual specifications.

"The plan designed by the Father contemplates that man and woman, husband and wife, working together, fit each child individually with a shield of faith made to buckle on so firmly that it can neither be pulled off nor penetrated by those fiery darts.

"It takes the steady strength of a father to hammer out the metal of it and the tender hands of a mother to polish and fit it on. Sometimes one parent is left to do it alone. It is difficult, but it can be done.

"In the Church we can teach about the materials from which a shield of faith is made: reverence, courage, chastity, repentance, forgiveness, compassion. In church we can learn how to assemble and fit them together. But the actual making of and fitting on of the shield of faith belongs in the family circle. Otherwise it may loosen and come off in a crisis" (in Conference Report, Apr. 1995, 8; or *Ensign,* May 1995, 8).

The following suggestions can help parents develop a more effective teaching partnership.

Taking Time to Plan Together

As parents, you should set aside specific times to discuss your children's needs and plan how to meet those needs. One busy couple discovered that holding weekly planning sessions together became one of the most valuable things they did as parents. They said:

"Although it took us almost a year to make our weekly planning session a habit, we now wonder how we ever got along without it. It helps us have more interest in what the other is doing. It helps us realize how important we are to each other and to our children. It gives us time to look at ourselves and at the children and decide on a course of action to meet our problems. We also plan our dates, special times with the children, details for family home evenings, and Sunday activities. It usually takes about 30 minutes, occasionally longer if big events or unusual problems need more talking over."

As you plan ways to teach your children, prayerfully consider the following questions:

- What should happen in the lives of our children as a result of our teaching?

- Which specific gospel principles should we teach in order to accomplish this?

- How should we teach these principles?

Suggestions for using these questions are found in "Preparing Lessons," pages 98–99,

and "Creating Lessons from Conference Talks and Other Resources," pages 100–101.

The Importance of Unity in Teaching Children

When fathers and mothers take time to counsel with one another, they are more likely to be unified in teaching their children, even in the unplanned teaching moments that occur in the ordinary flow of family life. Such unity is important because few things are more confusing to children than conflicting messages from the two people they love and respect most.

One couple shared the following story about an experience with their son:

Six-year-old Mike had worked hard most of the summer doing extra jobs at home and for the neighbors so he could earn money to spend when the family took their summer vacation. It was going to be a long trip, and his mother had said that if he wanted any treats or souvenirs along the way, he would need to buy those things himself. Even though she cautioned him almost daily to put his money in a safe place, Mike liked the feel of having money in his pocket. He carried it around with him constantly. Several times a day he would take it out and count it or show it to his friends.

On the day before the trip, Mike discovered that his money had fallen out of his pocket. Brokenhearted and crying, he went to his mother. She was sympathetic, and she helped Mike look in every place they could think of, but no money was to be found. "I'm so sorry your money is gone," she said. She resisted mentioning that she

had warned him many times, but she also resisted the temptation to make everything all better for her son. After all, she thought, playing with the money every day in spite of her warnings had been his choice.

A forlorn little Mike was sitting on the front steps when his father came home. After hearing the sad story, Mike's father reached in his pocket, pulled out the exact amount Mike had lost, and gave it to him. When the father saw the look of surprise on his wife's face, he remarked, "It's only a little money. What's the harm?"

As we consider this story, we might ask which parent was right. But that may not be the best question. It might be better to ask how Mike's parents could have been more unified in the way they handled the situation. They could have counseled together, considering Mike's needs.

They could have asked themselves, "What do we want to happen in Mike's life as a result of this situation? Does he need to learn greater responsibility? Does he need to feel more compassion and understanding from his parents? Does he need to learn not to show off in front of his friends? Does he need to learn the importance of following family rules?" This would have helped them determine what to teach their son and how to teach it.

Had Mike's parents spent time to be united in their approach to this situation, they could have found a good way to either replace Mike's lost money or not replace it. Instead, they responded in ways that taught conflicting lessons.

As you work together as parents, you can be one in teaching the gospel of Jesus Christ to your children.

5

TEACHING THROUGH PATTERNS OF GOSPEL LIVING

One of the ways the Lord teaches us is by guiding us to establish upright, worshipful patterns of living. He commands us to pray and read the scriptures every day, individually and as families. He commands us to attend church and partake of the sacrament weekly, to attend the temple as often as we can, and to fast and pay fast offerings each month. These patterns of living show us the way we should walk as His disciples.

Children learn to live as the Savior's disciples when they join with their families, from their earliest years onward, in repeating the patterns of worship, service, study, and work that He has ordained. If the family does not live by these patterns, the effectiveness of the parents' formal gospel teaching will be limited. If the parents' way of life is inconsistent with their spoken words, the children will tend to follow what the parents do more than what they say. But if the parents speak often of the Savior and establish His ways as their family pattern, they will teach their children "in the nurture and admonition of the Lord," as Enos said he had been taught by his father (Enos 1:1).

President Brigham Young stated: "In every nation, community, and family, there are peculiar traditions, and the child is trained in them. If the law of Christ becomes the tradition of this people, the children will be brought up according to the law of the celestial kingdom. . . . Children will then be brought up, under the traditions of their fathers, to do just right, and to refrain from all evil" (in *Journal of Discourses*, 3:327).

Our children are "brought up according to the law of the celestial kingdom" as we establish patterns of gospel living in our homes.

Specific Things We Can Do to Establish Patterns of Discipleship

We have the obligation to conscientiously choose and foster patterns of gospel living. For example, we can select art, music, and literature that will help our children develop a preference for that which uplifts and edifies. We can serve together in the Church and community. We can choose modest clothing for ourselves and help our children do the same. We can study the scriptures together and hold family home evening. We can foster a reverent attitude toward the Sabbath that will influence children's feelings about keeping it a holy day.

One of the most powerful ways to establish righteous patterns of living is to create and maintain family traditions. Children feel secure in knowing that no matter what happens in their lives, certain events in their family will remain the same. President Ezra Taft Benson counseled: "Foster wonderful family traditions which will bind you together eternally. In doing so, we can create a bit of heaven right here on earth within individual families. After all, eternity will be but an extension of righteous family life" (in Conference Report, Oct. 1989, 4; or *Ensign*, Nov. 1989, 5).

Many family traditions can be gospel centered. For example, in some families, children receive a new copy of the Book of Mormon on their eighth birthday. Some families celebrate Christmas by acting out the events surrounding the Savior's birth. In some families, the father administers a priesthood blessing to each of his children at the beginning of a new school year. Some families have annual reunions or meet together for holidays and baby blessings. These anticipated and beloved traditions strengthen families and individuals as they rejoice in repeating what is familiar and often sacred. Traditions can remind family members of their way of life as disciples of Christ, and they can often provide opportunities for instruction in gospel principles.

Changing Unwanted Patterns in Our Families

We can change unwanted patterns in our families. If we have come from a less-active family, we can change that pattern in our own lives and strive to regularly attend Church meetings. If we have criticized Church leaders or heard our parents do so, we can choose from now on to sustain our leaders through our language and actions. Such changes in the way we live will give our children a better pattern to follow.

A member of the Church shared the following story:

"My husband, Roger, was raised in a home with no patterns of gospel living. His father was addicted to alcohol, and the family suffered from this. His mother tried to be active in the Church, but his father wanted the family to do other things on Sunday. Roger became very active with friends as a teenager, and when he obtained his own testimony of the gospel, he began to keep a special loose-leaf notebook of what he wanted to have in his own family when he got married. He was about 17 at the time. He had one section in the notebook for what he would do with his children, one for what he wanted in a wife, one for how he wanted his house to be, and one for the kind of job he

would prepare himself for. He wrote all his ideas there, and he also included articles he found that were helpful. Some of what he wrote he learned from the negative example of the family in which he was raised; it taught him how he didn't want his own family to be. His father so objected to his Church activity that he needed to move out, and he lived with a religious family whom he admired, though they were not Church members. From them he got other ideas about his future family. So even at that early age, he wanted to be a turning point in his generation from a troubled past to a more blessed future.

"When we became engaged he showed me the notebook, and we would discuss the ideas and develop them until we shared our vision of what we wanted for our family. I remember the first thing we worked on was prayer. We taught our children to pray from the time they were very tiny, so it would be a deeply ingrained habit they wouldn't think of ignoring. We decided tithing would never be a question. We held family home evenings faithfully. And we established the tradition of scripture study every morning. At first we worked too hard to read a certain number of verses each time, but then we realized that the discussions we had when the children asked questions were more important than keeping strictly to a schedule. In the last few years we have added a hymn right after opening prayer, with all the verses. This wakes us up and brings a good spirit. These are only a few of the traditions around which our family has been built.

"I marvel that my husband decided to set up righteous traditions in his own family when he was so young and had such a poor example to follow. I also marvel and am grateful that he was so determined to work together to teach them to our family, mostly by just doing them on a faithful basis."

6

REGULAR OCCASIONS FOR TEACHING IN THE HOME

As parents, you should seek to establish regular occasions for teaching the gospel in the home. When you do this, your children consistently receive gospel teachings that apply in their lives and become a foundation for them. They are able to observe from your actions that believing the gospel means being guided by it in every aspect of life.

The following ideas can help you establish regular occasions for teaching your children the gospel.

Family Prayer

The Savior commanded, "Pray in your families unto the Father, always in my name, that your wives and your children may be blessed" (3 Nephi 18:21).

Family prayers are excellent occasions for showing children how to pray. As your children observe you earnestly speaking with your Father in Heaven, they will see your faith and righteous desires. They will learn to "counsel with the Lord in all [their] doings" so that He will "direct [them] for good" (Alma 37:37).

As you pray, you should use the words *Thee, Thou, Thy,* and *Thine* in place of *you* and *your.* This example will help your children learn the language of prayer, which expresses love and reverence for Heavenly Father.

Children can learn much of the gospel when they hear other family members pray. They learn the need for repentance as they hear others ask for forgiveness. They learn gratitude when they hear others thank Heavenly Father for their blessings. They

learn faith, humility, and obedience as they see that their parents continually seek guidance. They learn to honor and respect Church leaders as family members pray for them each day. They can gain a desire to serve missions and receive the blessings of the temple as parents ask Heavenly Father to help their children make choices that will keep them worthy to receive these blessings.

Children learn to have love and concern for others as they hear family members pray for other people. And children feel a great sense of love when they hear family members pray for them.

Each family member should be given an opportunity to lead the family in prayer. Small children can take their turns with help.

Family Scripture Study

Studying the scriptures daily is another powerful way to teach children the gospel. Whenever possible, families should read together at a regular time each day. For some, this is easiest to do early in the morning. For others, family scripture study is best done just before bedtime. Although it may sometimes be difficult to get family members to participate, your consistent efforts to study the word of God will bless your children's lives. Your children will learn the truth of Nephi's teaching: "Feast upon the words of Christ; for behold, the words of Christ will tell you all things what ye should do" (2 Nephi 32:3).

As children read the scriptures with their family members, they come to love

Because the family is the most important setting for learning the gospel, it is fitting for family members to share and discuss with one another the truths they learn in Church meetings, classes, and activities. This allows you as parents to be aware of your children's gospel learning, taking your rightful role as those most responsible to teach your children.

Most of the regular occasions for teaching in the family provide good opportunities to ask children about what they have learned at church. You should ask questions to encourage children to recall as much as they can, including stories and specific details. Do what you can to encourage all family members to discuss what has been shared (see "Conducting Discussions," pages 63–65).

the divine truths of the gospel. The language of the scriptures becomes familiar to them. They learn stories from the scriptures and see how to apply these sacred words in their daily lives. They can also learn to use the maps, the Topical Guide, the Bible Dictionary, and other study helps in the scriptures (see pages 56–58).

You may choose to read for a set amount of time each day. Each family member who can read should be given an opportunity to read from the scriptures. They can take turns reading a single verse or several verses at a time. Children who cannot read may still participate by repeating verses as others read them. If possible, younger children can look at the Church's illustrated books of scripture stories or pictures from the Gospel Art Picture Kit.

To help family members understand the scriptures, you can rephrase difficult passages in simpler terms or look up unfamiliar words in the Bible Dictionary. You can ask family members to summarize the main points of the day's reading. A young child can hold up a picture of the story being read.

You might ask a child to think of a situation in his or her life that is similar to the scripture story you are reading. For example, you could say, "We have just read about David and Goliath. What 'Goliaths' do you face in your life? What can you learn from David that will help you face these challenges?" Or you could say, "I noticed you were helping your younger sister clean her room. Did you realize that you were showing the same kind of love that Jesus spoke about in this story?"

If you are unfamiliar with the scriptures or have difficulty reading, you may feel uncomfortable or inadequate as you read with your children. There is no harm in letting your children know that you are all learning how to read the scriptures. If you postpone family study until you feel confident, you will deprive your children of much-needed spiritual nourishment. Remember that the Spirit can influence you regardless of your experience.

Family Home Evening

Family home evenings provide excellent opportunities for you to help your children understand and apply gospel principles. A family home evening may include family prayer, gospel instruction, hymns and Primary songs, and family activities.

In planning family home evenings, consider the current needs, concerns, and interests of family members. For example, does a child need to prepare for baptism or for ordination to an office in the priesthood? Has there been contention in the home? As you prayerfully consider the needs and challenges of family members, you will be able to better determine which gospel principles you should teach.

The principles of effective teaching presented in this book can help family members plan and present family home evenings. In addition, the Church has produced the *Family Home Evening Resource Book,* which contains lessons and ideas for making family home evenings successful. Church magazines are also helpful resources.

Families sometimes find it difficult to make family home evening a regular part of their lives. Sometimes the children are uncooperative, or the parents feel that they are too busy. However, efforts to plan and carry out family home evenings will bless all family members. One man recalled that his family had family home evening only twice as he was growing up. However, these experiences made such an impression on him that when he married he still remembered them and the gospel principles that he had learned. This led him and his wife to establish weekly family home evenings in his own family.

Family Mealtimes

Family mealtimes provide opportunities for you to teach valuable lessons and for all family members to participate in discussions. With otherwise busy schedules, mealtimes are often the only times you can gather with your children to share each day's events and discuss ideas together. You

can use these occasions to talk with your children about gospel principles, family values, messages shared in sacrament meeting and other Church meetings, school, upcoming activities, world events, and other topics of interest. It can be a time for you to learn more about your children's concerns, thoughts, and feelings.

Family mealtimes should be informal and cheerful occasions in which everyone feels welcome to participate in discussions. Where possible, this time should be free from other distractions. Such occasions can contribute to the unity and spiritual growth of the family.

Family Councils

You should call family members together in family council meetings. You may use family councils to set goals, resolve problems, discuss finances, make plans, and give support and strength. You may hold family councils in connection with family home evening or at other times. As you conduct family councils, you can teach your children how to listen and show respect for one another's feelings and opinions.

Private Visits

As you regularly talk with your children, you will draw closer to them. You may need to plan private times with each child to express love and encouragement and to teach gospel principles. You should allow each child to talk about the problems or experiences that are important

to him or her. As you show genuine consideration for your children's concerns and opinions, your children will learn to trust you and seek your advice. Then you can continue to teach them to make good decisions, pray, and study the scriptures for answers to their questions.

Use the scriptures to teach your children how to exercise their agency righteously. Elder Gene R. Cook suggested how a parent could use the scriptures to help a child who questions why the family doesn't do certain things on Sunday:

"You might be tempted to say, 'Because I said so,' or 'Because the Church says so.' But a more inspired parent might say, 'Well, you know that keeping the Lord's day holy is not something we just made up. Let me show you something.' Then you could open the Doctrine and Covenants to section 59 and read [verses 9 through 11]. . . .

"Then you could explain, 'As you can see, the Lord teaches that Sunday is a holy day. . . . It's a day to rest from our labors and "to pay our devotions to the Most High," meaning that we should go to our Church meetings, partake of the sacrament, do our other Church duties, and visit the sick, the poor, and the needy. It's a day consecrated to the Lord, and I bear testimony to you, my dear daughter, that this is true and that the Lord has blessed us greatly for keeping the Sabbath Day' " (*Raising Up a Family to the Lord* [1993], 19–20).

For ideas that can be applied in private visits with your children, see "Teaching in Interviews," page 153.

7

TEACHING MOMENTS IN FAMILY LIFE

As parents, many of your teaching opportunities come in unplanned moments—in conversations, as you work with your children, and as family members face challenges together. These opportunities can be powerful teaching moments because they are closely tied to what your children are experiencing. Because such opportunities may come and go quickly, you need to recognize them and be prepared to teach principles that your children are ready to learn. The following suggestions can help you look for teaching opportunities.

Addressing Children's Questions or Worries

All children have concerns about themselves and about the world. You can show them that the gospel provides answers and guidance for understanding and solving their problems. If a child is frightened by a storm, you can take that moment to encourage her to pray for comfort. If a teenage son is pressured to see a popular movie that may be inappropriate, you can discuss the matter with him and help him apply gospel principles in deciding whether or not to see it. If children are worried about an important decision, you can read Moroni 7:15–19 with them and discuss Mormon's counsel on "the way to judge." If a family member has died, you can teach your children about the spirit world and resurrection.

For suggestions about how you can counsel with your children, see page 139 in "Regular Occasions for Teaching in the Home."

Discussing Problems That Affect Children's Peers

From time to time, children may mention problems that affect their peers. Perhaps their friends have jobs that require them to work on Sunday. Perhaps they know a young man who is a member of the Church but has decided not to serve a full-time mission. Perhaps they have friends who use improper language or demonstrate a lack of courtesy for others. In discussing these situations with your children, you can use the scriptures to teach gospel principles. This can help you guide the children toward correct decisions in similar circumstances.

Sharing Opportunities to Make Correct Choices

When you have opportunities to make correct choices, you may want to share these experiences with your children. For example, if you are given too much change at a store, you can ask your children what you should do. This can lead to a discussion about topics such as honesty, agency, and the consequences of our actions.

Discussing Ideas Presented through the Media

You can talk with your children about the ideas promoted in popular movies, television shows, and music. News broadcasts also provide opportunities to discuss current events and issues. Such discussions can help children discern between uplifting entertainment and entertainment that presents philosophies and actions contrary to gospel standards.

Helping Children Learn from Mistakes

Mistakes can provide opportunities to teach. If a child has erred, you can forgive the child, talk about apologizing and repairing any damage done, and, if the child has disobeyed a commandment, teach about the path of repentance.

If you are in the wrong, you should apologize and ask for forgiveness. Your children can learn powerful lessons as

they see your efforts to overcome your own weaknesses. Consider the following experience shared by a Church member:

"I was about 10 years old when I did something that displeased my father. He was quite upset and decided to punish me. I was deeply hurt because I felt that he was disciplining me more than I deserved. I avoided him the rest of the day, and every time he tried to talk to me, I would turn away and run. The next day I was still upset at him, so I was surprised when he came into my room and told me that he was sorry he had disciplined me so strictly. He asked me if I would please forgive him. I learned then that you are never too old to apologize and admit you were wrong. That was an opportunity to learn the true value of repentance."

Explaining Reasons for Giving Service

As you serve in Church callings or in other ways, you can tell your children what you are doing and why you are doing it. This will help the children understand more fully how their beliefs and values affect their actions. If you make dinner for someone who is sick, you can explain why it is important to help that person. When children see you preparing to teach a lesson in church, you can talk with them about the importance of magnifying callings. You can discuss with your children why we raise our hands to sustain Church leaders and how we support those called by the Lord.

Helping Children Manage Their Emotions

When children become upset, frustrated, or angry, they may act in ways that are inappropriate. You can teach them to recognize and control impulses to hurt others or raise their voices. You can draw attention to the circumstances that provoked the anger and then discuss better ways to handle similar situations in the future.

Helping Children Recognize the Influence of the Spirit

You can help your children recognize the influence of the Spirit by drawing attention to their feelings. Elder Robert D. Hales related the following experience:

"After my baptism and confirmation, my mother drew me aside and asked, 'What do you feel?' I described as best I could the warm feeling of peace, comfort, and happiness I had. Mother explained that what I was feeling was the gift I had just received, the gift of the Holy Ghost. She told me that if I lived worthy of it, I would have that gift with me continually. That was a teaching moment that has lived with me all my life" (in Conference Report, Apr. 1999, 42; or *Ensign,* May 1999, 32).

Learning Lessons from Nature

You can use everyday observations of nature to teach the gospel to your children (see "Looking for Lessons Everywhere," pages 22–23; "Comparisons and Object Lessons," pages 163–64). For example, a child's comments about the beauty of spring flowers can lead to a discussion about the Resurrection of Jesus Christ. Planting seeds together is an excellent time to discuss how Alma compared the word of God to a seed (see Alma 32:28–43).

If you are alert, you can quietly and consistently turn many of your children's experiences into teaching moments.

8

THE TEACHING INFLUENCE OF OTHER FAMILY MEMBERS

Although parents have the primary responsibility for teaching the gospel to their children, other family members can be a great help. Parents should seek opportunities to have other family members teach and strengthen their children.

The Teaching Influence of Grandparents

Grandparents can strengthen and inspire their grandchildren as they share their experiences, testimony, and faith. Their true stories of obedience, learning from mistakes, making sacrifices to reach eternal goals, and cheerfully facing problems can help children as they face similar experiences. In addition to talking with their grandchildren, grandparents can record their testimonies and experiences in journals, which can uplift and teach family members now and in future generations.

Sister Susan L. Warner, who served as second counselor in the Primary general presidency, told the following story:

"I know a grandfather who, at a recent family gathering in the mountains, took his grandchildren for a walk. As they came to a clearing in the trees, he invited the young children to sit down on a log while he told them about a 14-year-old boy named Joseph Smith, who wanted to ask Heavenly Father some questions that were troubling him. The grandfather explained that the boy Joseph went to a grove of trees near his home to pray, having faith that God would answer him. The grandchildren quietly listened, but four-year-old Johnny,

who often has difficulty sitting still, could not contain himself. He blurted out, 'I've heard that story before.'

"The grandfather told of Joseph's sincere prayer and how it was answered with a glorious visitation from Heavenly Father and His Son, Jesus Christ. As he finished, little Johnny grabbed his grandfather's hand and said, 'That was a good testimony, Grandpa.' He loved hearing the story again.

"Though the grandfather had repeated this sacred account many times throughout his life, he said, 'Never did the Spirit of the Lord bear stronger witness than when I bore my testimony of Joseph Smith to my own grandchildren.' The grandfather and the children had felt the witness of the Holy Ghost" (in Conference Report, Oct. 1998, 85; or *Ensign,* Nov. 1998, 67).

Even if grandparents live far away from their grandchildren, they can still influence them for good. Through telephone calls or letters of praise and encouragement, they can inspire confidence and provide counsel.

The Teaching Influence of Brothers and Sisters

Parents should encourage their children to help one another learn and grow. Older siblings can often be positive examples to their younger brothers and sisters and can be assigned to teach them how to accomplish household tasks. When a son serves a full-time mission, he can, by his example and his letters, greatly influence a younger brother's desire to serve. When a sister marries in the temple, she can share her excitement and testimony with her brothers and

sisters. When children willingly help with the chores at home, they set good examples, teaching one another of service and responsibility. Their own learning is also reinforced.

The Teaching Influence of Uncles, Aunts, and Cousins

There may be times when uncles, aunts, or cousins can reach out and help a family member when parents cannot.

A father recalled how his son was influenced by a cousin. The son had refused to attend church for several weeks. General conference was approaching, and his cousin, excited to attend, arose early in the morning and stood in line to be seated in the Salt Lake Tabernacle. The son saw this example, was touched by his cousin's faith and enthusiasm, and was motivated to attend church again. That decision changed his life, and he later served a mission faithfully.

A mother told of the positive influence her brother and his family had when she and her husband sent her son to live with them and work at their gas station one summer. Another woman recalled with gratitude a conversation her

son had with a favorite uncle. Because of that discussion, her son chose to avoid friends who were influencing his behavior in damaging ways.

The Teaching Influence of Children

When parents listen to their children, they can learn a multitude of truths. Elder Russell M. Nelson described a time when he learned from one of his daughters:

"When our youngest daughter was about four years of age, I came home from hospital duties quite late one evening. I found my dear wife to be very weary. . . . So I offered to get our four-year-old ready for bed. I began to give the orders: 'Take off your clothes; hang them up; put on your pajamas; brush your teeth; say your prayers' and so on, commanding in a manner befitting a tough sergeant in the army. Suddenly she cocked her head to one side, looked at me with a wistful eye, and said, 'Daddy, do you own me?'

"She taught me an important lesson. I was using coercive methods on this sweet soul. To rule children by force is the technique of Satan, not of the Savior" (in Conference Report, Apr. 1991, 27; or *Ensign,* May 1991, 22).

HOME TEACHING AND VISITING TEACHING

I hope that home teachers and visiting teachers will experience two things: first, the challenge of the responsibility that is in their great calling, and second, the sweetness of results from their work, particularly with those among us who are less active.

President Gordon B. Hinckley

9

THE TEACHING PART OF HOME TEACHING

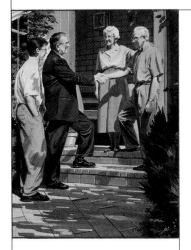

If you are a home teacher, you are a teacher of the gospel. In addition to looking after the welfare of the families to whom you and your companion are assigned, you bring a gospel message at least once each month. The scriptures teach that home teachers are to "warn, expound, exhort, and teach, and invite all to come unto Christ" (D&C 20:59).

In order to teach the families assigned to you, you need to prepare yourself spiritually and learn to apply the principles of gospel teaching discussed in this book. You should also strive continually to improve your teaching (see "Making a Plan to Improve Your Teaching," pages 24–27).

In your assignment as a home teacher, you have a special need for such preparation and continuing improvement. A knowledge of the basic principles of gospel teaching will help you teach messages in a way that will help all the individuals you teach, whether they are less-active members who are not accustomed to participating in gospel discussions or active, experienced Church members.

Remember that different people require different teaching approaches. You may need to present a message to a family in which there are children of many different ages. You may be assigned to fellowship new converts. Or you may have the opportunity to visit elderly members or single members.

One set of home teachers who thought carefully about their lesson appeared for their visit carrying fishing poles. Their pockets were stuffed with fishing lures. The family members wanted to know why, but the home teachers would not tell them before the time for their message. They had no trouble drawing the children around them and getting their attention. Then one of the home teachers demonstrated how a fisherman lures a fish into being caught. He explained that little fish are often more easily fooled than older and more experienced fish. He compared the fishing lures to Satan's temptations and taught the family that Satan uses cunning ways to try to catch us and take away our freedom. It was a memorable lesson for the family.

As a home teacher, you have special opportunities to show love for those you teach. As President Ezra Taft Benson taught, you should "do the little things, the small things that mean so much to a family. For example, know the names of all the family members. Be aware of birthdays, blessings, baptisms, and marriages. On occasion, write an appropriate note of commendation or make a phone call congratulating a member of the family on a special achievement or accomplishment" (in Conference Report, Apr. 1987, 61; or *Ensign*, May 1987, 50). You can help the family in time of need, support children and youth in their activities, and make certain that family needs are communicated to priesthood leaders.

Selecting the Message

As you select a message to share, remember the following instruction: "Home teachers usually present the First Presidency's message that is printed in the *Ensign* and the Church's International Magazines. Additional messages may come from the bishop or other local leaders. The head of the household also may request that home teachers give a special message. Home teaching messages should be based on the scriptures and the teachings of the latter-day prophets" (*Church Handbook of Instructions, Book 2: Priesthood and Auxiliary Leaders* [1998], 169).

Preparing the Message

Prepare each home teaching message as carefully as you would prepare a lesson for a Church class. The following suggestions may help you:

- Review the lesson. Counsel with your companion about what each of you will contribute to the presentation.

- If you present the First Presidency message or another topic for which a formal lesson plan is not provided, follow the suggestions found in "Creating Lessons from Conference Talks and Other Resources," pages 100–101.

- Adapt the message and the teaching methods to the background, age, and interests of the individual family members you teach. Make the lesson interesting and applicable to each family member.

- Ensure that the message will be brief enough to hold the interest of all present.

Delivering the Message

Remember that the head of the home should preside and conduct when you visit. Also keep in mind the following suggestions:

- Pray and read the scriptures together whenever possible. Use the scriptures at every appropriate opportunity. Bring them for each visit. Use them to answer questions or give counsel.

- Follow the promptings of the Spirit as you teach.

- Avoid lengthy conversations that are not interesting or helpful to all present. Be sensitive to the time constraints of the families you visit.

- Find ways to have each family member participate in the lessons. Show keen interest in each individual.

- Testify of the truths you teach. Share examples of how to apply those truths in everyday life.

10

THE TEACHING PART OF VISITING TEACHING

When you are assigned to be a visiting teacher, an important part of your responsibility is to "learn of the spiritual and temporal needs of the sister and her family" and to "give spiritual instruction through a monthly message" (*Church Handbook of Instructions, Book 2: Priesthood and Auxiliary Leaders* [1998], 203). You are a teacher of the gospel.

In order to teach the sisters assigned to you, you need to prepare yourself spiritually and learn to apply the principles of gospel teaching discussed in this book. You should also strive continually to improve your teaching (see "Making a Plan to Improve Your Teaching," pages 24–27).

This preparation will help you greatly because you may be called to teach sisters in many different situations. You may teach those who are young, elderly, married, single, divorced, newly converted to the gospel, very active in the Church, less active, well-educated, learning disabled, busy, lonely, welcoming, or resistant. Different sisters require different teaching approaches. Whatever the circumstances of the sisters you teach, you can help them know the Savior better and live His gospel more faithfully.

When Sister Elaine L. Jack was serving as general Relief Society president, she told the following story:

"Priscilla Samson-Davis, a sister in Ghana, has known struggles. There have been many rocks on the path of her life. As a teacher she has watched families nurse children through dysentery and malaria, work hard, barter daily for sacks of rice, onions, tomatoes—any food to keep their loved ones alive. She serves as a visiting teacher, regularly traveling on the bus to see a sister on the other side of town. When asked if this task were a burden, given all she had to manage, she simply replied, 'It's not hard. The woman I visit can't read. When I go, I read the scriptures to her.'

"Her simple answer testified of the faith and assurance she had that she was on the proper path. Though her bus route was halting and likely wound up and down streets, in the Lord's eyes it was truly straight and narrow, for she was going in the right direction. She was about her Father's business" (in Conference Report, Apr. 1994, 19; or *Ensign*, May 1994, 16).

Selecting the Message

As you select a message to share, remember the following instruction: "Visiting teachers give spiritual instruction through a monthly message. Messages that are published in the *Ensign* or the International Magazines are to be used as a guide and adapted to the needs of each sister" (*Church Handbook of Instructions, Book 2: Priesthood and Auxiliary Leaders* [1998], 203). Seek the guidance of the Spirit as you carefully review the monthly message with your companion and then consider prayerfully each sister you teach. In addition to the prepared message, you should use the scriptures and the teachings of latter-day prophets as your main resources in planning the message.

You may supplement these resources with other Church-produced materials.

Preparing the Message

Prepare each visiting teaching message as carefully as you would prepare a lesson for a Church class. The following suggestions may help you:

- Review the lesson. Counsel with your companion about what each of you will contribute to the presentation.

- Follow the suggestions found in "Creating Lessons from Conference Talks and Other Resources," pages 100–101.

- Adapt the message and the teaching methods to the circumstances, background, age, and interests of each sister you teach.

Delivering the Message

The following suggestions will help you as you teach the sisters you visit:

- Pray and read the scriptures together whenever possible. Use the scriptures at every appropriate opportunity. Bring them for each visit. Use them to answer questions or give counsel.

- Follow the promptings of the Spirit as you teach.

- Be sensitive to the time constraints of the sisters you visit.

- Find ways for the sisters you visit to participate in the lessons. Show keen interest in what they have to say.

- Testify of the truths you teach. Share examples of how to apply those truths in everyday life.

E

TEACHING IN LEADERSHIP SETTINGS

1

TO LEAD IS TO TEACH

*Elder Boyd K. Packer emphasized that all Church leaders serve as teachers: "The prophet is a teacher; his counselors are teachers; the General Authorities are teachers. Stake presidents and mission presidents are teachers; high councilors and quorum presidents are teachers; bishops are teachers; and so through all of the organizations of the Church. The Church moves forward sustained by the power of the teaching that is accomplished" (*Teach Ye Diligently, *rev. ed. [1991], 3–4).*

At a Church youth conference, an adult member of the Church witnessed an inspiring example of the influence that leaders can have when they teach true principles. He reported:

"At the end of the conference a dance was held. The dance band showed up without wearing shirts. As the adults watched, a group of youth approached the bandstand and made some sort of suggestion to the band, to which the band members were protesting. Soon some youth brought in shirts, and very reluctantly the band members put them on.

"When the music started, it was loud, and it kept getting louder. Just at the point where the adults were becoming concerned, a group of young people gathered in the middle of the floor and then approached the bandstand together. They asked for the music to be quieter. The band resisted, but the young people insisted, and so the band turned down the music. When the music again got louder, the youth gathered and confronted the band again. The same cycle repeated itself a third time. Finally the group came to the stake president. They said, 'We think this music is not appropriate. Rather than continuing to dance, those of us who care to would like to go to another building and have a fireside. We can do it ourselves, but if you adults want to come, that's fine.' The dance ended, and the young men and women met in another building.

"Afterward I asked the stake president how this had happened. He said that about

five years before, one of the members of the high council had said, 'If we want to teach standards to the young people, we have to know clearly what they should be. The first step is for the stake presidency to tell us.' It took some time for the stake presidency to gain a clear understanding of the standards and how they should be applied in their stake. Even more time was required to help the high council understand and become committed to these standards, and more time still to bring the bishops on board. Up until that time the parents and the youth had been receiving conflicting signals, but now, for the first time, the leaders were ready to teach the standards.

"And then they taught them, year after year, on every level throughout the entire stake. The result was what I witnessed that night at the youth conference dance.

"I learned that the influence of leaders can be very great when they conscientiously set out to fulfill their responsibility to teach the Saints. I learned also that a mixed message is no message at all, and that time spent becoming solidly rooted in what ought to be taught pays off. Finally, I saw for myself the maturity and wisdom and moral courage of youth who have been properly taught."

Your Responsibility as a Leader to Teach the Gospel

One of the most important ways you fulfill your responsibilities as a leader in the Church is through teaching (see *Church Handbook of Instructions, Book 2: Priesthood and Auxiliary Leaders* [1998], 305–7). Elder Gordon B. Hinckley taught, "Effective teaching is the very essence of leadership in the Church" ("How to Be a Teacher When Your Role as a Leader Requires You to Teach," General Authority Priesthood Board Meeting, 5 Feb. 1969; quoted by Jeffrey R. Holland in Conference Report, Apr. 1998, 31; or *Ensign,* May 1998, 26).

The Lord is the preeminent example of a leader serving as a teacher: "And Jesus went about all the cities and villages, teaching in their synagogues, and preaching the gospel of the kingdom" (Matthew 9:35). Elder Boyd K. Packer emphasized: "The Lord is our example. It would be hard to describe the Lord as an executive. Let me repeat that. It would be hard to describe the Lord as an executive. He was a *teacher!* That is the ideal, the pattern" (regional representatives' seminar, 6 Apr. 1984).

The scriptures contain numerous accounts of other leaders serving as teachers of the gospel. Adam and many of his descendants were "preachers of righteousness [who] spake and prophesied, and called upon all men, everywhere, to repent." Through their preaching, "faith was taught unto the children of men" (Moses 6:23). The early Apostles served "daily in the temple, and in every house, [and] they ceased not to teach and preach Jesus Christ" (Acts 5:42). King Mosiah testified, "And even I myself have labored with all the power and faculties which I have possessed, to teach you the commandments of God, and to establish peace throughout the land" (Mosiah 29:14).

Some Ways in Which You Teach as a Leader

Setting a Righteous Example

As a leader, you teach the gospel through the way you live. You are expected to keep the commandments, be kind, and be a faithful servant of the Lord and of those you lead. By setting a righteous example, you strengthen others in their resolve to live the gospel.

Following Church Policies and Procedures

As you faithfully follow the established patterns of Church government, you teach all who work with you. You help others see how to fulfill their duties. For example, Melchizedek Priesthood leaders who regularly hold home teaching interviews demonstrate how this is to be done.

Speaking Directly about Gospel Principles

Leaders have many regular opportunities to teach the gospel. These opportunities include leadership meetings (see page 152) and interviews (see page 153). You will see that other opportunities come spontaneously in the normal course of leading and interacting with others.

As a young bishop and a printer, Thomas S. Monson frequently worked with President J. Reuben Clark Jr., then a member of the First Presidency. As they worked together, President Clark often took advantage of opportunities to teach the gospel. Years later, President Monson told of one such occasion that had a great effect on him:

"[President Clark asked] me to read aloud the account found in Luke concerning the man filled with leprosy. Then he asked that I continue reading from Luke concerning the man afflicted with palsy and the enterprising manner in which he was presented to the attention of the Lord, who healed him. President Clark removed from his pocket a handkerchief and wiped the tears from his eyes. He commented, 'As we grow older, tears come more frequently.' After a few words of good-bye, I departed from his office, leaving him alone with his thoughts and his tears.

"Late one evening I delivered some press proofs to his office in his home in Salt Lake City. President Clark was reading from Ecclesiastes, and he was in a quiet and reflective mood. He sat back from his large desk, which was stacked with books and papers. He held the scriptures in his hand, lifted his eyes from the printed page, and read aloud to me: 'Let us hear the conclusion of the whole matter: Fear God, and keep his commandments: for this is the whole duty of man' (Ecclesiastes 12:13.) He exclaimed, 'A treasured truth! A profound philosophy!'

"What a blessing was mine to learn daily at the feet of such a master teacher. . . . Knowing that I was a newly appointed bishop presiding over a challenging ward, he emphasized the need for me to know my people, to understand their circumstances, and to minister to their needs.

"One day he recounted the Savior's raising from the dead the son of the widow of Nain, as recorded in the Gospel of Luke. When President Clark closed the Bible, I noticed that he was weeping. In a quiet voice, he said, 'Tom, be kind to the widow and look after the poor'" (*Inspiring Experiences that Build Faith* [1994], 233–34).

To lead in the Church is to teach, and to improve as a leader is to learn to teach more effectively—from the pulpit, in leadership meetings, and in one-on-one situations.

2

TEACHING IN LEADERSHIP MEETINGS

The Lord said: "And now, behold, I give unto you a commandment, that when ye are assembled together ye shall instruct and edify each other, that ye may know how to act and direct my church, how to act upon the points of my law and commandments, which I have given. And thus ye shall become instructed in the law of my church, and be sanctified by that which ye have received, and ye shall bind yourselves to act in all holiness before me" (D&C 43:8–9).

Referring to this revelation, Elder Jeffrey R. Holland stated, "In our administrative meetings let us both 'instruct and edify' as the revelations say, that even in these our teaching may ultimately be 'from on high' " (in Conference Report, Apr. 1998, 33; or *Ensign*, May 1998, 27; see also D&C 43:16).

Because time in leadership meetings is limited, time spent on teaching should be carefully planned. In some meetings the teaching may be a brief spiritual thought given at the beginning. In other meetings, one or more participants may be asked in advance to lead the group in a detailed study of selected topics. Those receiving such assignments should use the principles and methods of teaching recommended in this book.

Deciding What to Teach

In preparation for leadership meetings that will include detailed instruction, presiding leaders should prayerfully determine what should be taught and who should be asked to teach. They may select subjects that are doctrinal or that relate to Church government and the duties of those assembled. The Lord said:

"I give unto you a commandment that you shall teach one another the doctrine of the kingdom. Teach ye diligently and my grace shall attend you, that you may be instructed more perfectly in theory, in principle, in doctrine, in the law of the gospel, in all things that pertain unto the kingdom of God, that are expedient for you to understand" (D&C 88:77–78).

The scriptures are the basic resource for study in leadership meetings. "I give unto you a commandment," the Lord counseled, "that you rely upon the things which are written; for in them are all things written concerning the foundation of my church, my gospel, and my rock" (D&C 18:3–4). Other resources are the *Church Handbook of Instructions,* addresses from general conference, and other teachings of latter-day prophets (for assistance in developing lessons from such resources, see "Creating Lessons from Conference Talks and Other Resources," pages 100–101).

Inviting the Spirit through Reverence

We can teach and learn the gospel and be edified together when the Spirit attends us (see D&C 42:14; 50:17–24). We can invite the Spirit by our reverence (see "Inviting the Spirit As You Teach," pages 45–46; "Reverence," pages 82–83). In leadership meetings, those presiding and conducting can encourage reverence by being in their seats early. By their demeanor, they can help set the tone for meetings. Other leaders who attend can also come early; bring their scriptures, handbooks, and writing material; and prepare themselves quietly and prayerfully.

The prayer offered at the beginning of a leadership meeting can help establish reverence and invite the Spirit. A spiritual thought also provides a good opportunity for teaching and learning gospel principles. In some leadership meetings, appropriate prelude music and hymns sung during the meeting can help prepare the hearts and minds of those present.

3

TEACHING IN INTERVIEWS

President Thomas S. Monson shared the following experience:

"When I was approaching my eighteenth birthday . . . , I was recommended to receive the Melchizedek Priesthood. Mine was the task of telephoning my stake president, Paul C. Child, for an appointment and interview. He was one who loved and understood the holy scriptures. It was his intent that all others should similarly love and understand them. Knowing from others of his rather detailed and searching interviews, my telephone conversation with him went something like this:

" 'Hello, President Child. This is Tom Monson. I have been asked by the bishop to seek an interview with you.'

" 'Fine, Brother Monson. When can you visit me?'

"Knowing that his sacrament meeting time was six o'clock, and desiring minimum exposure of my scriptural knowledge to his review, I suggested, 'How would Sunday at five o'clock be?'

"His response: 'Oh, Brother Monson, that would not provide us sufficient time to peruse the scriptures. Could you please come at two o'clock, and bring with you your personally marked and referenced set of scriptures' " (*Inspiring Experiences that Build Faith* [1994], 193).

Young Thomas Monson discovered that an interview with the stake president was more than just an "interview"; it was an occasion for studying and learning the gospel.

Principles for Teaching in Interviews

If you conduct interviews, the following principles can help you.

"Treasure Up in Your Minds . . . the Words of Life" (D&C 84:85)

Remember that the Lord knows the members with whom you meet. He knows their needs, worries, strengths, and weaknesses. Often the Spirit will prompt and teach you as you prepare to help individuals and families.

The Lord said, "Treasure up in your minds continually the words of life, and it shall be given you in the very hour that portion that shall be meted unto every man" (D&C 84:85). As you study the scriptures, be open to the possibility that certain passages may be precisely what someone needs to hear in an interview. An experience shared by a bishop illustrates this truth:

"One Monday morning I was reading in the Doctrine and Covenants concerning repentance and forgiveness. Divine truth flooded into my mind and heart, especially concerning forgiving oneself. I had never considered that the truth 'I, the Lord, will forgive whom I will forgive, but of you it is required to forgive all men' (D&C 64:10) could apply to oneself.

"I finished my reading for that morning and went about my work. The next evening I met with a couple whose marriage was weak. As I spoke with them, the sister explained something that had occurred to her as a young girl when she broke a civil law, the consequences of which could have resulted in court action at that time. Thirty years had passed, and what occurred was of no consequence today, but she still felt the burden of guilt. Instantly this verse from the Doctrine and Covenants came to mind and brought peace to a troubled soul. What a testimony to me that daily scripture study paid such a quick dividend."

Bear Testimony of the Scriptures and the Principles They Teach

As you rely on the scriptures in conducting interviews, you should bear testimony of them. You may also share experiences to show how the principle being discussed has blessed your life and the lives of others.

4

WHEN LEADERS TEACH TEACHERS

If you are a leader in the Church, one of your most important responsibilities is to instruct the teachers in your organization in their duties and guide their efforts to improve. Sometimes you do this in leadership meetings (see page 152) and teacher improvement meetings, and sometimes it requires one-on-one teaching. Your efforts to fulfill this responsibility can make a significant contribution to the quality of teaching in the Church.

For instructions on what you should do to guide individual teachers, see the "Gospel Teaching and Leadership" section of the *Church Handbook of Instructions,* pages 305–6, and *Improving Gospel Teaching: A Leader's Guide,* pages 4–6. Following are five suggestions on how to provide the guidance described in these handbooks.

Love Each Teacher Purely

Sometimes we are inclined to criticize, thinking that if we point out others' shortcomings to them, they will want to change. This is seldom true. Criticism usually leads to defensiveness and discouragement. Teachers will be more receptive to your counsel when they feel your Christlike love for them and know that you truly want to help them. A sister who eventually became an effective leader of teachers had an experience early in her Church service that taught her this principle. This experience forever changed the way she thought about teaching:

"I was newly married and had an assignment in Relief Society to help improve

teaching. I did not recognize it at the time, but I cared too much for the task and not enough about the teacher whose class I observed. I told her, in so many words, 'You should have done it this way.' The response I received wasn't expressed in quite this way, but it came through unmistakably: 'Then you do it. If I'm not doing what you think should be done, then you take the class.' I learned right then that what I was missing was love. I didn't love her enough. I didn't respect her enough."

Point Out the Good Things the Teachers Are Doing

People tend to love doing things that they feel they do well. Your sincere compliments do what criticism cannot do to encourage teachers and help them continue to improve.

When you love the teachers with whom you serve, your compliments will be sincere. And you will find much to compliment, because every teacher has qualities that are worth noticing. A teacher may have a good speaking voice, a talent for directing discussions, or a good grasp of the scriptures or Church history. Another teacher may be organized, and another may have a humble, strong testimony.

Compliments should be specific. For example, you might say to a teacher, "I thought the picture you showed of the Savior reinforced your message very well" or "Your testimony at the end of the lesson helped me feel the Spirit" or "I like the way you handled that difficult question." Specific comments are usually more encouraging than general comments because they show that you care enough to observe attentively.

You will have many opportunities to point out the good things teachers do. You can do so in teacher improvement meetings and when you meet to counsel individually with teachers (see "Obtaining Support from Your Leaders," page 28). But you do not need to wait for such occasions. You can express compliments after a class, in the hallway, in a note, or in a telephone call. You may even express a compliment in front of the class if it will not embarrass the teacher.

Respect Each Teacher's Divine Potential

In addition to recognizing the present abilities of individual teachers, you should recognize teachers' divine potential. They are spirit children of Heavenly Father, and they have infinite capacity. With proper nurturing and their own humble dedication, they can improve and develop their talents and abilities.

Allow Teachers to Make Their Own Plans for Improvement

When teachers know that you love them and appreciate their efforts, they will feel more comfortable asking for help. When they counsel with you, help them make their own plans to improve. This approach honors the principle that teachers (and, in this case, leaders) should help others take responsibility for their own learning and growth (see "Helping Individuals Take Responsibility for Learning the Gospel," pages 61–62). People always learn best and grow most when they take the initiative. Usually it is better for teachers to develop slowly on the basis of their own plans than for leaders to push them to develop more rapidly (see "Making a Plan to Improve Your Teaching," pages 24–27).

Give Correction with Humility, Love, and the Guidance of the Holy Ghost

Although it is generally best to allow teachers to make their own plans for improvement, you may sometimes need to give correction. When you do so, be gentle and meek. Remember that reproving should be done only

"when moved upon by the Holy Ghost" and should be followed by an increase of love (D&C 121:43). The following story illustrates these important principles:

"Once as a bishopric member I had an assignment with one of the Aaronic Priesthood quorums. When I first went to quorum meeting I was greatly bothered. The adviser gave an excellent lesson and then at the end defeated all the good he had done by saying, 'Well, this is what we are taught, but that's not really the way it is.' I was very troubled by this, and, without making any criticism of the adviser, I bore my testimony, making sure the young men had a correct understanding. A few weeks later he did the same thing again. This time, after a good lesson, he questioned the importance of strict obedience to the principle he had been teaching.

"I waited for a few days and asked if I could visit him. I fasted and prayed before I went. I felt a great deal of love for this man and made sure I had no unkind feelings toward him. After we talked about the young men in the quorum, I told him I was concerned about some of his thoughts that were not quite what the lesson manual had outlined for us to teach. I told him that the young men were at an idealistic age and needed to understand the ideal so they would be able to try to live up to it. Tears moistened his eyes, and he began to share some of the difficulties he had had in life that led him to say what he said. In that talk together, we became very close. It was not the next week but a few weeks later that he mentioned in class that the things he had said earlier were wrong, and he apologized. I feel that love and the Spirit of the Lord were responsible for his remarkable change of heart. Needless to say, he got better and better as a teacher."

F

METHODS OF TEACHING

METHODS OF TEACHING

This part of *Teaching, No Greater Call* introduces many different methods for teaching the gospel. The methods are listed alphabetically. You should select methods carefully, always keeping in mind the principles you are teaching and the needs of learners. As you select methods, review the information in "Teaching with Variety" (pages 89–90), "Choosing Appropriate Methods" (page 91), and "Choosing Effective Methods" (page 92).

ACTIVITY SHEETS

See "Work Sheets," pages 183–84.

ACTIVITY VERSES

Little children enjoy poems and songs with simple actions. These poems and songs are often referred to as activity verses. You can use activity verses to help children learn gospel principles. You can also use them to help children feel welcome at the beginning of class, get ready to pray, or prepare to participate in a lesson.

It is helpful to have several activity verses ready to use whenever you see a need to change the pace of a lesson or include the children in an activity.

Ideas for activity verses and songs are included in the *Children's Songbook,* some Primary lesson manuals, and some issues of the *Friend.* You can create your own activity verses by adding simple actions to poems and songs.

Example of an Activity Verse

The following activity verse could be used to teach children to be thankful for God's creations. It is taken from the Primary song "The World Is So Big" (*Children's Songbook,* 235).

The world is so big and, oh, so round,
  [*form a large circle with arms*]
And in it God's creations are found;
Stars shining brightly through all the night,
  [*straighten and wiggle fingers*]
Sun in the day so warm and so bright.
  [*form a large circle with arms*]
The world is so big and, oh, so round.
God loves us all; our blessings abound.
  [*grasp arms and hug self*]

How to Teach an Activity Verse

Before teaching an activity verse, memorize the words and movements yourself. To teach an activity verse:

1. Say the words and show the actions to the children. Go slowly, and exaggerate the actions. This will help the children understand the words and actions.

2. Invite the children to do the activity verse with you.

3. If the children enjoy the activity verse, repeat it. If they become restless, shorten it. If the activity verse is long, you may want to help the children do the actions while you say the words by yourself.

You may occasionally want to use pictures to help present activity verses. Pictures from the Gospel Art Picture Kit, Church-produced lesson manuals, and Church magazines may be helpful. You may want to consider using a Primary Visual Aids Cutouts set (available through the *Church Materials Catalog*).

Some children may not participate in the activity verse but will enjoy watching others do the actions. They will join in when they are ready.

APPLICATION TECHNIQUES

As a gospel teacher, one of your most important goals should be to help others apply gospel principles in everyday situations. Application techniques can help learners discover the blessings that come when we live the gospel.

Below are some methods that can help those you teach live the principles you have taught. These and many other methods are described in this section of the book.

- Discuss situations similar to those the learners might experience. Use role plays, panel discussions, buzz sessions, games, work sheets, case studies, or brainstorming to discuss how to make correct choices in those situations.

- Prepare specific application questions to discuss with the class.

- Share a personal experience about how living a gospel principle has blessed your life. Invite those you teach to briefly share their own experiences.

- Encourage those you teach to set one or more goals that can help them live the principle you have taught. For example, in a lesson about prayer, you might encourage them to set a goal that will help them pray in a more meaningful way. You might ask them to share their feelings the next week.

- Share scripture passages that testify of the principle. Have those you teach share their favorite scriptures or scripture stories.

- Ask the learners to think of a song that helps them remember the principle. Suggest songs they might use.

- Encourage those you teach to share the message of the lesson with their families. For example, they might share an activity, song, work sheet, or scripture used in class. Have them discuss with their families how they can apply the principle.

- Have those you teach write a scripture, quotation, poem, or part of a song on a piece of paper that they can take home and have as a reminder of the lesson.

- Have children draw a picture of themselves living the principle.

- Help them memorize an article of faith that relates to the principle. With children, relate the principle to one of the items in "My Gospel Standards," on the back of the *My Achievement Days* booklet.

- A month in advance, assign a few learners to study a specific lesson and apply it in their lives. When you teach the lesson, have the assigned persons report on their experiences.

ATTENTION ACTIVITIES (ATTENTION GETTERS)

Attention activities can be used to create interest and to help learners focus their attention on the subject of the lesson. They should be brief and lead directly into the lesson. They are most often used at the beginning of lessons, but they can also be used to capture learners' attention during lessons and to make a transition from one part of a lesson to another. Many lessons in Church-produced lesson manuals include suggestions for attention activities.

For suggestions on using and developing attention activities, see "Beginning the Lesson," page 93, and "Helping Learners Be Attentive," pages 71–72.

AUDIOVISUAL MATERIALS (VIDEOCASSETTES AND AUDIO RECORDINGS)

You may occasionally use Church-produced videocassettes and audio recordings to help teach gospel principles. Some materials are designed to be used with specific lessons in specific courses of study. Others may be used with a variety of lessons. Refer to the current *Church Materials Catalog* for a list of available Church-produced audiovisual materials.

In Church settings it is often against copyright laws to use audiovisual materials that are not owned by the Church. For guidelines on copyright laws, see *Church Handbook of Instructions, Book 2: Priesthood and Auxiliary Leaders,* pages 322–23.

How to Use Audiovisual Materials

1. Watch or listen to the presentation before using it in class. Make sure that it reinforces or supports the lesson.

2. Prepare the presentation so that it will begin in the right place when you need it in the lesson. Generally, you should use only short segments; audiovisual presentations should not consume the entire lesson time.

3. Set up the equipment before class starts. Ensure that it works properly. Also ensure that all learners will be able to hear the presentation and see it from their seats.

When you use the presentation as part of the lesson, ensure that it is a teaching tool rather than entertainment. For example, you could encourage learners to look for specific principles or situations during a video presentation. Or you could have them summarize the message of an audio recording after it is over.

BRAINSTORMING

In a brainstorming activity, the teacher presents a question or situation and gives learners a short amount of time to freely suggest solutions or ideas.

Examples of Brainstorming Activities

You might use brainstorming to address a need in your family, quorum, or class. For example, you could have learners organize a service project, suggest ways to invite less-active members to an activity, or share ideas for improving home teaching efforts.

You may also use brainstorming to stimulate ideas on a specific topic in a lesson. For example, you could ask those you teach to spend a few minutes listing blessings they have received through the priesthood or things they can do to be good examples as Church members.

How to Conduct a Brainstorming Activity

1. Explain what it means to brainstorm. Tell those you teach that you will give them a short amount of time to contribute ideas. Ensure that they understand that you will not criticize or make fun of their ideas, and help them understand that they should not criticize or make fun of each other's ideas. Because of the nature of brainstorming, you may need to remind them to be reverent in their actions and suggestions.

2. Present a specific question or situation. Make sure learners know how much time they have to make suggestions.

3. Allow learners to contribute their ideas. If they are reluctant to begin brainstorming, you may need to get them started by suggesting a few ideas yourself. Look for ways to include individuals who seem hesitant to participate.

4. As learners offer suggestions, list the suggestions on the chalkboard or a piece of paper or have someone else list them.

5. When the time is up, discuss the suggestions learners have given. Invite them to refine their ideas and talk about how they relate to the lesson. If the purpose of the activity was to decide on a certain action to take, such as a service project or a plan to invite less-active members to an activity, help them select one of the suggestions. Then help them make plans to follow that suggestion.

6. If they share ideas that are sincere but that represent false doctrine, take time during the lesson to kindly correct those ideas.

BUZZ SESSIONS

Buzz sessions are activities in which learners are divided into small discussion groups. The groups talk about assigned topics and then share their ideas with the others. You can use buzz sessions to give a large number of people the opportunity to participate in a lesson. Individuals who are usually hesitant to participate might share ideas in small groups that they would not express in front of the entire group. This will help them see that their ideas are important to others.

At times, the groups may share their ideas by making posters or charts or drawing pictures. For example, you might ask them to draw different parts of the same scripture account or things for which they are thankful.

Example of a Buzz Session

In a lesson about preparing to serve full-time missions, an elders quorum instructor could divide quorum members into five groups and have each group prepare to report on one of the following questions:

- What can young men do to prepare to serve full-time missions?

- What can fathers do to help their sons prepare to serve full-time missions?

- What can home teachers do to help boys and young men prepare to serve full-time missions?

- What can Aaronic Priesthood advisers do to help young men prepare to serve full-time missions?

- What can adults do to prepare themselves to serve full-time missions?

You can use this same pattern to develop other topics for buzz sessions.

How to Conduct a Buzz Session

The following steps show how to conduct a buzz session. As you plan to conduct a buzz session, consider how long each of these steps will take. Ensure that the process will not consume too much lesson time.

1. Divide the class into groups of at least three people. (Or you may want to simply ask each learner to turn to the person sitting next to him or her for a quick discussion. If you choose this approach, you will need to adapt steps 2 through 6.)

2. Choose a leader for each group, or let the groups choose their leaders. Also assign a recorder for each group. Give each recorder a piece of paper and a pen or pencil. The recorders list their groups' responses during the discussion. The leaders keep the discussions going and later report the groups' ideas to the class. (If you conduct the kind of buzz session in which the groups draw pictures, give each group the materials they need, such as paper, pencils, and crayons.)

3. Assign each group a topic that relates to the lesson. You may ask all the groups to discuss the same topic, or you may assign each group a different topic. It may be helpful to give each group a piece of paper with a topic written on it.

4. Give the groups a set amount of time to discuss their topics. Make sure they stay on task. Alert them one or two minutes before they are to finish.

5. Invite each group leader to present the ideas generated from the group's discussion. (If all the groups have discussed the same topic, have the group leaders take turns sharing one idea. Otherwise, the first groups may share many ideas, leaving other groups with little to share.)

6. Summarize the presentations, making sure that the topic has been discussed sufficiently. Ensure that learners understand how their discussions relate to the gospel principles you are teaching.

CASE STUDIES

Case studies are true-to-life situations that prompt learners to ponder or discuss what they could do in similar situations. They can help show how gospel principles apply in everyday life. You might use case studies to encourage discussion, emphasize the main principle of a lesson, or conclude a lesson.

Case studies may be based on factual stories or realistic fictional situations. If you use a case study that is based on a true story, you may want to share the outcome of the story at some point in the lesson.

Examples of Case Studies

Following are four examples of case studies with discussion questions.

Treating Others with Kindness

You have been playing all morning with some friends in your neighborhood and have been having lots of fun. A girl who is visiting the family across the street comes outside and looks like she wants to play with you.

- What should you do?

Paying a Full Tithe

It is late December, and Brother and Sister Jones are looking at their month's finances. They realize that they cannot pay all their bills if they pay tithing.

- If you were in the position of Brother and Sister Jones, what would you do?

Sharing the Gospel

You have been planning for months to go to the temple with the other young men and women in the ward to perform baptisms for the dead. A friend who is not a member of the Church invites you to a party that same evening. You say that you can't go to the party, and your friend asks you what you will be doing that evening.

- How would you respond?

Making Correct Decisions

A friend has invited you to go to a movie that you know is inappropriate.

- What could you do to decline the invitation?

How to Create a Case Study

Some lessons in Church-produced manuals contain stories that could be used as case studies. However, at times you may want to create case studies on your own. To create a case study on your own, follow these steps:

1. Keep in mind the principles you are preparing to teach. Then think of situations that relate to those principles and that apply to the age-group you teach.

2. Prepare to present the situations realistically and in a way that will prompt thought and discussion (see "Conducting Discussions," pages 63–65; "Teaching with Questions," pages 68–70; "Stories," pages 179–82).

3. Consider what you can say or do to reinforce the principles after the discussion.

CHALKBOARDS

The chalkboard is one of the simplest, most readily available teaching tools. You can use the chalkboard to:

- Emphasize key facts or ideas and help learners remember them.

- Acknowledge learners' ideas by writing them down.

- Guide discussions by writing questions and listing learners' responses. For example:

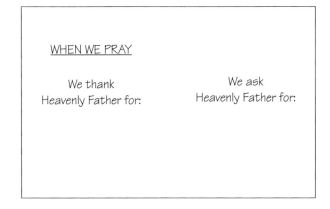

- Clarify concepts or stories by illustrating them in a simple way. For example:

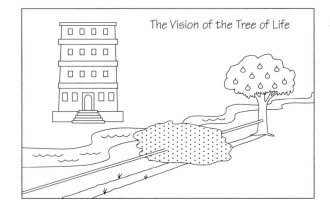

- Make outlines or lists to help learners follow a discussion.

- List assignments or scriptures related to the current lesson or the next lesson.

Guidelines for Using Chalkboards

The following guidelines can help you use the chalkboard as an effective teaching tool. These guidelines also apply to your use of overhead projectors and white boards.

- Plan and practice what you will write, deciding how you will organize the information or drawings. Practice drawing any illustrations you will use.

- If you plan to use an outline, a list, or an illustration on the chalkboard, you may want to do this before class and then cover it with paper, revealing it during the lesson at the appropriate time.

- Write clearly and large enough for all to see, making sure the material is well spaced, orderly, and easy to read. Write only key words or phrases.

- Use simple stick figures and shapes to illustrate stories or concepts. If you keep the figures and shapes simple, you will prevent them from becoming the main focus of the lesson.

- Hold the interest of those you teach by talking while you write.

- Avoid spending long periods of time at the chalkboard. This may cause learners to lose interest in the lesson.

- Do not apologize for your spelling, handwriting, or lack of artistic ability. Apologizing will only draw attention to that particular aspect of your writing or drawing. If you are uncomfortable at the chalkboard, ask someone to help.

- Occasionally ask someone to write on the chalkboard for you so you can maintain eye contact with learners. Make sure the person helping you understands what you want him or her to write and where he or she should write it on the chalkboard.

CHORAL READINGS (see also READERS' THEATERS; RECITATIONS)

In a choral reading, a group reads scripture passages, poetry, or prose together. A choral reading can be done in class or performed for an audience.

You can use this method to present scripture accounts, stories, poems, and other information. You can also use it as part of a special program for holidays or special events.

Example of a Choral Reading

Theme: Articles of Faith

Procedure: Have learners review the Articles of Faith and then repeat them back to you as a group.

How to Conduct Choral Readings

- Select material that supports the lesson topic. Appropriate materials may be found in the scriptures, Church-produced manuals, Church magazines, and the *Children's Songbook.*

- If you will be performing the choral reading for an audience, have the group practice reading the material so they learn to speak together. Make sure they speak clearly and use pauses and changes in the volume and speed of their voice to relay the meaning of the message. During the performance, lead them so they repeat their parts together.

COMPARISONS AND OBJECT LESSONS

It is often difficult to teach the intangible aspects of the gospel—principles such as faith, repentance, love, the Atonement of Jesus Christ, remission of sins, and redemption. Elder Boyd K. Packer said:

"In teaching the gospel, we do not re-create the material world around us; we deal with the intangible world within us, and there is a big difference. None of the ordinary tools are available to us. To convey to a youngster the idea of a cat is much simpler than to convey the idea of faith; faith is very difficult to describe.

"For instance, how big is faith? We soon learn that size is not helpful. Only vaguely can we talk to a youngster who knows nothing about faith by talking about an amount, such as much faith, or little faith. We can't tell him what color it is. We can't tell him what shape it is. We can't tell him what texture it is."

Then Elder Packer shared a teaching tool that we can use to teach about intangible principles: "Tie the invisible idea . . . to some tangible object the student already knows about and then build from that knowledge" (*Teach Ye Diligently,* rev. ed. [1991], 31–32).

You can use comparisons and object lessons to help learners understand intangible principles. Together with the use of stories and personal testimony, these methods give you an excellent set of tools for teaching the eternal realities that we cannot perceive with our senses.

As you use comparisons and object lessons, remember that they should always reinforce the lesson purpose and that they should not detract from the gospel principles you are teaching.

Comparisons

The Savior often referred to familiar earthly objects or experiences to help His listeners understand spiritual principles. He spoke of Himself as "the bread of life" (John 6:35) and "the good shepherd" (John 10:11, 14). He taught His followers to seek out the lost sheep (see Matthew 10:5–8) and to feed His lambs (see John 21:15–17). The Lord compared the kingdom of heaven to a treasure, a pearl, and a fishing net (see Matthew 13:44–48). He likened faith to a mustard seed (see Matthew 17:20). He said that people are known by their fruits (see Matthew 7:15–20). In His lessons, a narrow gate became the way of eternal life (see Matthew 7:13–14) and His disciples became fishers of men (see Matthew 4:18–19). He spoke of gathering His people as a hen gathers her chickens under her wings (see Matthew 23:37).

With practice and imagination, you can find gospel applications in familiar objects. For example, prayer can be compared to a radio, a patriarchal blessing can be compared to the Liahona, and hope can be likened to sunshine breaking through clouds. You might see lessons in the experiences you have at work, in routine household chores, or in your associations with other people (see "Looking for Lessons Everywhere," pages 22–23).

Elder Packer suggested a formula for finding comparisons:

_____ is like _____

As shown below, this formula could be used to teach about repentance. The intangible principle of repentance becomes clearer as we compare it to something simple and familiar. Elder Packer taught:

"Take the subject *repentance.*

" __Repentance__ is like _____

"What commonplace thing familiar to everyone could be likened to repentance? Suppose we use soap.

" __Repentance__ is like ____soap____ " (see *Teach Ye Diligently,* 36–37; see also page 34).

Other Examples of Comparisons

Following is a list of other comparisons you might use as you teach the gospel:

Scripture study is like a feast.

Children are like treasures.

Faith is like a shield.

The scriptures are like a life raft in troubled waters.

Sin is like quicksand.

Object Lessons

Like comparisons, object lessons relate intangible principles to familiar physical things. However, in an object lesson, you use actual objects rather than just talk about them. For example, to help learners understand the cleansing effect of repentance, a teacher could display a bar of soap and even use it to wash dirt from his or her hands.

Other Examples of Object Lessons

The following examples further illustrate how to use object lessons:

- To show that ordinances and covenants are inseparable, display a coin. Then ask which side of the coin is more important. (Neither side is more important.) Ask learners if they can separate the sides of the coin. Then explain that ordinances and covenants are inseparable, just as the two sides of a coin are inseparable. Also point out that ordinances and covenants are necessary for admission into God's presence, just as coins are sometimes needed for admission to events.

- To emphasize that each individual is important, have learners assemble a simple puzzle from which you have removed a piece. When they ask about the missing piece, give it to them. Ask them why the missing piece

is important. Then explain that each piece of the puzzle is like a family member or class member. Each person is important.

- To illustrate the importance of the gospel, display a map. Ask why we use maps. Then compare the map to the gospel. Explain that like a map, the gospel of Jesus Christ guides us. It helps us stay on the path that leads to eternal life with our Heavenly Father.

- To teach about nourishing the word of God after it has been planted in our hearts (see Alma 32:28–43), draw pictures of two plants—one that is healthy and has moist, rich soil and one that is unhealthy and has dry, poor soil.

When to Use Comparisons and Object Lessons

Comparisons and object lessons can be used in many ways, but they are especially helpful when you need to:

- Gain the attention of those you teach. You can use comparisons and object lessons to quickly create interest, focus the attention of learners, and introduce a subject or principle of a lesson.

- Provide a framework for a lesson. You might occasionally build an entire lesson around a comparison or object lesson.

- Conclude, summarize, and encourage. After teaching a gospel principle, you can use a comparison or object lesson to summarize what has been discussed and to motivate those you teach to make worthwhile changes in their lives.

DEMONSTRATIONS

Sometimes you may feel that the best way to teach a certain principle or skill is to demonstrate it. Demonstrations can be used to teach such skills as conducting songs and hymns, administering first aid, baking bread, tying a knot, using family history materials, or performing a priesthood ordinance. After you do a demonstration, the learners can then be given the opportunity to try the technique.

If you invite someone else to demonstrate a technique or skill, be sure to offer your assistance as he or she prepares.

How to Prepare and Present a Demonstration

To prepare a demonstration, follow these steps:

1. If you are doing the demonstration, practice it. Ensure that it will accomplish its objectives and that you will be able to present it in the time available. Also make sure it is appropriate for those you teach so they will not become frustrated trying the new skill.

2. Review any necessary materials and equipment. Make sure objects are large enough to be seen or that you can describe them if they are small. If you have asked someone else to do the demonstration and you do not expect that person to supply the needed materials and equipment, ask him or her to prepare a list of the necessary items for you to obtain. If you expect the learners to duplicate the process taught in the demonstration, have all the necessary equipment and materials ready for them to use. A review sheet might be provided for each person you teach. Any measurements or ingredients should be mentioned on the sheet and during the demonstration.

3. It may be helpful to have others who understand the technique assist while the learners practice the skill that has been demonstrated. If so, speak with these people in advance.

4. Arrange the classroom so everyone can see and hear.

5. If necessary, make arrangements to clean the area after the demonstration.

To present a demonstration, follow these steps:

1. Explain. Help learners understand the purpose of the demonstration and the reasons for the procedures. Also help them see how the technique, process, or skill will be useful to them.

2. Demonstrate. Show how to use the technique, process, or skill. This should provide an example, or model, for learners to follow.

3. Practice. Allow learners to practice the procedure. During the practice phase, you should observe, teach, and help when necessary. Be patient, understanding, positive, and encouraging.

To see an example of using a demonstration to teach a principle, see page 168.

DIORAMAS (see also PAPER STAND-UP FIGURES)

Dioramas are small scenes in which figures are displayed. Simple dioramas and figures can make stories memorable and interesting for children.

Examples of Dioramas and Figures

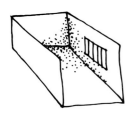 

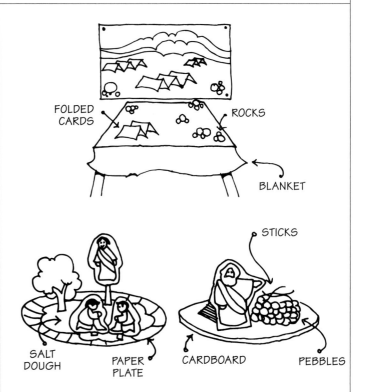

You may want to ask those you teach to help make dioramas and figures during class or to bring figures to use with dioramas that you have already made.

Recipe for Salt Dough

1 cup salt
4 cups flour
1 tablespoon cooking oil
2 cups water
Food coloring (optional)

Mix the salt and flour. In another bowl, mix the oil, water, and, if desired, food coloring. Then mix the oil and water into the flour and salt mixture. Knead the mixture into a dough. Put the dough into an airtight container to keep it soft.

Dioramas made of boxes and plates may be used for more than one story.

DISCUSSIONS

See "Conducting Discussions," pages 63–65.

DRAMATIZATIONS

In a dramatization, people act out a story. Those you teach can gain a greater understanding of gospel principles by dramatizing accounts from the scriptures, Church history, or Church magazines.

Types of Dramatizations

There are different types of dramatizations. For example, you may:

- Read an account (or have someone else read the account) while participants act it out silently.

- Relate an account and then have participants act it out with or without words. Little children often enjoy acting out a story several times, playing the roles of different people each time.

- Prepare scripts in advance for participants to read in class.

- Have some participants silently act out a familiar story and then have the others guess which story has been dramatized.

- Interview someone as if he or she is a person from the scriptures or Church history. For example, you could ask someone to play the part of Shem, one of Noah's sons. You could ask the person playing Shem to tell you about Noah's preaching, the flood, the ark, and the day that Noah and his family were able to walk on the land again. (If you plan to conduct such an "interview," you should talk to the assigned person in advance, telling him or her about the questions you will ask.)

How to Prepare and Conduct Dramatizations

Regardless of how dramatizations are conducted, they should relate clearly to the lesson. They should help learners remember gospel principles. They should communicate messages that are simple and direct. They should not detract from the sacredness of scriptural or historical events.

Simple costumes such as robes and hats can make dramatizations more interesting, especially for children. You may also find it helpful to use name tags to identify the people being portrayed by the participants.

Some learners may be reluctant to play the parts of people in the scriptures or Church history. You may be able to find ways for these learners to participate in dramatizations. For example, some little children may be more comfortable pretending to be animals. They may also enjoy making sound effects such as the sound of the wind or running feet. If some do not want to participate, do not pressure them to do so.

To conduct a dramatization:

1. Ask for volunteers to be in the dramatization. Assign them their roles.

2. Help the participants understand the story they are going to dramatize and the people they are going to portray.

3. During the dramatization, help the participants with their roles as necessary. They may need you to prompt them during the dramatization. If you are teaching little children, you may want to ask questions to prompt them, such as "What will you do next?" or "Now what will you say?"

Dramatizations should not take the entire lesson time. Be sure to leave enough time at the end of the dramatization to ask participants what they have learned. Help them relate the message of the dramatization to the lesson and to their own lives.

Cautions about the Portrayal of Deity in Dramatizations

"God the Father and the Holy Ghost are not to be portrayed in meetings, dramas, or musicals.

"If the Savior is portrayed, it must be done with the utmost reverence and dignity. Only people of wholesome personal character should be considered for the part. Only scriptures spoken by the Savior should be spoken by the person who portrays Him. The person who portrays the Savior should not sing or dance.

"At the end of the performance, the person should not wear the costume in the foyer or elsewhere. He should change immediately into street clothes.

"The Savior should not be portrayed by children in dramatization except in a nativity scene" (*Church Handbook of Instructions, Book 2: Priesthood and Auxiliary Leaders* [1998], 279).

You may want to ask a narrator to read words spoken by the Savior from the scriptures.

DRAWING ACTIVITIES

One way to help learners understand gospel principles is to have them draw pictures. Drawing allows them to explore and express their understanding and feelings of gospel stories and principles being discussed.

Examples of Drawing Activities

- Have learners draw pictures that relate to the theme of the lesson. For example, you could have them draw pictures about their homes, their families, a holiday, tithing, or preparing to go to the temple.

- Have learners make a mural or time line that relates to the lesson. Have them work together on one long piece of paper.

- Tell a story. Then have learners draw pictures that express their feelings about the story.

- After telling a story, ask each person to draw a picture about a specific part of the story. Have learners use their pictures to retell the story. You could connect the pictures and show them in a roller box (see "Roller Boxes," pages 178–79).

- Sing or play a recording of a hymn or Primary song. Have those you teach draw pictures showing what they think about or how they feel when they hear that hymn or song.

Guidelines for Conducting Drawing Activities

When you have people draw as part of a lesson, ensure that the activity relates to the principles you are teaching. However, do not allow the activity to become the focus of the lesson. Keep the project simple so learners can complete it in a short amount of time. Make sure you have all the necessary materials ready.

As learners draw, encourage them to use their imagination. Try not to make children feel that they have to draw a picture in a certain way. As they draw, praise them equally for their efforts. If you have a question about what someone is drawing, do not ask, "What are you drawing?" Instead, simply say, "Tell me about your picture."

Occasionally, you may use coloring pages from the *Friend*. When you have children color pictures of the Savior, remind them to be respectful and reverent.

When it is time to continue with the lesson, you may want to ask those you teach to tell each other about their pictures. Ask them how the pictures relate to the lesson. Invite them to share their feelings about what they have drawn. It is sometimes helpful to display the pictures during the rest of the lesson.

If you are teaching a Church class, encourage class members to show their pictures to their families. This will help them remember what they have learned. It will also give parents an opportunity to discuss gospel principles with their children.

EXAMPLES

Imagine explaining scripture marking to people who have never seen anyone mark the scriptures. They would have a hard time understanding if you tried to explain it using words only. But they would probably have no trouble at all if you showed them examples of marked pages in your scriptures. Imagine explaining tithing to children who do not understand the meaning of the term *one-tenth*. They would understand tithing more clearly if you showed them an example, spreading 10 coins on a table and putting one of them in a tithing envelope.

As a gospel teacher, you may often face the challenge of helping others understand something that they have not understood very well before. One way to accomplish this is to use examples. It is important to state principles and explain how to apply them, but your teaching will usually be more effective when you also give examples.

You should give examples often during lessons to help ensure that learners understand what you are teaching. On page 73 of this book, there is a story of a teacher who should have used an example in a Primary lesson on revelation. He carefully presented the lesson, using a variety of effective methods. Toward the end of the lesson, the teacher asked a review question: "Who has the authority to receive revelation for the Church?" All the children raised their hands. They all knew the answer: the President of the Church. But the teacher then discovered, almost accidentally, that the students did not know what he meant by the word *revelation*. If he had given a few simple examples early in the lesson, such as a personal experience in which he was guided by the Holy Ghost or the account of the Lord speaking to Joseph Smith in the First Vision, it would have made all the difference.

How to Use Examples

There are many ways to present examples. What is most important is that you use examples that will help learners clearly understand what you are teaching. Following are some ideas.

Familiar Examples of Unfamiliar Ideas

If you are discussing a concept that is unfamiliar to those you teach, you can use specific, familiar examples to help them understand. For instance, if you are talking about priesthood ordinances, you might say, "Baptism, the sacrament, and marriage in the temple for eternity are examples of priesthood ordinances." If you make reference to prophets, you could say, "Adam, Abraham, and Moses were prophets in ancient times. Some examples of prophets in the latter days are Joseph Smith, David O. McKay, Ezra Taft Benson, and Gordon B. Hinckley."

This may be difficult with intangible concepts, such as faith, remission of sins, or redemption. It is often better to teach such concepts with stories, comparisons, or object lessons (see "Comparisons and Object Lessons," pages 163–64).

Examples That Demonstrate Skills

Often the best way to teach a skill is to demonstrate how it is done. For example:

- To help others learn how to prepare a lesson, share an outline of a lesson you have prepared.

- Instead of simply telling others about the study helps available in their scriptures and giving an explanation of how to use them, have them open their scriptures to the Topical Guide, the Bible Dictionary, the footnotes, and other helps. Then show how to use them.

Examples That Demonstrate Principles

Some principles can be demonstrated. The following story shows how a Primary teacher demonstrated the principle of sharing:

"The teacher of a group of three-year-old Primary children spoke briefly about sharing and then told two short stories about children who shared. She then laid newspapers on the floor and gave each child a ball of clay. She observed that her ball of clay was much smaller than anyone else's and invited each child, one by one, to share with her. At first the children were reluctant, but when they saw her willingness to share with them, they began to enjoy sharing—not only with their teacher, but with each other. The lesson allowed the children not only to define the concept of sharing, but also to *experience* the feelings that are part of learning to share" (Janelle Lysenko, "Tools for Teaching Tots," *Ensign,* Mar. 1987, 71).

Stories That Give Examples of People Living Gospel Principles

Some principles, such as faith, love, loyalty, and repentance, cannot be demonstrated because they refer to spiritual realities that we cannot see. But with stories you can share examples of people living these principles. For instance, you could use the story of Joseph in Egypt fleeing from Potiphar's wife to teach about integrity. You could teach about loyalty by telling the story of John Taylor and Willard Richards, who voluntarily risked their lives to stay in Carthage Jail with the Prophet Joseph Smith and his brother Hyrum. You can also share your own personal experiences. Fictional stories, including parables, can provide examples of how to live gospel principles. (For guidelines and suggestions on using stories, see "Stories," pages 179–82.)

FLANNEL BOARDS

Flannel boards are portable boards on which figures are displayed, usually to tell a story. This teaching tool works well with children. If you use a flannel board, you may want to invite learners to help you put the figures on it. After using a flannel board to tell a story, you may want to allow the children to use the figures to retell the story.

How to Make a Flannel Board

To make a flannel board:

1. Cut a piece of heavy cardboard, thin plywood, or similar material.

2. Cut a solid-colored piece of flannel, felt, brushed nylon knit, or rough burlap large enough to overlap two inches on each side of the board.

3. With the outside of the fabric facing down, place the board in the center of the fabric. Wrap the edges of the fabric around the sides of the board, and secure the edges to the back of the board.

How to Make Flannel-Board Figures

To create your own flannel-board figures:

1. Draw a picture, or trace and color a picture from a Church magazine, manual, or other resource.
2. Cut out the picture.
3. Glue or tape the picture to heavier paper.
4. Attach a piece of flannel or a piece of sandpaper or other rough material to the back of the heavy paper. This will help the figure stick to the flannel board.

Pictures of people, animals, and objects can be ordered through the *Church Materials Catalog.* In the catalog they are called visual aids cutouts.

GAMES

Games give variety to lessons and allow learners to interact with each other. You can find ideas for games in Church-produced lesson manuals, Church magazines, and the *Family Home Evening Resource Book.*

How to Select Games

As you select games to use in lessons, ensure that they:

- Reinforce the gospel principles you teach.

- Are appropriate for the setting in which you teach.

- Are appropriate for the age of those you teach and the size of the group.

- Are easy to understand.

- Take only a small portion of the lesson. In some instances, a game may require a large portion of the lesson, but these instances are the exception, not the rule.

- Do not encourage competition. You should avoid giving rewards to people who "win."

- Give all learners the opportunity to participate and feel successful. You should praise learners equally for their good efforts.

Examples of Games

Matching Game

In this game, learners find sets of two cards with related information or pictures. Consider the following example, which could be used in a Primary class:

Obtain 12 pieces of paper of equal size that are large enough for everyone to see. On half of the papers, attach or draw pictures that relate to the lesson. On the other half, write descriptions of the pictures. On the sides that do not contain pictures or descriptions, number the papers 1 through 12. At the appropriate time in the lesson, lay the papers on the floor, with the numbered sides facing up, or tape them to a poster board. They do not have to be in numerical order.

To play the game, have each person take a turn choosing two pieces of paper. Turn the papers over to see if they contain a picture and its corresponding information. If they match, remove them from the others. If they do not match, put them back in place, with the numbered side facing up, and allow the next person to choose two pieces of paper. After all the pictures and descriptions have been matched, discuss how they relate to the lesson.

You may want to use one of the following variations to this game:

- Write half of a scripture verse on one piece of paper and the rest of the verse on another. Or write part of a scripture phrase on one paper and the rest on another. For example, some pairs could be "Restoration of" and "the gospel"; "Lehi's vision" and "of the tree of life"; and "iron" and "rod."

- Write the number of each article of faith on 13 different pieces of paper. On 13 corresponding papers, write key words from each article.

Guessing Game

In this game, the teacher gives a series of clues to help learners identify a certain person, place, object, scripture story, or principle. You may use this game to introduce a lesson or emphasize part of a lesson.

To play the game, give clues to help those you teach identify a person or object that relates to the lesson. Give one clue at a time, giving learners an opportunity after each clue to identify the person or object. Start with general clues. Make the clues more specific until someone guesses correctly. For example, the following clues could be used to help learners identify the prophet Moses:

I am an Old Testament prophet.
I spoke with God face to face.
I was raised by an Egyptian princess.
My spokesman was a man named Aaron.
I led the children of Israel out of captivity.

You may want to use one of the following variations to this game:

- Divide the class into partners. Give a word to one person in each partnership. The person who knows the word then gives one-word clues to help his or her partner guess the word. For example, if the person is given the word *baptism,* he or she could give clues such as *water, font,* or *immerse.* If the person is given the word *Noah,* he or she could give clues such as *flood, animals, ark, dove,* or *rainbow.*

- Give one person a word. Have the others guess the word by asking up to 20 questions. The questions must be answered *yes* or *no.*

- Have one person draw a picture to represent a certain subject, person, or story. Have the others guess what the picture represents.

Answer Game

On individual pieces of paper, write questions that will help learners review what they have learned at the end of a lesson. Put the pieces of paper into a jar or other container.

To review the lesson, toss a beanbag or other soft object to someone and have him or her draw a question from the container and answer it. Then have that person toss the beanbag to someone else, who will also draw a question from the container and answer it.

Board Game

In a board game, players advance game pieces from the starting point to the finish by answering questions and following instructions on prepared game cards. A board game, such as in the example on the next page, can be made out of a heavy board or could be drawn on a chalkboard. Coins or other small objects can be used as game pieces if you use a board. If you use a chalkboard, use the chalk to signal the advancement of the learners. The game cards should teach or review gospel principles. For example, you might prepare cards with the following statements:

- Your little brother brings home a toy that belongs to his friend John. He says, "John has lots of toys. He won't miss this one." You explain that since the toy belongs to John, it must be returned. You go with your brother to return the toy to his friend. Because this is the honest thing to do, move ahead six spaces.

- You have not studied for a certain test in school. During the test, you copy from the person who sits by you. Because this is not honest, move back three spaces.

To play the game, place the game cards face down. Then have the participants take turns selecting a card, reading the statement, and advancing their game pieces according to the statement.

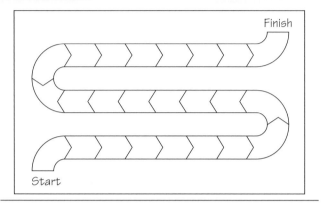

GUEST SPEAKERS

Occasionally you may want to invite a guest to speak to those you teach as part of a lesson. For example, an Aaronic Priesthood adviser could invite a returned missionary to talk to the young men about how they can prepare for missionary service.

How to Work with a Guest Speaker

You must ask your bishop for approval before inviting a guest speaker who is not a member of the ward (see *Church Handbook of Instructions, Book 2: Priesthood and Auxiliary Leaders* [1998], 325). When you have received your bishop's approval, follow these steps:

1. Invite the guest speaker in advance. Let him or her know about the subject of the lesson, the age-group of the people in the class, what you feel that class members should learn from the presentation, and the amount of time he or she should take. Give the speaker a copy of the lesson from the manual.

2. If you are preparing to ask the guest questions, prepare a list of the questions you will ask. Give a copy of the questions to the guest.

3. Introduce the guest before he or she speaks in class.

LECTURES

It is sometimes best to simply explain specific principles or historical events rather than conduct a discussion or other learning activity. Lecturing can be very effective if it is done at appropriate times, such as when you cover large amounts of material quickly, present information that is new to those you teach, or summarize a lesson.

How to Give Lectures

Lecturing is generally more effective with older learners than with very young learners, who may have difficulty sitting quietly when they are required to listen without doing anything else. However, even for adults, a lecture can become tiresome if it is not delivered well. The following guidelines can help you give effective lectures:

- Familiarize yourself with the lesson so you will not need to read the material word for word. This will help you maintain eye contact with learners.

- Use some visuals, such as pictures, posters, charts, maps, chalkboards, or overhead transparencies. These materials increase interest and encourage attention.

- Relate the lecture to daily situations so that learners can apply the principles in their lives.

- Use language that learners understand.

- Vary the pitch and tone of your voice to create variety and emphasize important points.

- Whenever possible, permit questions and discussion on the topic you are explaining. Even though a lecture enables you to cover more material than could be completed otherwise, most lessons should allow learners to participate in some way.

LIKENING

We should "liken all scriptures unto us, that it might be for our profit and learning" (1 Nephi 19:23). To liken the scriptures means to see how scripture accounts are similar to circumstances today and to show how the principles they teach are relevant in our lives. For example, in a lesson about standing up for the truth, you could liken the story of Abinadi in the court of King Noah to those you teach (see Mosiah 11–17). To teach about our spiritual blindness and the Savior's power to heal us and give us greater spiritual vision, you could liken the story of Christ healing the blind man (see John 9).

You will use this method most effectively when you give family members or class members an opportunity to ponder what they read. For example, after teaching about Joseph Smith's response when he was nearly overcome by the adversary in the Sacred Grove (see Joseph Smith—History 1:15–16), you could ask learners to recall and even write down an experience in which they were tried and tested. Then you could invite them to think about why it is important in times of trial to exert "all [our] powers to call upon God" (verse 16).

To help family members and class members see that the scriptures are relevant, you should teach in ways that connect the experiences of the prophets and people of the past to the experiences of individuals today. As you prepare each lesson, ask yourself how the principle (or story or event) is like something family members or class members have experienced in their own lives. For example, if you are teaching a lesson that includes a discussion of the Ten Commandments, you might wonder how to teach about the commandment against making and worshiping graven images (see Exodus 20:4–5). Most members of the Church have had little experience with the worship of graven images. However, there are many other things that people sometimes "worship." As you teach, you might liken the ancient commandment in Exodus 20:4–5 to something more familiar: modern society's worship of money, athleticism, pleasure, or popularity.

Almost every story in the scriptures can be likened to our lives. Consider the following story about a teacher who likened a scripture account to those she taught:

One ward was experiencing problems with Primary teachers providing treats every week during class. The treats detracted from the Spirit and focused the children's attention away from the lessons. The Primary president asked the ward teacher improvement coordinator to present a sharing time that would address the problem.

The teacher improvement coordinator pondered ways to present the ideas to both the teachers and the children. None of the approaches seemed to be quite right. Then as she reflected again on her assignment one morning, she was reminded of the account of Christ feeding the 5,000, which her family had recently read together. She remembered that after Jesus fed the multitude, there were people who followed Him because they wanted to be given food, not because they wanted to hear the gospel (see John 6:26–27).

That Sunday, the teacher improvement coordinator related this story. She used the story to teach the true reason for coming to Primary: to give and receive spiritual food.

Another way to help others liken the scriptures to themselves is to ask them to insert themselves into the scriptural text. For example, if someone places himself or herself in James 1:5–6, the teaching on prayer becomes as applicable to him or her as it was to Joseph Smith:

"If [I] lack wisdom, let [me] ask of God, that giveth to all men liberally, and upbraideth not; and it shall be given [me]. But let [me] ask in faith, nothing wavering."

Many times we can liken the scriptures to our lives by asking, "What did the prophet who recorded this account want us to learn from it? Why did he include these particular details?" When we ask these questions about the story of Enos, for example, we can discover applications to our own experiences with prayer. We can learn that praying sometimes takes much effort and that Heavenly Father answers our prayers. We can also learn that parents influence their children, even though it may take many years for the children to follow their parents' teachings.

As we liken the scriptures to ourselves and help others do the same, we will be able to see the power of the word of God in every aspect of our lives.

MAPS

You can find maps in the Latter-day Saint editions of the scriptures, Church-produced lesson manuals, Church magazines, and the meetinghouse library.

How to Use Maps

You may use maps in lessons by:

- Having learners locate cities that are mentioned in the accounts you study in the scriptures and Church history.
- Drawing simple maps on the chalkboard.
- Locating areas of interest, such as countries where full-time missionaries are serving or cities where temples are located.

MEMORIZATION

When we memorize scriptures, quotations, hymns, and Primary songs, they can be a source of comfort, guidance, and inspiration for us. As we recall them, they can help us feel the influence of the Holy Ghost wherever we may be.

Memorizing requires deliberate, concentrated effort. You can teach others helpful memorization techniques. You can also suggest inspiring material for them to memorize.

How to Help Learners Memorize

The following ideas can be useful in helping learners memorize. As you consider these ideas, remember that those you teach will remember material longer if it is meaningful to them. Be sure they understand the meaning of the words they are memorizing.

Write on the Chalkboard the First Letter of Each Word to Be Memorized

You might write the following letters on the chalkboard to help learners memorize the second article of faith:

W B T M W B P F T O S A N F A T

Point to the letters as you repeat each corresponding word.

Divide the Material into Short Phrases or Lines

Following are a few examples of how you could use this technique:

- Have everyone repeat short phrases together, one phrase at a time. For example, to memorize Proverbs 3:5–6, the learners could repeat the following portions of the passage: (1) "Trust in the Lord with all thine heart;" (2) "and lean not unto thine own understanding." (3) "In all thy ways acknowledge him," (4) "and he shall direct thy paths."

- Divide learners into groups. Give each group one of the phrases. As you point to each group, have them repeat their phrase. Occasionally you could have group members repeat the phrase silently in their minds rather than speak the words out loud. As the learners hear the phrases over and over, they will soon be able to repeat all the phrases in the proper order.

- Repeat the words phrase by phrase, stopping to let the learners say the next phrase.

- Prepare a written copy of the words, and cut the phrases into wordstrips. After saying the verse several times, display the wordstrips out of order. Have the learners put the scrambled wordstrips in order.

Write on the Chalkboard the Material to Be Memorized

Have learners read the material several times. Gradually erase or cover more and more words until the learners have memorized the material.

Use Music

You can use music to help learners memorize. For example, you could teach the books of the scriptures or the Articles of Faith from the *Children's Songbook,* pages 114–17, 119, 122–33. This can even be an interesting method for teaching adults and youth.

Practice the Memorized Material Several Times

It is important to practice the material we memorize. As you determine how to practice, consider the length of the material to be memorized. A short scripture could be learned all at once. A new song might be taught one line at a time. A part for a special program might take several practice periods. Review the material periodically with those you teach. Encourage individuals to practice on their own.

MUSIC

The First Presidency said:

"Inspirational music is an essential part of our church meetings. The hymns invite the Spirit of the Lord, create a feeling of reverence, unify us as members, and provide a way for us to offer praises to the Lord.

"Some of the greatest sermons are preached by the singing of hymns. Hymns move us to repentance and good works, build testimony and faith, comfort the weary, console the mourning, and inspire us to endure to the end" (*Hymns,* ix).

Hymns offer us great inspiration and comfort throughout our lives when we can memorize them and then recall them in times of need.

Elder Dallin H. Oaks encouraged all Church members to use hymns more often to strengthen themselves and others:

"I wonder if we are making enough use of this heaven-sent resource in our meetings, in our classes, and in our homes. . . .

"We need to make more use of our hymns to put us in tune with the Spirit of the Lord, to unify us, and to help us teach and learn our doctrine. We need to make better use of our hymns in missionary teaching, in gospel classes, in quorum meetings, in home evenings, and in home teaching visits" (in Conference Report, Oct. 1994, 10, 13; or *Ensign,* Nov. 1994, 10, 12).

Enhancing Lessons with Music

You can use music in a variety of ways to enhance your lessons and invite the Spirit. Following are a few examples.

Teaching or Reviewing a Gospel Principle

Most hymns can help you teach gospel principles or review principles you have already discussed.

When using a song to teach a principle, you might ask the learners questions to help them reflect on the message of the song or to encourage a discussion. For example, before having learners sing "Keep the Commandments" (*Hymns,* no. 303; *Children's Songbook,* 146–47), you might ask, "Why do you think we feel safety and peace when we obey the commandments?" You might use "I Lived in Heaven" (*Children's Songbook,* 4) to teach children about the plan of salvation. You could use "How Firm a Foundation" (*Hymns*, no. 85) to help those you teach understand that the Savior helps us face adversity. To teach about the comfort that we can receive at the death of a loved one, you could use "Where Can I Turn for Peace?" (*Hymns*, no. 129).

After teaching a gospel principle, you might ask those you teach, "What hymn could help us remember this principle?" Then sing one of the hymns they suggest. With children you might sing a song and then ask them how the song applies to the lesson. You could then invite them to sing the song with you.

Providing Insight into Scripture

Each hymn in the Church hymnbook is accompanied by scriptural references, which are indexed (see *Hymns*, pages 410–14). Most songs in the *Children's Songbook* also have scriptural references. You might refer to these references to find songs that would work well with a particular lesson. For instance, if you were teaching John 13:34–35, you might have learners sing "Love One Another" (*Hymns*, no. 308; *Children's Songbook*, 136), one of the hymns that corresponds to these verses.

Helping Learners Build and Express Their Testimonies

As learners sing hymns and other Church songs, the Spirit can bear witness to them of the truthfulness of the principles being taught. There are some songs whose very words are an expression of testimony, so that in singing them people can bear their testimonies together. Such songs include "I Know That My Redeemer Lives" (*Hymns*, no. 136); "I Am a Child of God" (*Hymns*, no. 301; *Children's Songbook*, 2–3); "We Thank Thee, O God, for a Prophet" (*Hymns*, no. 19); and "Did Jesus Really Live Again?" (*Children's Songbook*, 64).

President Gordon B. Hinckley explained how music strengthened his testimony of the Prophet Joseph Smith:

"Many years ago when at the age of twelve I was ordained a deacon, my father, who was president of our stake, took me to my first stake priesthood meeting. . . . Together these men lifted their strong voices, some with the accents of the European lands from which they had come as converts, all singing these words with a great spirit of conviction and testimony:

"Praise to the man who communed with Jehovah!
Jesus anointed that Prophet and Seer.
Blessed to open the last dispensation,
Kings shall extol him, and nations revere.
["Praise to the Man," *Hymns*, no. 27]

"They were singing of the Prophet Joseph Smith, and as they did so there came into my heart a great surge of love

for and belief in the mighty Prophet of this dispensation. In my childhood I had been taught much of him in meetings and classes in our ward as well as in our home; but my experience in that stake priesthood meeting was different. I knew then, by the power of the Holy Ghost, that Joseph Smith was indeed a prophet of God" ("Praise to the Man," *Ensign*, Aug. 1983, 2).

Concluding a Lesson and Encouraging Learners to Apply a Gospel Principle

At a lesson's conclusion, a hymn or song can summarize the principle taught and convey a motivating message. For example, at the conclusion of a lesson on keeping the commandments, you might have learners sing "Choose the Right" (*Hymns*, no. 239); "Keep the Commandments" (*Hymns*, no. 303; *Children's Songbook*, 146–47); "Dare to Do Right" (*Children's Songbook*, 158); or "Nephi's Courage" (*Children's Songbook*, 120–21).

Cultivating Feelings of Reverence

You and your family might sing hymns and other songs in family home evenings, family councils, and other gatherings to cultivate reverent feelings and enhance family gospel study. In a classroom setting, you might play recorded music or have someone play the piano as learners enter the classroom. This will help create a reverent atmosphere and prepare learners for the lesson.

Other ways you might cultivate reverence include playing music softly while you read a story or while children draw pictures about the lesson. Or you might have someone sing a song such as "Tell Me the Stories of Jesus" (*Children's Songbook*, 57) while learners view pictures of scripture stories.

Selecting and Preparing Appropriate Music

When selecting music for a lesson, refer to the indexes in *Hymns* and the *Children's Songbook* for hymns and songs that relate to the lesson topic. Audiocassette and compact disc recordings of music in *Hymns* or the *Children's Songbook* and of other Church music are listed in the *Church Materials Catalog*.

Make sure that any music you use that is not in Church-produced materials keeps with Church standards (see the "Music" section of the *Church Handbook of Instructions*). The ward music chairman or music director can help you select and prepare appropriate music.

If you plan to sing or lead a hymn or song, make sure you know the words well enough that you can pay attention to those you teach rather than to the hymnbook or songbook.

Suggestions for Conducting Songs

Review the sections "Using the Hymnbook" in *Hymns* (pages 379–86) and "Using the Songbook" in the *Children's Songbook* (pages 300–304). Learn the basic beat patterns for songs. Also consider the following suggestions:

- When leading a hymn or song, you may want to use your hands to indicate the pitch and the tempo, or speed, of the song. To indicate the pitch, hold your hand in a horizontal position, and while singing the words, move your hand up to indicate higher pitches and down to indicate lower pitches. As you do this, move your hand either slow or fast to indicate the correct tempo. You can also draw the pattern of a song on the chalkboard. For example, the melody pattern of the beginning of "I Am a Child of God" (*Hymns,* no. 301; *Children's Songbook,* 2–3) would look something like this:

$$— \quad — \quad — \quad \overset{\textstyle —}{child} \quad \overset{\textstyle of}{} \\ \underset{\textstyle I \ \ am \ \ a}{} \qquad\qquad \underset{\textstyle God}{—}$$

- Instead of using the beat pattern to conduct a song, consider using simple hand motions that reflect the words in the song.

Ask the ward music director for assistance if you feel you need additional help learning how to conduct music.

Using Music to Teach Children

Most children enjoy participating in musical activities. The appealing rhythms of music help children remember what they sing and the messages of the words. Music can increase children's understanding of gospel principles and strengthen their testimonies. You can also use music to greet children, prepare them for prayer, focus their attention on a lesson, or calm them after an activity. Music can change the pace of a lesson and allow children to use their extra energy.

Many lessons suggest songs that reinforce the principle being taught. Refer to the index of the *Children's Songbook* for other appropriate songs.

You do not need to be a skilled musician to use music in your teaching. If you are well prepared and you enjoy singing, the children will enjoy and learn from the music you use. Following are a few suggestions to help you use music to teach children. For additional suggestions, see *Children's Songbook,* pages 300–304, and the videocassette *How to Teach a Song to Children.*

The following example shows how a teacher could use the song "I Love to See the Temple" (*Children's Songbook,* 95) to teach about temples:

I know a beautiful song about temples. As we sing this song, listen carefully to find out what we do when we go to the temple.

Did you discover why we go to the temple? (Answers may include that we go to the temple to feel the influence of the Holy Ghost, to listen, to pray, to make covenants with Heavenly Father, and to be sealed as families.)

Now let's sing the song again. This time, listen to discover whose house the temple is.

Did you discover whom the temple belongs to? (It is the house of God.)

Continue with similar questions until you have emphasized the parts of the song that will help the children understand its message.

MUSIC WITH NARRATIVES (SING-A-STORY)

You can use music and narratives together to tell a story or share a gospel message that relates to a lesson. This method is sometimes referred to as a sing-a-story. During this activity, most of the story or message is expressed through songs that the family members or class members sing. Brief narratives connect the songs to one another.

You can also combine music and narratives to prepare holiday programs or other presentations.

Example of Music with Narratives

The following combination of music and narratives could be used in a lesson about gratitude:

Narrative: God loves His children very much. One way the Lord showed His love for us was by creating the earth for us. Psalm 136 instructs us to show gratitude to the Lord for His creation of the earth:

"O give thanks to the Lord of lords. . . .

"To him who alone doeth great wonders. . . .

"To him that by wisdom made the heavens. . . .

"To him that stretched out the earth above the waters. . . .

"To him that made great lights. . . .

"The sun to rule by day: . . .

"The moon and stars to rule by night" (verses 3–9).

Hymn: "For the Beauty of the Earth" (*Hymns,* no. 92)

Narrative: The earth that the Lord created for us provides abundantly for all our needs. We should praise God for the "harvest" of blessings we reap.

Hymn: "Come, Ye Thankful People" (*Hymns,* no. 94)

Narrative: We should also extend our deepest gratitude to the Lord for His Atonement, which can cleanse us of sin and give us eternal life. As we express thanks for His sacrifice, we more fully realize its power. This realization is overwhelming and humbling.

Hymn: "I Stand All Amazed" (*Hymns,* no. 193)

Narrative: The Lord expects us to share our blessings—to feed the hungry, clothe the naked, comfort the sick and afflicted, and teach those searching for truth. As we do these things, we show our most sincere gratitude to Him for the blessings He has given us.

Hymn: "Because I Have Been Given Much" (*Hymns,* no. 219)

Guidelines for Preparing Music with Narratives

- Refer to the topical index in the hymnbook and the *Children's Songbook* for a list of songs with similar themes that could be used for this activity. Use songs that are familiar to those you teach.

- If a piano will be used, work closely with the pianist to prepare the songs, or have the person leading the songs work with him or her. Make sure the pianist knows when to begin playing each song.

- Keep the narratives between the songs simple. They can be scriptures, brief stories, poems, personal experiences, or quotations. When using this activity with children, you may ask them questions and have the children answer them as part of the narrative. This will help the children understand the gospel message you are teaching.

- As appropriate, use pictures to help learners visualize the story or gospel message being presented. You may allow children to hold the pictures during the presentation.

OBJECT LESSONS

See "Comparisons and Object Lessons," pages 163–64.

OVERHEAD PROJECTORS (see also CHALKBOARDS)

Overhead projectors, which are available in some meetinghouse libraries, are machines that magnify and project images onto a screen or wall. They can be used as an alternative to the chalkboard. This is especially helpful if a class is too large for everyone to see the chalkboard. If your meetinghouse library has an overhead projector, ask your meetinghouse librarian how to use it.

PANEL DISCUSSIONS

A panel discussion consists of a group of two or more class members—or invited guests with specialized knowledge or experience—who are assigned a topic to discuss. A panel discussion is guided by a moderator, usually the teacher.

You can use panel discussions to present information or to discuss how to live a gospel principle or solve a problem. Panel discussions give class members an opportunity to express their thoughts on a wide variety of subjects. When you ask class members to present new material or to discuss problems of interest to the group, they will become more actively engaged in learning.

How to Prepare for a Panel Discussion

1. Select a topic that is appropriate to the lesson and the age of class members. Prepare questions about this topic that you can ask panel members.

2. In advance, choose panel members who feel comfortable answering questions in front of a group. Limit the number of panelists to between three and five. A panel of more than five may take up too much time, and individual panelists may not have sufficient opportunity to comment on topics. If you want to invite visitors with specialized knowledge or experience, remember that the bishop's approval is required before guest speakers may participate (see *Church Handbook of Instructions, Book 2: Priesthood and Auxiliary Leaders* [1998], 325).

3. Help the panel members prepare for the discussion. Consider the following suggestions:

   a. Help them understand what the discussion involves and what their responsibilities are, including any study or other preparation they should do. Also give them information on the age and needs of class members, the kind of presentation you would like to have, and the length of time they will be given to present their material.

   b. Help them obtain the information they need for their part in the discussion.

   c. If the panel will present new information or ideas, assign each panel member one aspect of the topic at least one week in advance so that he or she can prepare for the discussion. You may want to give panel members references from scriptures, lesson manuals, or other sources.

   d. If the panel members will focus on a problem, meet with them before the discussion and give them a list of questions to be discussed. Allow each person to choose two or three questions to which he or she would like to respond.

　e. Just before the presentation, give the panel members a few minutes to exchange ideas among themselves about the topics they will discuss.

How to Conduct a Panel Discussion

1. Arrange the room so panelists can be seen and heard.

2. When it is time for the panel discussion, introduce the panel members and the topic they will discuss.

3. As you or another assigned moderator guides the discussion and asks questions, be sure to give each panel member adequate time to respond. Much of the success of a panel discussion depends on the moderator. This person sets the spiritual tone for the presentation and guides the discussion by keeping the remarks focused on the topic or problem, picking up a lagging discussion, and helping all panel members participate in the discussion.

4. Allow class members to ask questions of the panelists.

5. After the discussion, summarize the points that have been shared.

PAPER STAND-UP FIGURES (see also DIORAMAS)

Teachers may use paper stand-up figures to help tell a story or illustrate a principle in a lesson.

How to Make a Paper Stand-Up Figure

1. Fold a piece of heavy paper in half.

2. With the folded side on top, draw the figure on the paper. Be sure to extend the top of the image to the fold. You may then have family members or class members color and decorate the figure.

3. Cut out the figure, making sure you do not cut along the fold where the image is extended.

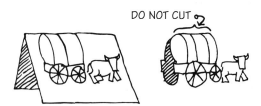

PICTURES (see also VISUALS)

Pictures are valuable tools for strengthening the main idea of a lesson and helping learners remain attentive. You can find pictures for gospel teaching in the meetinghouse library, the Gospel Art Picture Kit, Church-produced lesson manuals, and Church magazines.

Displaying Pictures

You may display pictures in various ways. For example, you may:

- Place them on the tray of the chalkboard, on an easel, or on a chair.

- Have individuals hold them.

- Hold them yourself.

Do not use tape to attach pictures to chalkboards or painted walls.

How to Teach with Pictures

Pictures can be an important part of telling a story. For example, you might help children review a story by asking them to place several pictures in sequence and then having each child tell part of the story.

Use pictures creatively. For example, you could display a picture of John the Baptist baptizing Jesus. Then you could say, "When Jesus lived on the earth, He set the example for us to follow. He knew that our Heavenly Father had commanded everyone to be baptized." Then you could ask the following questions:

- What is taking place in this picture?

- What did Jesus say is the right way to be baptized?

- Who baptized Jesus?

- Why did Jesus ask John to baptize Him?

- Why did Jesus and John go into the river?

- Why is it important for us to follow Jesus' example and be baptized as He was?

After discussing these questions, you could summarize learners' answers and relate them to the main idea of the lesson.

Remember that artists take some liberties when they create pictures. Therefore, not all elements within a picture should be taken literally. Rely on the account in the scriptures for the background and setting of an event.

PUPPETS

Puppets can be used to dramatize parts of a lesson or story, welcome children to class, give instructions, sing songs, help with role playing, ask questions, or help children remain attentive.

Examples of Puppets

GLUE OR STAPLE

CLOTH OR PAPER →

SEW, GLUE, OR STAPLE

BACK   FRONT

SMALL PAPER SACK

PAPER →

← STICK

QUESTIONS

See "Teaching with Questions," pages 68–70.

READERS' THEATERS (see also CHORAL READINGS; RECITATIONS)

In a readers' theater, participants use a script to tell a story. A readers' theater can be done in class or performed for an audience.

You can use this method to present scripture accounts, stories, poems, and other information. You can also use it as part of a special program for holidays or special events.

Example of a Readers' Theater

Story: Abinadi, King Noah, and Alma

Procedure: Explain that God sent a prophet named Abinadi to warn King Noah's people to repent of their sins. Then have learners read the words of King Noah, his wicked priests, Abinadi, Alma, and the Nephites in Mosiah 17:1–19 and 18:1, 7–11, 17, 30. Also have someone act as narrator, reading the story line between the statements of the people in the account.

How to Conduct Readers' Theaters

- Select material that supports the lesson topic. Appropriate materials may be found in the scriptures, Church-produced manuals, and Church magazines.

- Divide the material into parts. Assign the parts to the participants. Give each participant the part of a character or narrator. Make sure the participants have enough time to study their parts and that they understand their roles.

- If you will be performing the readers' theater for an audience, have participants practice reading the material. Make sure they speak clearly and use pauses and changes in the volume and speed of their voices to relay the meaning of the message.

RECITATIONS (see also CHORAL READINGS; READERS' THEATERS)

In a recitation, participants repeat material, which is usually memorized. A recitation can be done in class or performed for an audience.

You can use this method to present scripture accounts, stories, poems, and other information. You can also use it as part of a special program for holidays or special events.

Example of a Recitation

Theme: The Ten Commandments

Procedure: On the Sunday before a lesson about keeping the commandments, give each person a copy of the song "The Commandments" (*Children's Songbook,* 112–13). Assign each of them a line from the song to memorize. During the next lesson, have each person recite his or her part in turn.

How to Conduct a Recitation

- Select material that supports the lesson topic. Appropriate materials may be found in the scriptures, Church-produced manuals, Church magazines, and the *Children's Songbook.*

- Divide the material into parts, and assign the parts to the participants. Give each participant the part of a character or narrator. Make sure the participants understand their parts and that they have enough time to study them.

- If you will be performing the recitation for an audience, have participants practice reading the material. Make sure they speak clearly and use pauses and changes in the volume and speed of their voices to relay the meaning of the message.

ROLE PLAYING

In role playing, participants act out a situation or problem that occurs in everyday life. Role playing helps people apply gospel principles to real-life situations as they find solutions to problems, consider the consequences of different choices, and come to understand other people's points of view. Role playing can be used to introduce or summarize a lesson or to stimulate discussion about a principle in the lesson.

Note: A role play is not the same as a case study. In a case study, learners *discuss* a situation or problem. In a role play, participants *act out* how people might behave in a certain situation.

Examples of Role Playing

- A child has promised his parents that he will help clean the house. As he is getting ready to work, some friends come over and ask him to play. They want him to go with them now and do his work later. Role-play what he should say to his parents and what he should say to his friends.

- A group of friends are walking down the street. They find a wallet with some money in it, but they do not know whose it is. Each of the friends wants to do something different with the wallet. Role-play what they should do.

How to Use Role Playing

1. Prepare those you teach for role playing by briefly explaining the problem or situation. Give them enough information so they will be able to act out their roles thoughtfully. Emphasize that they are to play a role and not act as themselves.

2. Select the participants or ask for volunteers. Indicate who will play each specific part. Arrange for as many participants as possible, since allowing several people to role-play a situation often tends to be more successful than having just one person act out what might happen. (Role playing could be repeated to help more people participate and to discover other solutions.)

3. Give the participants a few minutes to plan what they are going to do.

4. To involve all those present, invite those not participating to watch carefully.

5. After role playing, discuss and evaluate what happened by asking questions such as "How did you feel about the problem?" or "Could this happen in real life?" or "How does this exercise help you know what to do if this really happens?" Allow those you teach to determine ways to solve similar problems in their own lives. Discuss various solutions.

General Guidelines for Role Playing

- Participation in role playing should be voluntary. Do not force anyone to participate.

- Role-play real-life situations that relate to the lesson and that are important to those you teach.

- People relate better to role plays of situations they have experienced personally. However, exercise caution in selecting situations to role-play. While it is important that the problems should be as real and significant as possible, no participants should be placed in a position where they might be acting out their own life.

- As the teacher, be sensitive to the learners' feelings and attitudes. Accept mistakes, and teach them to appreciate each other's points of view. Do not permit criticism of the participants.

- Simple props such as hats or name tags may add interest to role playing, especially if you teach children.

ROLLER BOXES

As shown below, a roller box is a container used to display pictures that have been joined together on a roll. This teaching tool provides a fun way for children to view illustrations, especially if they have drawn the illustrations themselves.

Roller boxes can be used to show different aspects of a gospel principle, such as different ways to keep the Sabbath day holy. They also can be used to show a story from the scriptures or Church history.

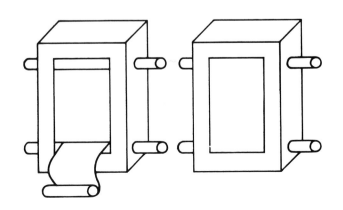

How to Make a Roller Box

1. Cut an opening in the side of a large box or carton. The opening should allow one picture to be displayed at a time.

2. Cut two sticks about six inches longer than the width of the box. You might use broom handles or paper-towel tubes.

3. Cut two holes for the sticks on each side of the box, as shown in the illustration on page 178.

4. Push the sticks through the holes.

5. Give each child a piece of paper and pencils or crayons. Have each child draw a different aspect of a gospel principle or a different segment of a story. When the pictures are drawn, tape the ends of the pictures together in the proper sequence so they form a single roll. Or you may have the children draw on different sections of one long piece of paper.

6. Attach the ends of the roll to the sticks.

Children can use small boxes, pencils, and long strips of paper to make their own roller boxes.

SCRIPTURES, MARKING AND WRITING MARGIN NOTES

See pages 58–59.

SCRIPTURES, MEMORIZATION OF

See "Memorization," pages 171–72.

SCRIPTURES, READING ALOUD

See page 56.

SCRIPTURES, STUDY HELPS IN

See pages 56–58.

SCRIPTURES, TEACHING FROM

See "Teaching from the Scriptures," pages 54–59.

SING-A-STORY

See "Music with Narratives (Sing-a-Story)," pages 174–75.

STATIONS

Stations are places where different teachers conduct learning activities. Learners divide into equal groups and rotate between the stations. In each station a person leads a learning activity and remains in that area to give the same information or demonstration to each group that comes to the station.

You or the leader of each station should keep track of the time to ensure that the groups spend the same amount of time in each learning activity. You may want to play music to indicate when it is time for the groups to rotate to the next station. Allow time to summarize the experience with the entire class.

Examples of Stations

- Display items that pertain to a certain topic, and have people explain the items. For example, you might have stations for home production and food storage, water storage, fuel supplies, and emergency kits.

- Have teachers at different stations discuss aspects of family relationships, such as the role of parents, discipline, or communication.

- Have someone at each station portray a different person from the scriptures. Have each person discuss how the person he or she portrays is an example of someone who faithfully lives the gospel.

- Have stations with simple crafts, games, or activities of pioneer children.

STORIES

Everyone likes good stories. Stories enrich lessons and capture the interest of learners as few other teaching methods can. Stories can be used to answer questions, introduce or reinforce principles, or summarize lessons. They can be especially effective to clarify and teach gospel principles by giving examples of righteous living, reaching all listeners on their own level of understanding.

When stories are used well, they engage learners' values and emotions. They can help learners apply gospel principles as they share in great scriptural events, moments of decision, hardships and struggles, and the blessings of living the gospel of Jesus Christ. They make principles easier to understand and remember. They show in vivid and inspiring ways how gospel principles can be applied in our lives. For example, to teach about faith, you might share Alma's explanation that if we have faith we "hope for things which are not seen, which are true" (Alma 32:21). But you would make your teaching more complete if you also told a story in which someone exercises great faith, such as the story of David going forth to battle Goliath (see 1 Samuel 17:20–50, particularly verses 26, 32–37, and 45–47).

The Savior is the Master Teacher and the example we should follow in all our gospel teaching. He frequently used stories in His teaching. His parables are excellent examples of using stories to teach. For example, a lawyer asked Him, "Who is my neighbour?" He answered by telling a story about a man who was beaten and robbed as he traveled from Jerusalem to Jericho. Two men passed by the wounded man, but a third, a Samaritan, stopped and took care of him (see Luke 10:29–35). When Jesus finished the parable, He asked the lawyer, "Which now of these three, thinkest thou, was neighbour unto him that fell among the thieves?" The man answered, "He that shewed mercy on him." Then Jesus responded, "Go, and do thou likewise" (Luke 10:36–37).

Selecting Stories

When selecting a story, ask yourself the questions listed below to make sure the story is appropriate and effective. These questions and others are found in "Choosing Appropriate Methods" (page 91) and "Choosing Effective Methods" (page 92).

- Will the story invite the Spirit?
- Does the story match the sacredness of what I am teaching?
- Will the story edify and strengthen those I teach?
- Will it help learners better understand the principle being taught?
- Will it make wise use of lesson time?

Different Kinds of Stories

You can use stories from your own experience. You can also use stories about others, such as stories from the scriptures, from the lives of Church leaders, and from the lives of others you know or have read about. For certain purposes, you may want to use stories that are fictional, such as parables or folktales.

Personal Experiences

Relating personal experiences can have a powerful influence in helping others live gospel principles. When you tell about what you have experienced yourself, you act as a living witness of gospel truths. If you speak truthfully and with pure intent, the Spirit will confirm the truth of your message in the hearts of those you teach. The personal experiences of those you teach can also have a powerful influence for good.

Elder Bruce R. McConkie taught, "Perhaps the perfect pattern in presenting faith-promoting stories is to teach what is found in the scriptures and then to put a seal of living reality upon it by telling a similar . . . thing that has happened in our dispensation and to our people and—most ideally—to us as individuals" ("The How and Why of Faith-promoting Stories," *New Era,* July 1978, 5).

In relating personal experiences, you and those you teach should remember the following cautions:

- Do not speak of sacred things unless you are prompted by the Spirit. The Lord said, "Remember that that which cometh from above is sacred, and must be spoken with care, and by constraint of the Spirit" (D&C 63:64).
- Avoid sensationalism, which means saying something in order to produce a startling effect. Also avoid trying to produce strong emotions in the people you teach.
- Do not embellish your experiences for any reason.
- Do not tell of experiences in order to draw attention to yourself.
- Do not talk about past sins or transgressions.

Stories about Others

The scriptures and Church history are filled with stories about men, women, and children who have applied gospel principles in their lives. For example, you could teach about prayer by telling the story of Enos pleading with the Lord for himself, his people, and his enemies. You could also teach about prayer by using the story of Joseph Smith's supplication in the Sacred Grove. And there are many instructive, moving stories from the lives of faithful Latter-day Saints today that you could share. When sharing stories about others, remember the following guidelines:

- As with personal experiences, be sure you are acting in accordance with the Spirit. Avoid sensationalism, and do not embellish the stories you share.
- Make sure you tell the stories accurately. Do not share stories about others that may not be true or that may have elements that are not true. Before sharing a story, go to the source to confirm that what you say is factual.
- If a story has not been printed or shared publicly, obtain permission from the person whose story it is before you tell it.

Fictional Stories

There is a place for fictional stories in gospel teaching. You can learn how to use fictional stories by studying how the Savior used parables in His teaching. He spoke of a wise man who built his house on a rock and a foolish man who built his house on the sand (see Matthew 7:24–27), of a woman who swept her house to find the coin she had lost (see Luke 15:8–10), and of a prodigal son who squandered his inheritance but was welcomed home by his father (see Luke 15:11–32). If we are receptive to the Spirit, we can learn great truths from these parables and the many others that the Savior taught.

As the Bible Dictionary explains, parables are comparisons. They teach spiritual truths by comparing them to material things or situations (see Bible Dictionary, "Parables," 740–41). This is true of all fictional stories that appropriately teach gospel principles. Stories can make gospel principles plain to the understanding, vivid to the imagination, and memorable. For suggestions on using comparisons to teach gospel truths, see "Comparisons and Object Lessons," pages 163–64.

As you prepare to use fictional stories, remember the following guidelines:

- Make sure that those you teach understand that the stories are not true.

- As with other kinds of stories, make sure that fictional stories are appropriate, tasteful, and in accordance with the Spirit.

The *Friend* and *New Era* magazines often contain fictional stories that can be used to supplement and enrich lessons. For examples of the effective use of stories in gospel teaching, study general conference talks.

Guidelines for Preparing and Telling a Story

- Have a reason for telling a story. Do not use a story merely to entertain those you teach. Connect the story with a gospel principle that is part of the lesson's main idea or objective.

- If a story is not factual, explain that to the class.

- Select uplifting stories from your life, the scriptures, Church magazines and manuals, Church history, and the lives of General Authorities. In sharing stories from your life, avoid telling about past misdeeds or sins.

- Remember to use stories that are appropriate for the age-group you are teaching.

- Before sharing a story with those you teach, read it thoughtfully several times to become familiar with it. As you do this, determine whether or not you will tell the story in your own words. Stories that are filled with expressive dialogue and descriptions may be more effective if they are read.

- Determine how much time you will have to tell the story. If the story needs to be shortened, include only

those characters and events that are necessary for the story to be easy to follow.

- If you are telling a story in your own words, outline on paper or in your mind the sequence of events in the story. Practice telling the story out loud in your own words. Use words and descriptions that add interest and color.

- Plan how you will help listeners visualize the story in their minds. You can create interest in the story by using pictures or other visual materials such as drawings on the chalkboard or objects that relate to the story. For example, before telling the story of the coming forth of the Book of Mormon, you could show a picture of Moroni hiding the gold plates in the Hill Cumorah. You could ask questions such as "What is happening in this picture?" or "Why is Moroni doing this?"

- Begin the story in an interesting way, using words that produce a vivid picture of the characters and setting. For example, to introduce the account of the Savior calming the storm, you could read from the scriptures: "And, behold, there arose a great tempest in the sea, insomuch that the ship was covered with the waves" (Matthew 8:24).

- Enjoy telling the story. Tell it in a natural tone of voice, with interest and conviction.

- After telling the story, discuss with learners how the principle taught in the story applies in their lives.

Additional Suggestions for Telling a Story to Young Children

- Keep in mind the ages of the children, adapting the story to their attention span and understanding.

- Plan ways to involve the children in the story. For example, you could have them hold pictures or repeat phrases.

- Before you tell the story, explain words in the story that the children might not understand. This will help you tell the story without interruption.

- If you read from a book with pictures, stop frequently to show the children the pictures of the story. Display the pictures long enough for everyone to see them before you proceed with the story.

- If the children make comments or ask questions, give simple, concise answers. Then continue with the story.

- Young children enjoy having stories repeated. If you are repeating a story, start it and then ask, "What happened next?" You could toss a beanbag or soft toy to one child and ask him or her to say one thing about the story. That child would then toss the beanbag to another child, and so on, until the story is finished.

- Put various passages from a scripture account together. Assign different learners to read the scriptures in sequence.

- Children may enjoy sitting on the floor in front of you as you tell a story.

- Children may enjoy dramatizing a story after they have heard it.

VISUALS (see also PICTURES)

We learn through all our senses. In formal teaching settings we tend to rely heavily on the spoken word. But teachers who desire to increase learners' ability to understand and learn will also use visuals. Most people will learn better and remember longer when you present ideas by using pictures, maps, word groupings, or other visuals rather than merely speaking.

The following examples show some things you can accomplish with visuals.

Clarify Relationships between Ideas, People, or Places

A Relief Society teacher wanted to help the sisters better understand how Romans 5:3–4 shows the relationship between tribulations and hope. She drew a simple diagram:

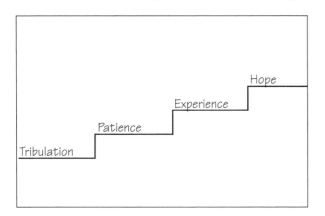

She then asked the sisters to discuss how tribulation brings patience, inviting them to give specific examples from their own lives. As the sisters continued through the simple diagram, they discovered how tribulation, patience, experience, and hope were significant in their individual lives.

A Sunday School class was studying the story of the road to Emmaus (see Luke 24:1–35). The teacher used a map in the scriptures to help the class members understand the distance between Jerusalem and Emmaus. He then showed them a map of their own city with a similar distance between two places familiar to the learners. This helped the learners understand approximately how long it would take to walk that distance, helping them to better appreciate what occurred in the conversation between the disciples and Jesus.

Convey Emotion and Provide Spiritual Reassurance

One teacher used a chalkboard to illustrate Doctrine and Covenants 84:88 to a class of missionaries. He wanted the missionaries to feel that the Lord's influence could encircle them. He illustrated each phrase from the scripture as follows:

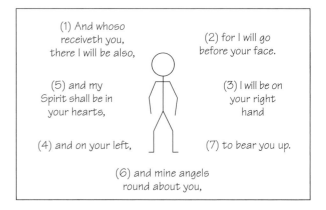

This simple arrangement of the words of the scripture verse allowed the missionaries to feel the protective promise of the Lord in a profound way. An interesting discussion followed as the learners were invited to discuss their fears concerning missionary work and their confidence in the Lord's promise to help them.

Help Learners Understand Sequence

Visuals can help those you teach understand the sequence of certain events. For example, time lines can help learners understand the sequence of events as they study such subjects as the ministry of Jesus, the missionary travels of Paul, or early Church history.

Help Learners Understand Principles

When learners visualize scriptural sequences, they can often understand principles more clearly. Most Church members have been taught the plan of happiness visually. Picturing a diagram of premortal life, earth life, life after death, judgment, and the three kingdoms of glory is useful in helping us understand the sequence of the plan.

Visuals can increase learners' understanding of intangible principles. For example, you could represent the mediating power of Christ's Atonement with the following illustration:

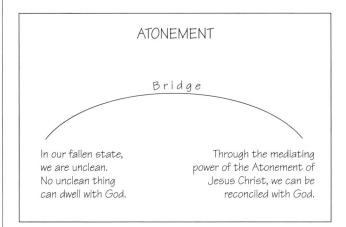

ATONEMENT

Bridge

In our fallen state, we are unclean. No unclean thing can dwell with God.

Through the mediating power of the Atonement of Jesus Christ, we can be reconciled with God.

Help Learners Remember

A lesson about helping the poor and needy might be enhanced by using the picture Christ and the Rich Young Ruler. In this picture, the Savior points the young man toward people in need as He says, "Go thy way, sell whatsoever thou hast, and give to the poor, and thou shalt have treasure in heaven: and come, take up the cross, and follow me" (Mark 10:21). This picture can help learners remember to give service to those in need.

WHITE BOARDS

See "Chalkboards," pages 162–63.

WORK SHEETS

Work sheets provide written activities that help learners assess their understanding of a gospel principle, learn new information, or review key concepts. You can prepare a work sheet in order to introduce, emphasize, or review important parts of a lesson. A work sheet can also provide a reminder of a lesson for those you teach to take home and share with their families.

Examples of Work Sheets

Assessment Work Sheet

You can use a work sheet to help people assess how a gospel principle is currently part of their lives and discover areas in which they can improve. Use a work sheet like the following at the beginning of a lesson. Explain that if anyone answers *no* to any of the questions, the lesson will help him or her understand how to better live the principle and will suggest one or two ways to improve.

What Kind of Example Am I?

Yes	No	
☐	☐	Do I listen with respect to others' opinions?
☐	☐	Do I always speak positively about others?
☐	☐	Do I treat my family members with love?
☐	☐	Am I honest in my work?
☐	☐	Am I a good sport?
☐	☐	Do I keep my language clean and pure?
☐	☐	Is my appearance neat and clean?
☐	☐	Do I keep the commandments?
☐	☐	Do I read the scriptures regularly?
☐	☐	Am I cheerful about helping others?
☐	☐	Do I watch only wholesome movies and television programs?
☐	☐	Do I read only uplifting books or magazines?
☐	☐	Am I unselfish with my time and talents?
☐	☐	Am I dependable?

Matches

List various names of prophets in one column and list what they are noted for in another column. Have learners match the prophets with the events, as shown below.

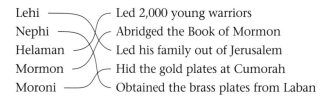

Lehi	Led 2,000 young warriors
Nephi	Abridged the Book of Mormon
Helaman	Led his family out of Jerusalem
Mormon	Hid the gold plates at Cumorah
Moroni	Obtained the brass plates from Laban

You can have learners match items from any number of gospel subjects. For example, they could match the Articles of Faith with the correct numbers, or they could match priesthood duties with the correct priesthood offices.

Chronology

Prepare a work sheet that lists several historical facts or parts of a scripture story. Have learners number them in the proper order. For example:

Christ visited the Nephites. (3)

Mormon died. (4)

Lehi left Jerusalem. (2)

The Jaredite civilization flourished. (1)

Joseph Smith received the gold plates. (5)

Fill In the Blanks

Provide sentences with some words missing. Have learners fill in the blanks with the correct words. Provide the answers in a key in scrambled order. For example:

"If any of _____ lack _____ , let him _____ of God, that _____ to all _____ liberally, and _____ not; and it _____ be _____ him" (James 1:5).

Answers: upbraideth, you, given, men, shall, wisdom, giveth, ask

Scripture Application

You can use work sheets to review and apply material from current and previous lessons. Select several scriptures that relate to gospel topics recently studied. Review the scriptures with those you teach, ensuring that they understand them. Then write the scripture references on the chalkboard. Present a short case study (see "Case Studies," pages 161–62). Ask those you teach to select at least one of the scriptures and apply it to the case study. Give each person a piece of paper and a pen or pencil. Have learners write the passage or passages they select, what those passages teach, and how they apply to the case study.

Scrambles

Scrambles can be used in different ways. For example:

- Scramble letters in words. Have learners unscramble them to spell the words. The following work sheet contains scrambled words associated with skills that missionaries need:

TSYUD (Study)	EWS (Sew)
OKOC (Cook)	TUEGDB (Budget)
RNOI (Iron)	AETHC (Teach)
CXEEISER (Exercise)	ANSRMNE (Manners)
NOMYTTIES (Testimony)	CNAEL (Clean)

- Scramble words and have learners unscramble them to complete a phrase, a scripture, a song title, or an article of faith. For example:

together be forever can families ("Families can be together forever" [*Hymns,* no. 300; *Children's Songbook,* 188].)

go the I which commanded will and Lord the hath things do ("I will go and do the things which the Lord hath commanded" [1 Nephi 3:7].)

Guidelines for Creating and Using Work Sheets

- Information and ideas from lesson manuals and Church magazines can be adapted into interesting work sheets.

- Work sheets should be suitable for the age of the learners. They should instruct and be enjoyable. They should not be too difficult.

- Learners can work individually, or the class can be divided into small groups, with each group contributing to a work sheet. The information from a work sheet could be written on the chalkboard, and the class could complete it together.

- Have enough pencils or pens for all the learners.

- Work sheets should not take a long time. However, you should allow enough time for class members to complete them.

- After giving everyone a certain amount of time to finish a work sheet, review the answers.

- Help everyone feel successful in completing a work sheet. Help anyone who seems to be having difficulty.

G

THE TEACHING THE GOSPEL COURSE

Helps for the Course Instructor

Purpose of the Course

This course provides a foundation that will help Church members become more effective gospel teachers in their homes and in the Church. The lessons in the course are designed to be taught as part of an organized class. They may also be studied individually or as a family.

Course Overview

The Lord has commanded us to "teach one another the doctrine of the kingdom" (D&C 88:77). As the Master Teacher, He has set the example for us to follow. In latter-day revelations, He has given us specific commandments about how we should teach (see, for example, D&C 42:12–14; 50:13–22; 52:9; 88:122). His example and His commandments guide us as we strive to improve as teachers.

Lesson 1, "The Importance of Gospel Teaching in God's Plan," sets the tone for the entire Teaching the Gospel course. It focuses on the Lord's grand design to teach us the plan of redemption. The lesson teaches that we can assist in this sacred work.

Lessons 2, 3, and 4 present three fundamental principles of gospel teaching: "Love Those You Teach," "Teach by the Spirit," and "Teach the Doctrine."

Lesson 5, "Invite Diligent Learning," focuses on helping individuals take responsibility for learning the gospel. Lessons 6 and 7, both titled "Create a Learning Atmosphere," show how to prevent and solve problems that can arise in teaching situations. In lessons 8 and 9, both titled "Use Effective Methods," you will teach and discuss the effective use of a variety of teaching methods. Lesson 10, "Prepare Every Needful Thing," shows how to plan lessons.

In lessons 11 and 12 you will help class members apply everything that they have learned in the first 10 lessons. Lesson 11, "Improve upon Your Talents," helps class members make a personal plan for improvement and shows how the many resources available in the ward can help them carry out this plan successfully. Lesson 12, "Go Forth and Teach," gives class members the opportunity to teach one another by sharing what they have learned during the course.

Format of the Course

For information on when the course should be held, who should attend, and adaptations that can be made, see *Improving Gospel Teaching: A Leader's Guide,* page 10.

Preparing to Teach the Course

It is recommended that you read all 12 lessons before the course begins. This will help you see how the lessons work together to provide a foundation for gospel teaching. It will also alert you to principles of gospel teaching that you should exemplify as you teach the course.

Using Church-Produced Materials

In addition to this book, you will need the scriptures and the "Gospel Teaching and Leadership" section of the *Church Handbook of Instructions.* You may also want to refer to the materials listed in "Church Resources for Teaching the Gospel," page 105 in this book.

Contact the meetinghouse librarian to learn of the resources available in the meetinghouse library.

Working with Class Members

Materials Class Members Will Need

Class members should bring their scriptures to class. In addition, they should bring a notebook or journal in which they can write notes, assignments, and insights. Each class member should bring a copy of this book to class.

Helping Class Members Participate in Class

Each lesson includes instructions to help class members play an active part in the learning experience. For example, class members may be invited to write in their notebooks, express their ideas, or share personal experiences. As you prepare lessons, ensure that you plan enough time for class members to participate in these activities.

Assignments

The lessons in this course contain two different types of assignments:

1. Invitations to prepare a portion of the lesson. These assignments are listed in the "Preparation" section of many of the lessons. They give class members opportunities to participate and to teach one another. You should prayerfully consider which class members should be given these assignments. In extending the assignments, give class members time to prepare.

2. Assignments to practice specific principles outside of class. These assignments are an important part of the course because they will help class members continue to improve as teachers. You should give these assignments at the conclusion of each lesson.

Supporting Individual Class Members

In addition to teaching the lessons in the course, you should take time to support class members individually. Class members will experience greater success as you contact them between lessons to offer encouragement and assistance. They may want to talk about the experiences they are having as they apply the principles taught in the lessons.

The Promise of Divine Assistance

Ponder the note to the teacher on page 234. As you exercise faith, pray for assistance, and apply the principles you will be teaching in the course, you will help class members become "instrument[s] in the hands of God to bring [others] to the knowledge of the truth" (Alma 17:9).

Personal and Family Study of the Course

If the Teaching the Gospel course is not currently offered in your ward or if you are unable to attend, you can study the lessons on your own or with family members. However, personal or family study is not intended to be a replacement for participating in the course when you are invited. You will gain much more as you meet with others to share ideas and learn together about how you can improve as teachers.

Keys to Studying on Your Own or with Your Family

Read "Helps for the Teacher," on pages 186–87. Adapt the suggestions to your own situation.

Make a personal commitment. Your study will be more productive if you begin with a personal commitment to improve and a willingness to diligently complete the course.

Study the lessons in sequence, and do not try to cover more than one lesson per week. You will need time between lessons to apply what you have learned.

Keep a notebook. Making a record of your progress is an important part of the Teaching the Gospel course. In the lessons there are opportunities to record notes, impressions, plans, experiences, and progress related to the course.

Complete the assignments. Your efforts to improve will be successful only when you implement what you have learned. Each lesson has assignments to help you apply the principles in actual teaching opportunities. Complete these assignments faithfully. Record in your notebook your evaluation of your efforts and progress.

If you are studying with family members, organize your study as if you were in a class. You might take turns conducting discussions. Read the scriptures suggested in the lessons, discuss the questions, and do the assignments.

If you are studying alone, imagine that you are in a class. What would you add to a discussion of the lesson topics? How would you respond to the questions asked? Record your insights in your notebook. See "Developing a Personal Plan for Studying the Gospel," pages 16–17, for suggestions on carrying out your study effectively.

If you are studying alone, find someone to whom you can report. Your personal study will improve if there is someone with whom you can share your insights and ideas. Perhaps you can ask a family member, a friend, or a priesthood or auxiliary leader. Share with this person your goals and plans and the results of your efforts.

The Importance of Gospel Teaching in God's Plan

Purpose	To help class members increase their desire to assist in the Lord's work by teaching His gospel.

Note to the Teacher

In His loving-kindness, our Father in Heaven has provided teachers to help His children learn what they must do to receive eternal life. Each of us is a beneficiary of gospel teaching, and each of us has been commanded to teach the gospel to others. Your efforts in teaching this course are part of this great work.

The following statements by President Gordon B. Hinckley reflect a message that you should communicate to class members throughout this course:

"We must strengthen ourselves and our people to get our teachers to speak out of their hearts rather than out of their books, to communicate their love for the Lord and this precious work, and somehow it will catch fire in the hearts of those they teach" (*Teachings of Gordon B. Hinckley* [1997], 619–20).

"We have work to do, you and I, so very much of it. Let us roll up our sleeves and get at it, with a new commitment, putting our trust in the Lord. . . . We can do it, if we will be prayerful and faithful. We can do better than we have ever done before" (in Conference Report, Apr. 1995, 117; or *Ensign,* May 1995, 88).

With this message as its focus, this lesson sets the tone for the entire Teaching the Gospel course.

Preparation

1. Prayerfully study the scripture passages in this lesson. Seek to apply them to the purpose of the lesson.

2. Study the section of this book titled "The Importance of Gospel Teaching in God's Plan" (pages 2–10).

3. Encourage class members to come to class with their scriptures and a notebook. If necessary, meet with a member of the bishopric to make arrangements to provide notebooks for class members.

4. Obtain enough copies of *Teaching, No Greater Call* to give to class members who have not yet received it.

Suggested Lesson Development

Welcome class members to the course. If you do not know them or if they do not know each other, invite them to briefly introduce themselves.

Ensure that each class member has a notebook to use during the lesson. Explain that the purpose of the notebooks is to record notes, impressions, plans, experiences, and progress related to the Teaching the Gospel course.

Teachers of the gospel influence the lives of many people.

Story

Share the following story told by President Thomas S. Monson:

"There was a Sunday School teacher—never to be forgotten, ever to be remembered. We met for the first time on a Sunday morning. She accompanied the Sunday School president into the classroom and was presented to us as a teacher who actually requested the opportunity to teach us. We learned that she had been a missionary and loved young people. Her name was Lucy Gertsch. She was beautiful, soft-spoken, and interested in us. She asked each class member to introduce himself or herself, and then she asked questions that gave her an understanding and an insight into the background of each boy, each girl. She told us of her childhood. . . . She never raised her voice. Somehow rudeness and boisterousness were incompatible with the beauty of her lessons. . . . She made the scriptures actually come to life. We became personally acquainted with Samuel, David, Jacob, Nephi, and the Lord Jesus Christ. Our gospel scholarship grew. Our deportment improved. Our love for Lucy Gertsch knew no bounds. . . .

"The years have flown. . . . The boys and girls who learned, who laughed, who grew under the direction of that inspired teacher of truth have never forgotten her love or her lessons" (in Conference Report, Apr. 1992, 81–82; or *Ensign,* May 1992, 59–60).

Testify to class members that their efforts to teach the gospel of Jesus Christ can likewise touch the lives of many people. Express your feelings about the importance of the call to teach.

Quotation

Have a class member read the following statement by Elder Jeffrey R. Holland:

"For each of us to 'come unto Christ,' to keep His commandments and follow His example back to the Father, is surely the highest and holiest purpose of human existence. To help others do that as well—to teach, persuade, and prayerfully lead them to walk that path of redemption also—surely that must be the second most significant task in our lives" (in Conference Report, Apr. 1998, 31; or *Ensign,* May 1998, 25).

Gospel teaching plays an essential role in Heavenly Father's plan.

Scripture Discussion

Point out that teaching has always played an important role in God's plan of redemption. Have class members read the scripture passages listed below. It may be helpful for you to explain the background of each passage (for example, you could explain that Doctrine and Covenants 138 contains an account of President Joseph F. Smith's vision of the spirit world). Ask class members to share insights they gain from these passages about the role that teaching plays in Heavenly Father's plan.

a. Doctrine and Covenants 138:56. (We "received [our] first lessons in the world of spirits.")

b. Alma 12:27–32. (After Adam and Eve were cast out of the Garden of Eden, God helped them learn of the plan of redemption. He sent angels to teach them, and He answered their prayers. He gave them commandments *after* they had been taught the plan of redemption.)

c. Moses 6:57–58. (The Lord commanded Adam and Eve to teach the gospel freely to their children.)

Summarize the discussion by reading Romans 10:13–15, 17 and 2 Nephi 2:8. Bear your testimony of the role of gospel teaching in Heavenly Father's plan.

We have many opportunities to learn the gospel and teach it to others.

Quotations

Point out that Church members teach the gospel in many different roles. Then ask five different class members to read the statements below. Note that each statement is directed to a specific group of people.

To Parents

The First Presidency said:

"We call upon parents to devote their best efforts to the teaching and rearing of their children in gospel principles which will keep them close to the Church. The home is the basis of a righteous life, and no other instrumentality can take its place or fulfill its essential functions in carrying forward this God-given responsibility.

"We counsel parents and children to give highest priority to family prayer, family home evening, gospel study and instruction, and wholesome family activities. However worthy and appropriate other demands or activities may be, they must not be permitted to displace the divinely-appointed duties that only parents and families can adequately perform" (First Presidency letter, 11 Feb. 1999).

To Priesthood and Auxiliary Leaders

Elder Gordon B. Hinckley said: "Effective teaching is the very essence of leadership in the Church. Eternal life will come only as men and women are taught with such effectiveness that they change and discipline their lives. They cannot be coerced into righteousness or into heaven. They must be led, and that means teaching" ("How to Be a Teacher When Your Role as a Leader Requires You to Teach," General Authority Priesthood Board Meeting, 5 Feb. 1969; quoted by Jeffrey R. Holland in Conference Report, Apr. 1998, 31; or *Ensign,* May 1998, 26).

To Teachers in Church Classrooms

President Thomas S. Monson taught:

"The classroom at church adds a vital dimension to the education of every child and youth. In this setting each teacher can provide an upward reach to those who listen to [the] lessons and feel the influence of [the teacher's] testimony. In Primary, Sunday School, Young Women meetings and those of the Aaronic Priesthood, well-prepared teachers, called under the inspiration of the Lord, can touch each child, each youth, and prompt all to 'seek . . . out of the best books words of wisdom; seek learning, even by study and also by faith' (D&C 88:118). A word of encouragement here and a spiritual thought there can affect a precious life and leave an indelible imprint upon an immortal soul. . . .

"The humble and inspired teacher in the church classroom can instill in . . . pupils a love for the scriptures. Why, the teacher can bring the Apostles of old and the Savior of the world not only into the classroom but also into the hearts, the minds, the souls of our children" (in Conference Report, Oct. 1991, 92; or *Ensign,* Nov. 1991, 68).

To Home Teachers and Visiting Teachers

President Spencer W. Kimball said: "When you go into [people's] homes, . . . you are going to save souls. . . . Who can tell but that many of the fine active people in the Church today are active because you were in their homes and gave them a new outlook, a new vision. You pulled back the curtain. You extended their horizons. You gave them something new" (*The Teachings of Spencer W. Kimball,* ed. Edward L. Kimball [1982], 526).

To All Church Members

President Lorenzo Snow said, "Though one teach with the eloquence of an angel, yet one's good practice, good examples, one's acts constantly manifesting whole-heartedness for the interests of the people, teach much more eloquently, much more effectually" (*The Teachings of Lorenzo Snow,* comp. Clyde J. Williams [1984], 78–79).

Teacher Presentation

Suggest that class members consider the different teachers described in the statements that have been read: parents, priesthood and auxiliary leaders, teachers in Church classrooms, home teachers, visiting teachers, and those who teach by example. Invite each class member to briefly tell about someone who, in one or more of these roles, has helped him or her gain a better understanding of the gospel and a greater desire to live according to its principles.

Testimony

Speak briefly about the blessings that come to us because of our many opportunities to learn and teach the gospel—in our homes, in the Church, and in our everyday associations. Express your gratitude for these opportunities. Emphasize that the Lord provides these opportunities to help us resist the evil teachings and influences that surround us. Share the following statement by President Gordon B. Hinckley:

"There is hunger in the land, and a genuine thirst—a great hunger for the word of the Lord and an unsatisfied thirst for things of the Spirit. . . . The world is starved for spiritual food. Ours is the obligation and the opportunity to nourish the soul" ("Feed the Spirit, Nourish the Soul," *Ensign,* Oct. 1998, 2).

The purpose of the Teaching the Gospel course is to help us improve as teachers.

Teacher Presentation

Read the statements by President Gordon B. Hinckley included in "Note to the Teacher" on page 189.

After reading President Hinckley's statements, point out that the purpose of the Teaching the Gospel course is to help us teach the gospel of Jesus Christ "better than we have ever done before."

Explain that resources for the course are the scriptures, *Teaching, No Greater Call,* and the "Gospel Teaching and Leadership" section of the *Church Handbook of Instructions.*

Give copies of *Teaching, No Greater Call* to class members who have not yet received it. Tell class members that this book contains materials that relate to the lessons in the course. They will benefit from reading these materials before and after each lesson.

Explain that this course builds a foundation for gospel teaching. It focuses on principles and teaching methods that apply to all age-groups and cultures. There are 12 lessons in the course. The titles of the upcoming 11 lessons show what class members can expect from the course. Have class members turn to page vi of this book to see the titles of the lessons.

Offer to help class members as they strive to apply the principles taught in the course. In addition, encourage each class member to:

a. Study the scriptures; *Teaching, No Greater Call;* and the "Gospel Teaching and Leadership" section of the *Church Handbook of Instructions.*

b. Bring the scriptures to class each week.

c. Bring their notebooks to class each week.

d. Come to class each week prepared to participate in the lessons and contribute to the learning of others in the class.

e. Ponder and pray about opportunities to teach.

f. Begin to develop and implement a personal plan for improving as a teacher.

Conclusion

Quotation

Invite a class member to read the following statement by Elder Boyd K. Packer:

"It has been said that the responsibility of Church members is divided into three main categories: to provide for the salvation of the living members of the Church, to accomplish the necessary work for our kindred dead, and to preach the gospel to all the world. All of these responsibilities require learning, and all that is learned must somehow be taught. We are among those who must teach it" (*Teach Ye Diligently,* rev. ed. [1991], 7).

Summary

Summarize the principles you have discussed.

Testimony

Share your testimony as prompted by the Spirit.

Assignments

Encourage class members to:

1. Write in their notebooks about teaching and learning opportunities that come as they participate in the course.

2. Seek the guidance of the Spirit (the Holy Ghost) in connection with an upcoming family home evening lesson, Church assignment, or other opportunity to teach. Remember the Lord's words: "The Spirit shall be given unto you by the prayer of faith" (D&C 42:14). Write in their notebooks about their experiences with this assignment. (As part of lesson 3, some class members will be asked to report on these experiences.)

3. Review the principles taught in this lesson by studying the section of this book titled "The Importance of Gospel Teaching in God's Plan" (pages 2–10).

Lesson
2

Love Those You Teach

Purpose	To help class members seek to be filled with Christlike love for those they teach.

Note to the Teacher	In the final hours of His mortal ministry, Jesus taught and strengthened His Apostles (see John 13–17). As part of these teachings, He commanded His disciples to love one another as He loved them (see John 13:34; 15:12, 17). Their obedience to this commandment would show that they truly were His disciples (see John 13:35). All they were to do, including their commission to go forth and teach all nations, was to be done with love. In the latter days, the Lord has taught us similarly: "No one can assist in this work except he shall be humble and full of love" (D&C 12:8).

As you teach this lesson, help class members understand how to be filled with Christlike love toward those they teach. As class members follow the counsel in this lesson, they will teach more effectively. They will also find more joy as teachers. |

Preparation	1. Prayerfully study the scripture passages in this lesson. Seek to apply them to the purpose of the lesson. Become familiar enough with 3 Nephi 11–17 that you can briefly relate the parts of the account that are outlined on page 195 of this book.

2. Study the section of this book titled "Love Those You Teach" (pages 30–39).

3. If the following materials are available, prepare to use them as part of the lesson:

    a. The pictures Jesus Teaching in the Western Hemisphere (62380; Gospel Art Picture Kit 316); Jesus Healing the Nephites (62541; Gospel Art Picture Kit 317); and Jesus Blesses the Nephite Children (Gospel Art Picture Kit 322).
    b. "My Joy Is Full," a four-minute segment of *Book of Mormon Video Presentations* (53911).

4. Assign a class member to prepare to talk briefly about how he or she has been influenced by the love of a gospel teacher (such as a parent, a teacher in a Church classroom, or a Church leader). Ask this class member to address the following questions as part of the presentation:

How did you know that this person loved you?

How did this person's love affect your feelings about learning the gospel?

5. A week or more in advance, arrange to have a soloist or a small group of adults or children sing "Love One Another" (*Hymns*, no. 308) at the end of class. If this is not possible, prepare to have class members sing the hymn together. |

Suggested Lesson Development	**Teachers with Christlike love make a difference in the lives of those they teach.**
Scripture Account and Pictures	Display the picture of Jesus teaching the Nephites. In your own words, briefly relate the account of the resurrected Savior's visit to the Nephites. Be sure to include the following:

The resurrected Savior appeared to the Nephites in the land Bountiful. He invited them to come and feel His side and the nail prints in His hands and feet. Then He taught them at length. After teaching them, He urged them to go to their homes and ponder the things that He had said. He was about to return to the Father when He saw them in tears, desiring that He stay longer with them. (See 3 Nephi 11–16; 17:1–5.)

Display the picture of Jesus healing the Nephites. Then invite a class member to read 3 Nephi 17:6–10.

Chalkboard

After the class member has read the passage, write on the chalkboard *He did heal them every one.*

Scripture Account and Picture

In your own words, continue relating the account. Be sure to say that after Jesus had healed the people, He asked them to bring their little children to Him (see 3 Nephi 17:11–12).

Display the picture of Jesus blessing the Nephite children. Then invite a class member to read 3 Nephi 17:21–25.

Chalkboard

After the class member has read the passage, write on the chalkboard *He took their little children, one by one, and blessed them.*

Video Presentation

If you are using the video presentation "My Joy Is Full," show it now.

Discussion

Ask class members to ponder the love that the Savior showed toward the Nephites. Also invite them to think about what the Nephites might have felt as Jesus ministered to them one by one.

- In what ways might a teacher's Christlike love influence those who are being taught? (Answers may include that a teacher's Christlike love can invite the Spirit, help people overcome fear, and lead people to be more receptive to the gospel.)

Quotation

Following a brief discussion of this question, have a class member read the statement by the Prophet Joseph Smith on page 30 of this book.

Class Member Presentation

Ask the assigned class member to talk about how he or she has been influenced by the love of a teacher.

Teacher Presentation

Explain that this lesson includes teachings from the scriptures that can help us be filled with Christlike love for those we teach. It also includes a discussion on how our Christlike love influences our service as teachers.

We can be filled with Christlike love for those we teach.

Scriptures and Notebook Activity

Invite different class members to read the scripture passages listed below. After each passage is read, ask class members to identify principles in the passage that can help them be filled with Christlike love. Encourage class members to write in their notebooks any thoughts they have as they participate in this discussion. Explain that they will be given an opportunity to share these thoughts toward the end of class.

John 15:10 (Keeping the commandments)
Ephesians 4:32 (Forgiving others)
Mosiah 2:17 (Serving)
Mosiah 4:11–12 (Repenting, being humble, and exercising faith)

Alma 38:12 (Bridling passions)

3 Nephi 11:29–30 (Ceasing contention)

Moroni 7:48 (Praying to be filled with the pure love of Christ)

Our Christlike love for those we teach should be reflected in our preparation, our teaching, and our everyday lives.

Notebook Activity and Discussion

Point out that when we are filled with Christlike love for those we teach, our love is reflected in our preparation, our teaching, and our everyday lives. Then write the following on the chalkboard. Ask class members to copy it in their notebooks.

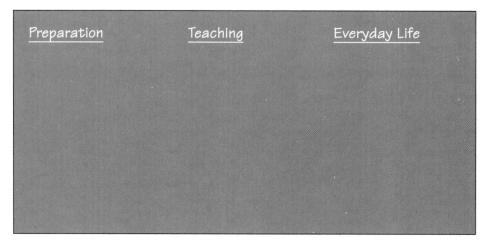

Preparation	Teaching	Everyday Life

Have class members think of specific people whom they teach (such as family members, class members, or quorum members). Then ask them to consider the following question, writing their ideas under the appropriate headings in their notebooks:

▪ What are some things you can do to show Christlike love for these people? (Note that some ideas are listed in the following chart. Other ideas are included in "Love Softens Hearts," "Understanding Those You Teach," and "Reaching Out to the One," pages 31–36 in this book.)

Preparation	Teaching	Everyday Life
Pray for them.	Greet them warmly at the beginning of class.	Pray for them.
Be aware of their needs and interests.	Express your love for them.	Be friendly when you see them.
Be well prepared to teach them.	Listen attentively.	Be aware of their activities and accomplishments.
	Respond respectfully as they participate in class.	Attend activities in which they are participating.
	Encourage them to live the principles you teach.	Compliment them when appropriate.
	Compliment them when appropriate.	Show concern and give encouragement when they experience trials.

Invite class members to discuss some of the ideas that they have written in their notebooks. Write their ideas on the chalkboard.

Conclusion

Summary and Quotation

Briefly summarize the lesson, using the following statement by Elder Joseph B. Wirthlin:

"The compassion of Christlike friends deeply touches and changes our lives. . . . Love is the very essence of the gospel of Christ. In this Church, prayers for help are often answered by the Lord through the simple, daily service of caring brothers and sisters. In the goodness of genuine friends, I have seen the reflected mercy of the Lord Himself" (in Conference Report, Oct. 1997, 42; or *Ensign,* Nov. 1997, 32).

Testimony

As prompted by the Spirit, bear your testimony and express your love for class members.

Music

Have the assigned soloist or small group sing "Love One Another" (*Hymns,* no. 308). If this is not possible, invite class members to sing the hymn together.

Assignments

Encourage class members to:

1. Select at least one idea from the notebook activity on page 196. Use this idea in a teaching opportunity during the coming week. Write in their notebooks about the results of this action.

2. Continue last week's assignment to seek the guidance of the Spirit in connection with an upcoming family home evening lesson, Church assignment, or other opportunity to teach. Remember the Lord's words: "The Spirit shall be given unto you by the prayer of faith" (D&C 42:14). Write in their notebooks about their experiences with this assignment. (As part of lesson 3, some class members will be asked to report on these experiences.)

3. Review the principles taught in this lesson by studying the section of this book titled "Love Those You Teach" (pages 30–39).

Lesson 3

Teach by the Spirit

Purpose	To help class members seek the Spirit's guidance and teach in a way that will help others feel the influence of the Spirit.
Note to the Teacher	We learn the truths of the gospel by the power of the Holy Ghost, or the Spirit (see Moroni 10:5). The Lord described the importance of teaching by the Spirit when He said, "The Spirit shall be given unto you by the prayer of faith; and if ye receive not the Spirit ye shall not teach" (D&C 42:14). As both teachers and learners live worthy of being led by the Spirit, "both are edified and rejoice together" (see D&C 50:13–22).
	Some class members—especially those with little Church experience—may feel that they are incapable of teaching by the Spirit. As you teach this lesson, help class members see that they *can* teach by the Spirit. Help them understand that the qualifications for teaching by the Spirit are not eloquence, education, or long experience, but prayer, diligence, reverence, and humility.
Preparation	1. Prayerfully study the scripture passages in this lesson. Seek to apply them to the purpose of the lesson.
	2. Study the section of this book titled "Teach by the Spirit" (pages 40–48).
	3. Ask two or three class members to prepare to talk briefly about their experiences as they have sought the guidance of the Holy Ghost in their teaching. (At the end of lessons 1 and 2, class members were assigned to write in their notebooks about such experiences.)
	4. Bring to class a pitcher of water and a transparent glass.
	5. Before class, write the following question on the chalkboard: *In our efforts to teach the gospel, what matters most?*
Suggested Lesson Development	Before the opening prayer, invite class members to sing "Help Me Teach with Inspiration" (*Hymns,* no. 281) or another reverent hymn. Following the hymn, ask the class member offering the prayer to ask for the guidance of the Holy Ghost during the lesson.
	"It is the Spirit that matters most."
Quotation	Direct class members' attention to the question that you have written on the chalkboard. Invite class members to think about the question without answering aloud. Then tell them that an answer to the question is found in the following statement by President Ezra Taft Benson:

"If there is one message I have repeated to my brethren of the Twelve, it is that it's the Spirit that counts. It is the Spirit that matters. I do not know how often I have said this, but I never tire of saying it—it is the Spirit that matters most" (mission presidents' seminar, 3 Apr. 1985).

Explain that we often refer to the Holy Ghost as "the Spirit." Teaching by the Spirit is the most powerful kind of teaching because it is only through the influence of the Spirit that we can understand the things of God (see 1 Corinthians 2:11).

As we learn and teach the gospel, the Spirit will attend us in many ways.

Scripture
Discussion

Emphasize that the Spirit is usually manifested quietly and simply rather than in spectacular displays of power (see 1 Kings 19:9–12). Then have class members read the scriptures listed below. Ask them to explain what each passage teaches about how the Spirit can attend our gospel teaching. Write their answers on the chalkboard.

a. John 14:26. (Teaches us all things and brings all things to our remembrance.)
b. John 15:26. (Testifies of Christ.)
c. 2 Nephi 33:1. (Carries the truth to our hearts.)
d. Doctrine and Covenants 6:14–15, 22–23. (Enlightens and brings peace to our minds.)
e. Doctrine and Covenants 11:13. (Fills our souls with joy.)
f. Doctrine and Covenants 50:21–22. (Edifies.)

Class Member
Presentation

Invite the assigned class members to talk about their experiences as they have sought the guidance of the Holy Ghost in their teaching (see "Preparation," item 3).

There are specific things we can do to invite the Spirit.

Chalkboard
Discussion

- What can we do in our teaching to invite the Spirit? (Write class members' answers on the chalkboard. Encourage class members to write these things in their notebooks.)

If class members do not mention some items from the following list, add them to the list on the chalkboard:

a. Pray.
b. Teach from the scriptures.
c. Testify.
d. Use hymns, Primary songs, and other sacred music.
e. Express love for others and for Heavenly Father and Jesus Christ.
f. Share insights, feelings, and experiences that relate to the principles in the lesson.

- Which of these have we done in class today? Have we done anything else in class to invite the Spirit?

Notebook Activity

Ask class members to think about a teaching opportunity that they will soon have. Invite them to consider how they can use some of the suggestions written on the chalkboard as they teach. Give them a few minutes to write their ideas in their notebooks.

Our best efforts will be enough when the influence of the Spirit is present.

Object Lesson

Write *Who can teach by the Spirit?* on the chalkboard.

Display the pitcher of water and the glass. Explain that in this demonstration, the glass represents us as teachers of the gospel. Then fill the glass partway. Explain that the water you have poured into the glass represents our best use of our talents.

Express that we may think that we could be truly effective in our teaching if only we had more talents. However, this glass cannot be filled by our talents alone. To be truly effective teachers of the gospel, we must teach by the power of the Holy Ghost. The miracle is that no matter who we are and no matter how talented we seem to be, the best we can do will be enough when the influence of the Spirit is present. As you explain this, fill the glass to the top.

Quotation

Have a class member read the following statement by Elder Henry B. Eyring:

"It is wise to fear that our own skills are inadequate to meet the charge we have to nourish the faith of others. Our own abilities, however great, will not be enough. But that realistic view of our limitations creates a humility which can lead to dependence on the Spirit and thus to power" (in Conference Report, Oct. 1997, 114; or *Ensign*, Nov. 1997, 82–83).

Each of us can qualify to teach by the Spirit.

Scripture Discussion and Chalkboard

Conduct the discussion below to help class members understand how they can qualify to teach by the Spirit.

Ask a class member to read Doctrine and Covenants 42:14.

Write the following on the chalkboard:

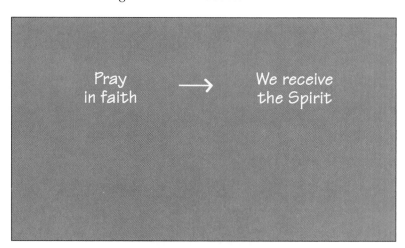

Ask a class member to read Doctrine and Covenants 88:77–78.

- What does the Lord promise if we diligently teach the doctrine of the kingdom? (His grace will attend us.)

Write the following on the chalkboard:

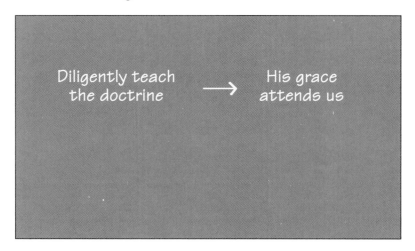

Diligently teach
the doctrine   →   His grace
attends us

Explain that grace is an enabling power. It is divine help and strength given through the mercy and love of God. Through the Lord's grace, we can do good works that we cannot do on our own (see Bible Dictionary, "Grace," 697).

Have a class member read Doctrine and Covenants 100:7–8.

- What do these verses tell us about how we should declare the gospel? ("In solemnity of heart," and "in the spirit of meekness.")

Explain that *solemnity* means reverence and dignity. Then, to help class members understand the meaning of the word *meekness,* read the following statement by President Gordon B. Hinckley:

"Meekness implies a spirit of gratitude as opposed to an attitude of self-sufficiency, an acknowledgment of a greater power beyond oneself, a recognition of God, and an acceptance of his commandments" ("With All Thy Getting Get Understanding," *Ensign,* Aug. 1988, 3–4).

- What does the Lord promise if we teach His gospel with solemnity and meekness? (See D&C 100:8. The Holy Ghost will bear record of the principles we teach.)

Write the following on the chalkboard:

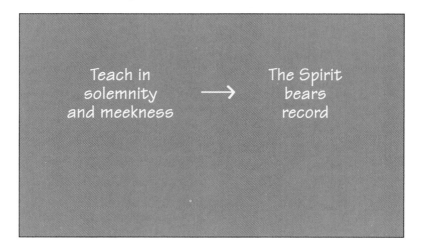

Teach in
solemnity
and meekness   →   The Spirit
bears
record

| Participation | Direct class members' attention to the principles that you have written on the chalkboard. Emphasize that as we pray in faith and teach the doctrine diligently and in solemnity and meekness, we will receive the Spirit, which will bear record of the truths we teach. Invite class members to tell about times when they or others have invited the Spirit by following these principles. |

Conclusion

| Summary and Quotation | Briefly summarize the lesson. Then have a class member read the following statement by President Thomas S. Monson: |

"Some of you may be shy by nature or consider yourselves inadequate to respond affirmatively to a calling. Remember that this work is not yours and mine alone. It is the Lord's work, and when we are on the Lord's errand, we are entitled to the Lord's help. Remember that whom the Lord calls, the Lord qualifies" (in Conference Report, Apr. 1996, 62; or *Ensign,* May 1996, 44).

| Testimony | Bear testimony as prompted by the Spirit. |

| Assignments | Encourage class members to: |

1. Reflect further on the ideas about teaching by the Spirit that they have written in their notebooks. Use one of these ideas in connection with an upcoming teaching opportunity.

2. Continue to record their progress in their notebooks.

3. Review the principles taught in this lesson by studying the section of this book titled "Teach by the Spirit" (pages 40–48).

Teach the Doctrine

Lesson

4

Purpose	To help class members understand the power that comes from studying and teaching the doctrines of the gospel, which are found in the scriptures and the teachings of latter-day prophets.
Note to the Teacher	As you prepare to teach this lesson, pray for guidance to teach effectively from the scriptures and the teachings of latter-day prophets. As prompted by the Holy Ghost, talk about the effect the doctrines of the gospel have had in your life as you have studied and taught them.
Preparation	1. Prayerfully study the scripture passages in this lesson. Seek to apply them to the purpose of the lesson. 2. Study the section in this book titled "Teach the Doctrine" (pages 49–59) and the following in the "Gospel Teaching and Leadership" section of the *Church Handbook of Instructions*: "Teach the Saving Doctrines and Ordinances of the Gospel" (page 301), "Teach from the Scriptures and the Teachings of Latter-day Prophets" (page 302), and "Use Church-Approved Lesson Materials" (page 304). 3. Invite a class member or another member of the ward to come to class prepared to talk about how learning a specific doctrine of the gospel has influenced his or her life. 4. If current Church-produced lesson manuals are available, bring a few of them to class. 5. Before class, write the following on the chalkboard:

> "I give unto you a commandment that you shall teach one another the doctrine of the kingdom" (D&C 88:77).
>
> How does learning the doctrine of the kingdom affect us?
>
> How is learning true doctrine different from learning other things?

Suggested Lesson Development

The Lord has commanded us to "teach one another the doctrine of the kingdom." The doctrine can have a powerful effect on our minds and hearts.

Chalkboard and Scripture Discussion

Direct class members' attention to the scripture and questions that you have written on the chalkboard (see "Preparation," item 5).

Explain that in the scripture written on the chalkboard, the phrase "doctrine of the kingdom" refers to the revealed truths of the gospel.

Direct class members' attention to the questions that you have written on the chalkboard. Before asking class members to discuss the questions, invite them to read the following scripture passages aloud:

a. Enos 1:1–4. (The doctrines of the gospel sink deep into our hearts and lead us to humble ourselves before God.)
b. Alma 31:5. (The word of God leads people to do good and has a "powerful effect" on the mind.)
c. Alma 32:28. (The word of God enlarges our souls, enlightens our understanding, and becomes delicious to us.)
d. Joseph Smith—History 1:11–12. (The word of God comes "with . . . power to the heart.")

Ask class members to discuss the questions on the chalkboard.

Class Member Presentation

Invite the assigned class member or other member of the ward to talk about how learning a specific doctrine of the gospel has influenced his or her life.

We should focus our teaching on the doctrine.

Case Study

Ask class members to imagine that they are members of a Young Men, Young Women, or Sunday School presidency. A teacher in their organization says to them, "When I teach the youth I spend a lot of class time talking about things like sports, dating, and movies. I feel like class members will lose interest if I spend too much time teaching from the scriptures."

Discussion and Quotations

- What counsel could you give to help this person teach the doctrine from the scriptures?

As part of this discussion, invite three different class members to read the statements below. Emphasize the importance of teaching the word of God to Church members of all ages.

To Teachers of Adults

President Joseph Fielding Smith said, "It is not pleasing to me when I attend a service and someone is called upon to speak who stands before the people and presents, though it be in a pleasing way, some platitudes, some philosophy of men—the ideas of those who today mould the thought of the world, but who in their own hearts have no faith in or love for Jesus Christ—or who discuss questions at variance with the fundamental principles of the gospel" (*Doctrines of Salvation*, comp. Bruce R. McConkie, 3 vols. [1954–56], 2:342).

To Teachers of Young Men and Women

President J. Reuben Clark Jr. taught:

"The youth of the Church are hungry for the things of the Spirit; they are eager to learn the gospel, and they want it straight, undiluted. . . .

"You do not have to sneak up behind [them] and whisper religion in [their] ears; . . . You do not need to disguise religious truths with a cloak of worldly things; you can bring these truths to [them] openly" (*The Charted Course of the Church in Education,* rev. ed. [pamphlet, 1994], 3, 9).

To Teachers of Small Children

Elder Ezra Taft Benson counseled, "All we ask of you [is] that in the hearts of these children who come under your watchcare and direction, you will so inspire them that nothing in this world will be dearer to them than the Gospel" ("Our First Obligation," *Children's Friend,* Oct. 1950, 454).

To All Gospel Teachers

Elder Boyd K. Packer said:

"True doctrine, understood, changes attitudes and behavior.

"The study of the doctrines of the gospel will improve behavior quicker than a study of behavior will improve behavior" (in Conference Report, Oct. 1986, 20; or *Ensign,* Nov. 1986, 17).

We should ensure that we teach correct doctrine.

Quotations and Discussion

Read the following statement by President Marion G. Romney:

"When I drink from a spring I like to get the water where it comes out of the ground, not down the stream after the cattle have waded in it. . . . I appreciate other people's interpretation, but when it comes to the gospel we ought to be acquainted with what the Lord says" (address to religious educators, 13 Apr. 1973; quoted by J. Richard Clarke in Conference Report, Oct. 1982, 19; or *Ensign,* Nov. 1982, 15).

▪ To what sources should we turn to help those we teach "be acquainted with what the Lord says"? (Answers should include the scriptures and the teachings of latter-day prophets.)

▪ How can we ensure that we are teaching correct doctrine?

As part of this discussion, have class members read Doctrine and Covenants 42:12–13 and 52:9. Emphasize that we can ensure that we are teaching correct doctrine by being consistent with the scriptures and the teachings of latter-day prophets. Invite a class member to read the following statement by President Spencer W. Kimball:

"No one has the right to give his own private interpretations when he has been invited to teach in the organizations of the Church; he is a guest, . . . and those whom he teaches are justified in assuming that, having been chosen and sustained in the proper order, he represents the Church and the things which he teaches are approved by the Church" (*The Teachings of Spencer W. Kimball,* ed. Edward L. Kimball [1982], 532–33).

If you have brought current Church-produced lesson manuals to class, display them now.

Point out that Church-produced manuals contain suggestions for application questions, activities, and audiovisual materials that help us focus our teaching on the scriptures and the words of latter-day prophets.

The Lord promises us great blessings as we diligently learn and teach His doctrine.

Quotation

Point out that we must study the doctrines of the gospel before we can teach them effectively. Then read the following statement by President Spencer W. Kimball:

"It is a common thing to have a few passages of scripture at our disposal, floating in our minds, as it were, and thus to have the illusion that we know a great deal about the gospel. In this sense, having a little knowledge can be a problem indeed. I am convinced that each of us, at some time in our lives, must discover the scriptures for ourselves—and not just discover them once, but rediscover them again and again" ("How Rare a Possession—the Scriptures!" *Ensign,* Sept. 1976, 4).

Chalkboard and Scripture Discussion

Erase the chalkboard, and draw the following chart. Explain that the chart will show the Lord's promises to teachers who "rediscover [the scriptures] again and again." Ask class members to copy the chart in their notebooks. (Do not have them turn to this page in their books.)

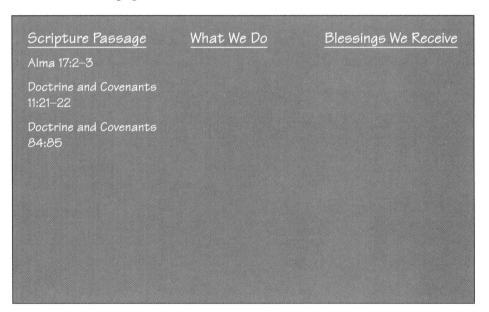

Scripture Passage	What We Do	Blessings We Receive
Alma 17:2–3		
Doctrine and Covenants 11:21–22		
Doctrine and Covenants 84:85		

Have class members read the scripture passages outlined in the chart. After each passage is read, ask class members to identify things we can do and blessings that we will receive as a result of those actions. Write their insights in the appropriate columns. Encourage class members to write these insights in their notebooks. Some possible answers are given in the following chart.

Scripture Passage	What We Do	Blessings We Receive
Alma 17:2–3	Search the scriptures diligently	Receive the spirit of prophecy and revelation
Doctrine and Covenants 11:21–22	Pray and fast	Teach with power and authority of God
Doctrine and Covenants 84:85	Obtain the word of God through study	Receive the guidance of the Spirit
	Prepare to teach by "treasur[ing] up . . . continually the words of life"	Teach with the power to convince others
		Teach with inspiration

Application Ask class members to write in their notebooks one specific thing they will do to follow the counsel in these scripture passages. Also, ask them to write about how they feel this action will help them receive the Lord's blessings in their responsibilities to teach.

Conclusion

Testimony As prompted by the Spirit, testify of the power that comes from studying and teaching the doctrines of the gospel.

Assignments Encourage class members to:

1. Study the scriptures diligently every day. (You may want to encourage them to read "Developing a Personal Plan for Studying the Gospel," pages 16–17 in this book.)

2. In connection with the notebook assignment during the lesson, strive to do one thing in the coming week to improve their personal gospel study. Write about their progress related to this goal.

3. Review the principles taught in this lesson by studying the section in this book titled "Teach the Doctrine" (pages 49–59).

Lesson 5

Invite Diligent Learning

Purpose	To help class members understand that individuals are responsible to learn the gospel; to help them see how they as teachers can help others fulfill that responsibility.

Note to the Teacher

The Lord has commanded us to "seek learning, even by study and also by faith" (D&C 88:118). As President Spencer W. Kimball taught, this commandment should be obeyed diligently: "One cannot become a 'doer of the word' without first becoming a 'hearer.' And to become a 'hearer' is not simply to stand idly by and wait for chance bits of information; it is to seek out and study and pray and comprehend" ("How Rare a Possession—the Scriptures!" *Ensign,* Sept. 1976, 2).

An individual's decision to study the gospel diligently is a righteous use of agency. Teachers who understand the doctrine of agency will not try to force others to learn the gospel. Instead, they will strive to teach in a way that will encourage others to put forth diligent effort to learn the gospel.

Preparation

1. Prayerfully study the scripture passages in this lesson. Seek to apply them to the purpose of the lesson.

2. Study the section of this book titled "Invite Diligent Learning" (pages 60–74). Also study "Principles of Conversion," page 300 in the "Gospel Teaching and Leadership" section of the *Church Handbook of Instructions.*

3. In advance, ask three class members to help you present the readers' theater on pages 209–10. Ask one to read the part of the narrator, another to read the part of the Zoramite, and a third to read the part of Alma.

4. Make three large name tags for the participants in the readers' theater. Write *Narrator* on one name tag, *Zoramite* on another, and *Alma* on the other.

Suggested Lesson Development

Each individual is responsible to learn the gospel.

Readers' Theater

Ask the participants in the readers' theater to come to the front of the class. Give them their name tags. Then explain that these three class members have agreed to present a readers' theater. The purpose of this presentation is to examine the responsibility individuals have to learn the gospel.

Write the following scripture references on the chalkboard: *Alma 32:27–28, 33, 38, 41.* Explain that these scripture references correspond with the teachings of Alma that will be used in this presentation. Encourage class members to follow along in their scriptures as Alma's part is read.

Narrator: As Alma and his brethren were preaching among an apostate people called the Zoramites, they entered one of the Zoramites' synagogues. There they heard the Zoramites declare that "there [would] be no Christ" (Alma 31:16).

              After hearing this false teaching, Alma and his brethren separated to preach the word of God and testify of Christ. A great multitude of Zoramites approached Alma, and one of these Zoramites spoke to him. (See Alma 31:37–38; 32:1.)

Zoramite: (Read Alma 32:5, beginning with the words "Behold, what shall these my brethren do.")

Narrator: (Read Alma 32:6.)

Chalkboard   Write the following on the chalkboard:

> ### The Individual's Responsibility
> Be in a preparation to hear the word (be teachable).

Point out that the Zoramites responded to their afflictions by choosing to be humble. They sought out a man who could teach them the word of God.

Readers' Theater   Narrator: Seeing that the Zoramites were in a preparation to hear the word of God, Alma taught them how to truly receive the word and gain a testimony of its truth.

Alma: (Read Alma 32:27–28, 33.)

Chalkboard   Add to the list on the chalkboard as shown below:

> ### The Individual's Responsibility
> Be in a preparation to hear the word (be teachable).
> Give place for the word.

Readers' Theater | Narrator: | Toward the end of his discourse Alma explained to the Zoramites that after they gained a testimony of the word, there would remain more to do. In giving this explanation, he compared the word to a tree that has grown from a seed.

Alma: | (Read Alma 32:38, 41.)

Chalkboard

Add to the list on the chalkboard as shown below:

<u>The Individual's Responsibility</u>
Be in a preparation to hear the word (be teachable).
Give place for the word.
Nourish the word.

Invite the class members who participated in the readers' theater to return to their seats.

Teacher Presentation

Explain that Alma taught the Zoramites that they were individually responsible to learn the gospel. We are all individually responsible to learn the gospel. Individuals who are just beginning to accept this responsibility are "in a preparation to hear the word" (Alma 32:6). Others are experimenting on the word and giving place for the word to be planted in their hearts (see Alma 32:27–28). Still others are already nourishing the word with faith, diligence, and patience (see Alma 32:41).

Individuals learn the gospel through their faith, diligence, and patience.

Discussion

- What are some specific things people can do to "nourish the word"? (Write class members' answers on the chalkboard. Note that some possible answers are listed below.)

a. Study and ponder the scriptures daily.
b. Search the scriptures for specific answers to questions.
c. Study addresses from general conference.
d. Study articles in Church magazines.
e. Fast and pray for understanding.
f. Seek understanding while doing temple work.
g. Discuss gospel principles with family members and friends.
h. Follow the guidance of the Spirit.
i. Strive faithfully to obey the commandments.

- What blessings have come to you as a result of your diligent efforts to learn the gospel?

Teachers should help individuals exercise their agency to learn and live the gospel.

Teacher
Presentation

Remind class members that God has given us agency—the power to choose good or evil (see D&C 29:35). We exercise our agency when we choose whether or not we will learn and live the gospel.

Quotation

Read the following statement by Elder James E. Faust:

"Agency, given us through the plan of our Father, is the great alternative to Satan's plan of force. With this sublime gift, we can grow, improve, progress, and seek perfection" (in Conference Report, Oct. 1987, 42; or *Ensign,* Nov. 1987, 35).

Discussion

- What difference does it make in our teaching to realize that individuals have agency and are responsible for their own learning? (You may want to write class members' responses on the chalkboard.)

Help class members see that they should focus on those they teach, not just on their teaching. Effective gospel teachers do not merely think about what they will teach. They ask themselves, "How will I help those I teach desire to learn and discover what they need to know?" In doing so, teachers respect the agency of those they teach and help them find joy in accepting their responsibility to learn.

Suggest that as we strive to help others accept their responsibility to learn the gospel, we should invite and encourage them rather than push them. We should ponder and pray about our plans to help each person we teach.

We should not do anything that could detract from others' desire to learn the gospel.

Discussion

- What are some things teachers might do that could detract from people's desire to learn the gospel? (Give class members time to ponder and discuss this question. Encourage them to discuss the question in general terms rather than criticize individual teachers. Note that some possible ideas are listed below.)

  a. Read lessons to them from the manual.
  b. Spend most of the lesson time lecturing.
  c. Try to impress them with knowledge or teaching skills.
  d. Criticize or treat lightly their questions and comments.
  e. Make comments or ask questions that might undermine their faith.
  f. Use language or examples that could cause the Spirit to withdraw.
  g. Fail to center lessons on gospel truths.

Quotation

Conclude this discussion by having a class member read the following statement by Elder Dallin H. Oaks:

"Every gospel teacher who seeks to follow the Master will *focus all of his efforts on others and never on himself.* Satan said, 'Send me, . . . I will redeem all mankind, . . . and surely I will do it; wherefore give me thine honor.' Contrast that proposal with the example of the Savior, who said, 'Father, thy will be done, and the glory be thine forever' (Moses 4:1–2). A gospel teacher will focus his teaching on the needs of the sheep and the glory of the Master. He will avoid the limelight. He will teach the flock that they should always look to the Master. He will never obscure their view of the Master by standing in the way or by casting a shadow of self-promotion or self-interest" (address given 31 March 1998).

There are many things we can do to invite diligent learning.

Notebook Activity

Have class members turn to page 60 in this book. Ask one class member to read aloud the statement on that page. The statement lists three general things that we can do to invite diligent learning. Point out that in each of these areas there are many simple, specific things we can do.

Have class members review the following list in their books. Invite them to choose one idea from the list that they will apply in an upcoming teaching opportunity. If time permits, allow them to briefly write in their notebooks about how they will use this idea. You may also want to ask them to share their plan with other class members. If there is not time for them to write in their notebooks and discuss their plans, encourage them to write in their notebooks at home.

a. Ask someone to prepare to assist with a lesson. Help him or her prepare.

b. Ask someone to prepare an object lesson.

c. Share personal experiences as appropriate.

d. Ask those you teach to ponder the blessings the Lord has given them and their families.

e. Teach how to read the scriptures with understanding.

f. Acknowledge the worth of each individual's contribution to the lesson. Listen to and make use of ideas expressed during discussions.

g. Ask questions that stimulate thought and invite contributions to discussions.

h. When someone asks a question, invite others to suggest answers.

i. Ask those you teach to think about how they can apply the things they have learned.

Conclusion

Remind class members that gospel teachers should exemplify diligent gospel learning. Encourage them to evaluate their own efforts to learn the doctrines of the gospel. Invite them to determine what they can do to follow Alma's counsel to nourish the word with faith, diligence, and patience (see Alma 32:37, 41–42).

Encourage class members to remember the sacredness of each individual's agency. Then read the following statement by President Spencer W. Kimball:

"The treasures of both secular and spiritual knowledge are hidden ones—but hidden from those who do not properly search and strive to find them. . . . Spiritual knowledge is not available merely for the asking; even prayers are not enough. It takes persistence and dedication of one's life" (*The Teachings of Spencer W. Kimball,* ed. Edward L. Kimball [1982], 389–90).

Testimony

Bear testimony as prompted by the Spirit.

Assignments

Encourage class members to:

1. Write in their notebooks about their experiences as they carry out their plans to invite diligent learning (see "Notebook Activity," above). As appropriate, talk about these experiences with a leader, another class member, or a family member.

2. Review the principles taught in this lesson by studying the section of this book titled "Invite Diligent Learning" (pages 60–74).

Create a Learning Atmosphere
Part 1

Purpose	To help class members understand how teachers and learners can work together to create an atmosphere of gospel learning.

Note to the Teacher	In lesson 5, class members discussed the individual's responsibility to be diligent in learning the gospel. This week's lesson focuses on a responsibility that teachers and learners share: creating a learning atmosphere. It will help class members apply gospel principles in their efforts to prevent distractions in the classroom and help solve discipline problems that may already exist.
	With this lesson as a foundation, class members will be prepared to suggest solutions to specific problems. This will be done as part of lesson 7.

Preparation	1. Prayerfully study the scripture passages in this lesson. Seek to apply them to the purpose of the lesson.
	2. Become familiar with the stories in the lesson. Practice reading them in a way that will keep class members' interest.
	3. Bring the following items to class:
	a. A large piece of paper (or several smaller pieces of paper).
	b. Three marking pencils.
	4. Study the section of this book titled "Create a Learning Atmosphere" (pages 75–87).

Suggested Lesson Development	**The School of the Prophets provides an example of how to create an atmosphere of gospel learning.**
Quotations	Share the following statement:
	"In the early days of this dispensation the Lord commanded the brethren to 'teach one another the doctrine of the kingdom.' They were to learn all things pertaining to the gospel and the kingdom of God that it was expedient for them to know, as also things pertaining to the arts and sciences, and to kingdoms, and nations. They were to 'seek learning, even by study and also by faith,' and were to build a holy sanctuary or temple in Kirtland, which among other things was to be 'a house of learning.' (D. & C. 88:74–81, 118–122.)
	"As part of the then existing arrangement to fulfil these commands, the Lord directed the setting up of the *school of the prophets* (D. & C. 88:122, 127–141)" (Bruce R. McConkie, *Mormon Doctrine,* 2nd ed. [1966], 679).
	Explain that the purpose of the school of the prophets was "to prepare selected members of the priesthood to preach the gospel of Jesus Christ to all the world" (Ezra Taft Benson, in Conference Report, Apr. 1983, 69; or *Ensign,* May 1983, 53).

By revelation, the Lord taught the members of the school how to conduct themselves. Three elements of His instructions can help families and Church classes establish a learning atmosphere.

Chalkboard

Write the following list on the chalkboard:

> 1. Everyone contributes.
>
> 2. There is a bond of friendship in the gospel that unites all who are present.
>
> 3. Each individual is attentive and ready to focus on the contributions of others.

Scripture

Have class members turn to Doctrine and Covenants 88:122–23, 125. Explain that the three elements that you have written on the chalkboard are taught in this scripture passage. Have class members read the passage aloud. As they read, ask them to look for commandments from the Lord that can help us maintain these three elements of a learning atmosphere.

Emphasize that when people come together to learn the gospel, each person has something worthwhile to contribute. Each can be prompted by the Spirit to share insights and experiences that will edify the others. All who are present should listen to one another so that "all may be edified of all" (D&C 88:122).

Teachers and learners share the responsibility to create an atmosphere of gospel learning.

Teacher Presentation and Scripture

Point out that the first five lessons in this course included discussions about teachers' responsibilities. One lesson, lesson 5, also included discussion about individuals' responsibility to learn the gospel for themselves. Today's lesson focuses on a responsibility that is shared by both teachers and learners: the responsibility to create an atmosphere in which we can successfully learn the gospel together. To fulfill this responsibility, teachers and learners must help one another and be unified in purpose.

Explain that Alma spoke of this unity when he taught the people who had been baptized in the waters of Mormon. Have a class member read Mosiah 18:18–22.

Story

Share the following story, related by a woman who was concerned about the Sunday School class she attended. Ask class members to listen for ways in which the learners and the teacher in the story worked together to help create a learning atmosphere.

"In our new ward my husband and I discovered that the Gospel Doctrine class wasn't very effective. As the teacher talked, some class members read their scriptures; others just kept their heads down. I could tell that this bothered the teacher. Once he even asked, 'Is anybody listening?'

"Soon we learned that a number of people in the ward attended the Gospel Principles class instead of Gospel Doctrine. We heard that the teacher of that class was excellent. We attended the class and found it to be lively, insightful, and rewarding. But walking home from Church one day, we confided to each other that we both felt that what we were doing wasn't quite right. We needed to support our bishop by supporting the teacher he had called to teach us. So we began talking about what we could do to enrich the Gospel Doctrine class. We realized that we had placed all the responsibility for a good class experience on the teacher, as if we were daring him to get our attention and hold our interest.

"We prayed for guidance during the week and went to the Gospel Doctrine class on Sunday with a different spirit. A few minutes into the lesson, my husband asked a question, and the teacher invited other class members to offer answers. A good discussion ensued, to which several class members contributed. Later in the lesson, the teacher made a point that wasn't clear to me, so I asked him to help me understand. He responded by pointing out a scripture that I had never noticed before. Then a sister told a story that reinforced his point, and another class member offered another scripture. We felt the influence of the Spirit in that classroom. The teacher became more relaxed. I could see him gain strength and confidence from our simple gestures of interest and participation. The lesson concluded with a prayer of gratitude and a resounding 'Amen' from the class.

"Since that day most class members have been participating with great interest. Our teacher seems energized by their enthusiasm, and he often expresses gratitude for the support he feels. Sunday School keeps getting better and better."

Group Discussions

Divide the class into three groups. Give each group a marking pencil and a large piece of paper (or several smaller pieces of paper). Ask each group to choose one person to be a scribe. Then assign each group one of the following questions:

1. What are some things teachers and learners can do to encourage everyone to contribute?

2. What are some things teachers and learners can do to develop friendships among themselves?

3. What are some things teachers and learners can do to help everyone be attentive and listen to one another?

Inform the groups that they will have three minutes to discuss their questions. As they do so, they should consider their own experiences and the story that you have just shared with them. The scribe in each group will write the group's ideas on the large piece of paper. Then he or she will display the list for everyone else to see.

After two or three minutes have passed, have them display their lists. Briefly review the ideas in the lists. Encourage class members to write these ideas in their notebooks.

If class members do not include the following suggestions in their lists, you may want to mention them:

1. What are some things teachers and learners can do to encourage everyone to contribute?

   a. Teachers and learners should apply the principles they discuss.

b. Where possible—such as in Melchizedek Priesthood, Relief Society, and Gospel Doctrine classes—learners should read the lesson material before coming to class.

c. Learners should contribute willingly to discussions. They should raise their hands to help the teacher know that they are ready to ask questions or share comments.

d. Individual learners should be careful not to dominate discussions.

e. Learners should complete assignments diligently.

2. What are some things teachers and learners can do to develop friendships among themselves?

a. Teachers and learners should be aware of each other's abilities and needs.

b. They should support one another in class and outside of class.

c. As appropriate, they should verbally express their concern and love for one another.

3. What are some things teachers and learners can do to help everyone be attentive and listen to one another?

a. Teachers and learners should listen carefully and respectfully to each other.

b. Teachers and learners should arrive on time.

c. They should remain alert and focused on the lesson.

d. Learners should ask appropriate questions when they do not understand what is being taught.

e. Where possible, learners should be present throughout the lesson.

Teachers help learners understand and fulfill their responsibility to create a learning atmosphere.

Stories and Discussion

Explain that you are going to share two stories. Ask class members to think about how the teachers in these stories helped others contribute to a learning atmosphere. Then share the following story told by President Thomas S. Monson:

"One winter day, I thought back to an experience from my boyhood. I was just eleven. Our Primary president, Melissa, was an older and loving gray-haired lady. One day at Primary, Melissa asked me to stay behind and visit with her. There the two of us sat in the otherwise-empty chapel. She placed her arm about my shoulder and began to cry.

"Surprised, I asked her why she was crying.

"She replied, 'I don't seem to be able to encourage the [boys] to be reverent during the opening exercises of Primary. Would you be willing to help me, Tommy?'

"I promised Melissa that I would. Strangely to me, but not to Melissa, that ended any problem of reverence in that Primary. She had gone to the source of the problem—me" (in Conference Report, Oct. 1987, 82–83; or *Ensign*, Nov. 1987, 69).

▪ In this story, what did the Primary president do to help create a learning atmosphere? (She helped young Tommy Monson understand and fulfill his responsibility.)

- After hearing this story, are there any suggestions that you would like to add to lists you have made? (You may also want to suggest that class members add these suggestions to the lists in their notebooks.)

Story and Discussion   Indicate that you will now share a story about a teacher in the Young Women organization:

"Come with me into a classroom of 12- and 13-year-old young women. Listen as you hear the learners discover doctrine. Notice the experience the teacher provides for the learners so that they can connect the doctrine to the reality of their lives. Feel the accompanying witness of the Spirit:

"Our teacher moves her chair closer into the semicircle of five girls. 'We have a guest waiting outside,' she begins. 'It is Sister Jonas. She has agreed to show us her tiny baby and tell us how she feels about being a new mother. As you watch this new little baby, would you also notice his mother—how she treats the baby, what she does, what she says. We'll talk about her visit after she leaves.'

"Sister Jonas comes in, spends seven or eight minutes talking about her baby and answering questions. The girls thank her, and she leaves the classroom.

" 'The baby was darling, wasn't he?' our teacher responds to the delighted hum of the class. 'But what did you notice about the mother?'

"A minute of silence and then a response: 'Well, she was happy.' Another: 'She kind of rocked back and forth the whole time she was holding him.' A few more responses, and then Katie slowly begins, 'She—ummm—she talked really quietly.'

" 'Could you say more about that?' the teacher coaxes.

" 'Well, her voice reminds me of my mother's voice when she called from the hospital to tell us we had a new baby sister last year.'

"The teacher, turning to the other girls: 'What do you think? Did anyone else notice her voice?'

"The girls become more thoughtful and begin to reply with words like 'reverence,' 'heaven,' 'love.'

"The teacher: 'I think I understand. I believe those words come to our minds because we are recognizing a great gift from our Heavenly Father. He loves us and trusts us so much that He is willing to share His creative powers with us. We feel such gratitude and reverence for this trust. Motherhood is a *divine* role.'

"After this clear statement of doctrine and testimony, our teacher moves on to an activity where the girls identify qualities their own mothers exhibit that show an understanding of the divinity of motherhood. 'Could each of you prepare for motherhood right now by practicing one of these very virtues—maybe being more patient, kinder, or more positive this week?'

"Each girl talks about her choice. Our teacher bears personal testimony. The closing prayer is offered" (Virginia H. Pearce, in Conference Report, Oct. 1996, 14–15; or *Ensign,* Nov. 1996, 13).

- In this story, what did the teacher do to help create a learning atmosphere? (Answers may include that she invited a guest to share a personal experience, asked insightful questions, listened attentively, responded to class members' comments with follow-up questions, taught the doctrine, and helped the young women apply the doctrine in their lives.) What did the class members do? (Answers may include that they listened and participated thoughtfully.)

- How might the atmosphere of learning developed in this classroom help prevent future difficulties?

- After hearing this story, are there any suggestions that you would like to add to the lists you have made? (You may also want to suggest that class members add these suggestions to the lists in their notebooks.)

When we help learners become engaged in creating a learning atmosphere, we are teaching them to be followers of Jesus Christ.

Teacher Presentation

Point out that the stories that you have shared show some ways to both prevent problems and solve them. Have class members turn to the section of this book titled "Create a Learning Atmosphere," beginning on page 75. Point out that pages 76–83 discuss creating a learning atmosphere and preventing disruptions and that pages 84–87 give specific suggestions on how to deal with disruptions if they occur. Explain that whether we seek to prevent problems or solve them, our goal should be the same: to teach the gospel of Jesus Christ and to help learners understand and fulfill the responsibility that they share to create a learning atmosphere.

This goal is the key to discipline in the classroom. As we keep the goal in mind, we are not merely correcting behavior or keeping the classroom quiet. Instead, we are teaching others to be followers of Jesus Christ.

Sometimes teachers think that they are failing if they cannot quickly find a way to create an atmosphere of gospel learning. However, such an atmosphere is seldom created quickly. People develop one step at a time—line upon line and precept upon precept (see 2 Nephi 28:30). Constant effort is required. The key is to work faithfully, diligently, and patiently, always being guided by true principles.

Conclusion

Testimony

Bear testimony as prompted by the Spirit.

Assignment

Inform class members that next week's lesson will focus on a number of specific things that teachers can do to prevent distractions and solve discipline problems. Ask them to think of a situation that can detract from a learning atmosphere and to think of a possible solution. The solution should be specific and practical. They should write about both the situation and the solution in their notebooks, and they should be prepared to take two or three minutes in next week's class to talk about what they have written.

In considering possible solutions, class members should study the section of this book titled "Create a Learning Atmosphere" (pages 75–87).

Create a Learning Atmosphere
Part 2

Purpose	To help class members apply the principles they learned in lesson 6.

Note to the Teacher	At the conclusion of lesson 6, you asked class members to prepare to talk about ways to prevent distractions and solve discipline problems (see page 218). Because teachers desire to learn practical, specific ways to deal with problems, you should plan this lesson so that you will spend most of the class time on this application activity.
	As you direct the discussions in this lesson, help class members become more confident in their ability to create a learning atmosphere.

Preparation	1. Prayerfully study Doctrine and Covenants 12:8. Seek to apply it to the purpose of the lesson.
	2. Prepare to talk about how to prevent or solve a specific distraction or discipline problem. Make sure your solution is practical.
	3. Make sure class members are also prepared to talk about how to prevent distractions and solve discipline problems (see the assignment on page 218). Remind them to make their solutions specific and practical.
	4. Continue studying the section of this book titled "Create a Learning Atmosphere" (pages 75–87).

Suggested Lesson Development	**Our success in influencing others depends on our humility and love.**
Teacher Presentation and Scripture Discussion	Remind class members that in lesson 2 they discussed the importance of loving those we teach. This principle should govern all we do as we try to create a learning atmosphere, especially as we work individually with class members.
	Have a class member read Doctrine and Covenants 12:8.
	▪ Why are humility and love important in influencing others for good?
	Suggest that as class members talk about how to prevent distractions and solve discipline problems, they should keep in mind the importance of this principle.
Quotation	Share the following statement by President Howard W. Hunter:
	"God's chief way of acting is by persuasion and patience and long-suffering, not by coercion and stark confrontation. He acts by gentle solicitation and by sweet enticement. He always acts with unfailing respect for the freedom and independence that we possess. He wants to help us and pleads for the chance to assist us, but he will not do so in violation of our agency. He loves us too much to do that" (in Conference Report, Oct. 1989, 21; or *Ensign,* Nov. 1989, 18).

We can help others understand and fulfill their responsibility to contribute to a learning atmosphere.

Teacher Presentation

Refer to the assignment that you extended to class members last week. Inform class members that you have also worked on that assignment. Then share the problem that you have considered and your solution to it. Indicate which of the three elements of a learning atmosphere would be strengthened by your solution (for a review of these elements, see page 214). After sharing your solution, ask the following questions:

- What is effective about this solution?

- What cautions should be taken in using this solution?

- What other possible solutions can you think of?

Class Member Presentations

Have class members take turns talking about the problems they have considered and their suggestions on how to solve the problems. Ensure that each class member has the opportunity to contribute. As time permits, follow each presentation with the three questions above.

Teacher Presentation

Explain that in preventing distractions and solving discipline problems, it is often necessary to work with class members one by one. However, we can also teach class members of their responsibilities while they are assembled together. One good way to do this is to begin by sharing our feelings about our callings and our responsibilities as teachers. Then we can outline class members' responsibilities, teaching about the three elements of a learning atmosphere that were discussed in last week's lesson (see page 214). Finally, we can emphasize that we need their help because a class can be successful only when the teacher and the learners work together. (For an example of such a presentation, see the story on page 78 of this book. You may want to read this story with class members.)

We should find ways to reduce distractions.

Object Lesson

Ask a class member to stand in front of the class. Have the class member stretch his or her arms out, and put a heavy book or other object in each hand. Ask him or her to teach the other class members about the First Vision while continuing to hold the objects in this position. As the individual's arms begin to drop, remind him or her to keep them up. After about 30 seconds, have the individual put the objects down and return to his or her seat.

Point out that while this person was trying to teach, class members did not concentrate fully on what was being said. Their attention was drawn instead to the effort to hold up the books.

Teacher Presentation

Emphasize that in addition to problems that we have already discussed, the physical setting can also distract from teaching and learning. When class members enter a classroom or other teaching setting that is disorderly or uncomfortable, they are less likely to give their full attention to the message of the lesson.

Carefully planned physical arrangements can help reduce distractions. For example, we should arrange chairs so learners will be able to see us, the chalkboard, and each other. Such a classroom arrangement enhances the teacher's ability to teach and the learners' ability to participate and learn. Controlling the temperature of the room, where possible, can help everyone be comfortable. More suggestions for preparing the physical setting are found in "Preparing the Classroom," page 76 in this book.

We can prevent and solve discipline problems by following basic principles of gospel teaching.

Teacher Presentation

Point out that when we create and maintain a learning atmosphere, we help prevent distractions and solve discipline problems. The most important thing we can do to accomplish this is to implement the principles of gospel teaching that are taught in this course. These principles are:

1. Love those you teach.

2. Teach by the Spirit.

3. Teach the doctrine.

4. Invite diligent learning.

5. Prepare every needful thing.

6. Use effective methods.

As teachers, we should regularly examine ourselves and our teaching to make sure that we are applying each of these principles.

Conclusion

Testimony

Bear testimony as prompted by the Spirit.

Assignments

Encourage class members to:

1. Continue studying the section of this book titled "Create a Learning Atmosphere" (pages 75–87). Consider their own teaching, identifying things they can do to help create a learning atmosphere.

2. Review the list on page 210 about how to invite diligent learning. Choose one item in the list, and apply it in an upcoming teaching opportunity. Write about the experience in their notebooks.

Lesson
8

Use Effective Methods
Part 1

Purpose	To help class members select teaching methods and use those methods effectively.

Note to the Teacher	The quality of gospel teaching and learning improves as methods are selected carefully and used effectively. Teachers should select methods that (1) help those they teach gain a clear and memorable understanding of gospel doctrines and principles and (2) are appropriate for the content of the lesson and the age-group of those they teach.
	In this lesson and lesson 9, class members will learn about the following fundamental teaching methods: using object lessons, making comparisons, using the chalkboard, sharing stories, asking questions, and conducting discussions.

Preparation	1. Review the section of this book titled "Use Effective Methods" (pages 88–95). Also review part F, "Methods of Teaching" (pages 157–84).
	2. Bring to class one cup that is clean outside and inside and a similar cup that is clean outside but dirty inside.
	3. Prepare a demonstration in which you use the chalkboard to teach a gospel principle. You may want to use one of the examples on page 162, or you may develop an example on your own.

Suggested Lesson Development	**We should use teaching methods that help individuals understand, remember, and apply gospel principles.**
Story	Share the following story. Explain that this is an experience that President Boyd K. Packer and his wife had when he was serving as a mission president.
	"We scheduled zone conferences. For each one, Sister Packer baked a three-tiered cake, . . . decorated beautifully—thick, colorful layers of frosting, trimmed beautifully, and with 'The Gospel' inscribed across the top. When the missionaries were assembled, with some ceremony we brought the cake in. It was something to behold!
	"As we pointed out that the cake represented the gospel, we asked, 'Who would like to have some?' There was always a hungry elder who eagerly volunteered. We called him forward and said, 'We will serve you first.' I then sank my fingers into the top of the cake and tore out a large piece. I was careful to clench my fist after tearing it out so that the frosting would ooze through my fingers, and then as the elders sat in total disbelief, I threw the piece of cake to the elder, splattering some frosting down the front of his suit. 'Would anyone else like some cake?' I inquired. For some reason, there were no takers.

222

"Then we produced a crystal dish, a silver fork, a linen napkin, and a beautiful silver serving knife. With great dignity I carefully cut a slice of the cake from the other side, gently set it on the crystal dish, and asked, 'Would anyone like a piece of cake?'

"The lesson was obvious. It was the same cake in both cases, the same flavor, the same nourishment. The manner of serving either made it inviting, even enticing, or uninviting, even revolting. The cake, we reminded the missionaries, represented the gospel. How were they serving it?

"After the demonstration we had no difficulty—in fact, some considerable enthusiasm—for the effort to improve the teaching of the discussions. A few months later I thought the missionaries might well be reminded of the lesson, so I sent out a bulletin with a sketch of the cake.

"When I met the missionaries again, I said, 'You received a bulletin recently, didn't you?'

" 'Yes indeed.'

" 'And what did it say?'

"Invariably the missionaries said, 'It reminded us to sharpen up on presenting our lessons and to do more studying, to learn the lessons carefully, and then to help one another in our procedure for having them taught.'

" 'You got all that out of a picture?'

" 'Yes, that's one lesson we won't soon forget!'

"I should, of course, add that I was very happy where necessary to pay the bill to clean the elder's suit!" (*Teach Ye Diligently,* rev. ed. [1991], 270–71).

Note: If you desire to model President Packer's object lesson yourself, you might consider serving the cake by grabbing a piece of it with your hand and squeezing it onto a plate rather than throwing it on a class member.

Discussion
- What can we learn from this story about how we should present the gospel?

- What evidence is there that President Packer's lesson was effective?

Emphasize that the missionaries in President Packer's mission *understood* the lesson, *remembered* it, and *applied* it in their lives. It is not enough to help those we teach to simply understand gospel principles. We also need to help them remember them and apply them.

Have class members turn to page 158 in this book. Explain that this page contains a list of methods that can be used to teach the gospel. Today's lesson and next week's lesson will include demonstrations of a few of the methods in the list. Emphasize that we should select methods that lift those we teach and that do not detract from the principles we teach.

Using object lessons

Demonstration and Discussion
Point out that in the story you have shared, President Packer used an object lesson to remind missionaries to teach effectively. We can use object lessons to teach a variety of gospel principles.

Display two cups—one that is clean outside and inside and one that is clean outside but dirty inside. Then ask the following question:

- Which of these two cups would you rather drink from?

Explain that Jesus once compared a group of people to a cup that is clean outside but dirty inside. Invite a class member to read Matthew 23:25–26.

- What gospel principle does this object lesson teach? (It is not enough to simply *appear* righteous; we need to be righteous and clean in our hearts.) What do you feel is particularly effective about this object lesson?

Teacher Presentation

Point out that pages 163–64 in this book provide material that can help teachers develop effective object lessons. Invite class members to turn to page 164. Review the suggestions for developing and using object lessons. Then share any additional suggestions you may have on using object lessons.

Making comparisons

Quotations

Point out that object lessons are effective because they relate spiritual principles to familiar, physical objects. We can also achieve this by making simple comparisons.

Have different class members read the following comparisons (additional comparisons are found on pages 163–64 of this book):

President Gordon B. Hinckley taught:

"Faith is like the muscle of my arm. If I use it, if I nurture it, it grows strong; it will do many things. But if I put it in a sling, and do nothing with it, it will grow weak and useless" (in *Church News*, 6 June 1998, 2).

Elder Russell M. Nelson said:

"The verb *to inoculate* . . . literally means 'to put an eye within'—to monitor against harm.

"An affliction like polio can cripple or destroy the body. An affliction like sin can cripple or destroy the spirit. The ravages of polio can now be prevented by immunization, but the ravages of sin require other means of prevention. Doctors cannot immunize against iniquity. Spiritual protection comes only from the Lord—and in his own way. Jesus chooses not to inoculate, but to indoctrinate" (in Conference Report, Apr. 1995, 41–42; or *Ensign*, May 1995, 32).

Elder Joseph B. Wirthlin said:

"Giant oak trees . . . have deep root systems that can extend two-and-one-half times their height. Such trees rarely are blown down regardless of how violent the storms may be.

"Faithful members of the Church should be like oak trees and should extend deep roots into the fertile soil of the fundamental principles of the gospel" (in Conference Report, Oct. 1994, 98; or *Ensign*, Nov. 1994, 75).

Scripture Discussion

Invite a class member to read Matthew 13:44.

- What can we learn from this comparison?

Teacher Presentation	Emphasize that comparisons are effective only when we refer to things that are familiar to those we teach. Point out that pages 163–64 in this book provide material that can help teachers develop effective comparisons.

Using the chalkboard

Demonstration	Explain that the chalkboard can be used effectively to emphasize key ideas, focus class members' attention, and simplify complicated concepts. Tell class members that you will demonstrate how to use the chalkboard. Then do the demonstration that you have prepared (see "Preparation," item 3).

Discussion	Ask class members the following questions:

- What did you learn from this demonstration? How did the use of the chalkboard help you learn these things?

- From this demonstration, what did you learn about how we should use the chalkboard as a teaching tool?

If class members do not mention the following suggestions, mention them yourself:

1. Write clearly and large enough for all to see. It is usually more effective to write a few key words rather than complete sentences.

2. Talk while you write. This will help you keep the attention of the class members.

3. Avoid spending long periods of time at the chalkboard.

4. Plan ahead. Practice drawing any figures, maps, or diagrams you plan to use.

5. Do not apologize for your handwriting or lack of artistic ability.

6. Use simple stick figures and shapes to illustrate stories or concepts.

7. Occasionally allow class members to write on the chalkboard. This can help increase participation.

Point out that class members can find additional suggestions on pages 162–63 of this book.

As we prepare to teach, we can choose from a variety of teaching methods.

Teacher Presentation	Point out that a variety of methods can enhance and enliven gospel teaching and learning. However, we should not use different methods solely for the sake of variety. We should select methods that (1) help those we teach gain a clear and memorable understanding of gospel doctrines and principles and (2) are appropriate for the content of the lesson and the age-group of those we teach.

Application	Ask a class member to share a specific doctrine or principle from a lesson that he or she is preparing to teach. Then have class members turn to page 158 and review the list of methods. Invite them to suggest methods that might be used to effectively teach that doctrine or principle. As class members suggest particular methods, ask them to explain why they have suggested those methods.

Conclusion

Quotation

Have a class member read the following statement by Elder Boyd K. Packer:

"When we teach moral and spiritual values, we are teaching things that are intangible. Perhaps no teaching is so difficult to accomplish, nor so rewarding when successfully done. There are techniques to employ and tools to use. There are things that teachers can do to prepare themselves and their lessons so that their students . . . can be taught, and their testimonies can be conveyed from one to another" (*Teach Ye Diligently,* 62).

Emphasize that methods are important but that they should not be the focus of the lessons we teach. They are tools to help those we teach focus on the saving doctrines of the gospel and apply them in their lives.

Testimony

Bear testimony as prompted by the Spirit.

Assignments

Encourage class members to:

1. Consider methods they might use to teach gospel principles more effectively.

2. Write in their notebooks about their experiences with selecting and using different teaching methods.

3. Review the section of this book titled "Use Effective Methods" (pages 88–95). Also review part F, "Methods of Teaching" (pages 157–84).

Use Effective Methods
Part 2

Purpose	To help class members apply the principles they learned in lesson 8.

Note to the Teacher

This lesson is a continuation of lesson 8. In preparation for this lesson, you will invite a few class members to teach gospel principles by using the following methods: sharing stories, asking questions, and conducting discussions (see "Preparation," item 1, below). You should ensure that this experience is uplifting for them and that it helps them gain confidence in their ability to use different teaching methods. You should be especially sensitive to the needs and feelings of class members who are less experienced teachers.

Preparation

1. Speak with three class members in advance, asking each of them to prepare one of the demonstrations listed below. Encourage them to refer to the scriptures and *Gospel Principles* (31110) for help with the subject matter of the demonstrations and to this book for help on how to use the methods they have been assigned.

   Demonstration 1: Tell a true story to teach about the power of personal prayer. Be prepared to share a few insights on how to effectively use stories in gospel teaching.

   Demonstration 2: Use questions to teach about the blessings of keeping the Sabbath day holy. Be prepared to share a few insights on how to effectively use questions in gospel teaching.

   Demonstration 3: Conduct a discussion to teach about why we should be willing to make sacrifices. Be prepared to share a few insights on how to effectively conduct discussions in gospel teaching.

2. As necessary, help the assigned class members prepare their demonstrations.

Suggested Lesson Development

Remind class members that in the previous lesson they saw demonstrations on using object lessons, comparisons, and the chalkboard to teach gospel principles. Today they will see demonstrations in which assigned class members will teach gospel principles by sharing a story, asking questions, and conducting a discussion.

Sharing stories

Demonstration and Discussion

Invite the assigned class member to present the first demonstration (see "Preparation," item 1). After this demonstration, have class members discuss the following question:

- How did the use of this story help you better understand the power of personal prayer?

Invite the assigned class member to share a few insights that he or she has gained about how to use stories to teach gospel principles.

Teacher Presentation

Have class members turn to the "Stories" entry on pages 179–82. Review "Guidelines for Preparing and Telling a Story," page 181.

Asking questions

Demonstration and Discussion

Invite the assigned class member to present the second demonstration (see "Preparation," item 1). After this demonstration, have class members discuss the following question:

- In what ways did the questions in this demonstration help you better understand the blessings of keeping the Sabbath day holy?

Invite the assigned class member to share a few insights that he or she has gained about how to use questions to teach gospel principles.

Teacher Presentation

Help class members understand that the questions that we use as teaching tools should:

1. Stimulate thought and discussion. To find out what people know, think, or feel, ask questions that begin with *what, where, when, why, how,* or *in what way.* Generally, questions that can be answered *yes* or *no* are not effective unless they lead to other questions or to commitments.

2. Help class members see how to apply gospel principles in their lives.

3. Encourage class members to share personal insights and experiences that relate to the principles being taught.

Point out that we should not be concerned if those we teach are silent for a few seconds after we have asked a question. They may need time to think of responses.

Explain that class members can find additional suggestions in "Teaching with Questions," on pages 68–70 in this book.

Conducting discussions

Demonstration and Discussion

Invite the assigned class member to present the third demonstration (see "Preparation," item 1). After this demonstration, have class members discuss the following question:

- How did this discussion help you better understand why we should be willing to make sacrifices?

Invite the assigned class member to share a few insights that he or she has gained about how to conduct discussions.

Teacher Presentation

Help class members understand that in conducting discussions, we should:

1. Help learners feel comfortable sharing their testimonies, insights, experiences, questions, and ideas.

2. Acknowledge learners' contributions with appreciation and respect.

3. Be sensitive to learners who are hesitant to participate. It may be helpful to talk with them privately to assess their feelings about reading aloud or participating in class. It may also be helpful to allow them to prepare for class discussions by assigning scriptures that they can read and ponder before class.

4. Redirect learners' comments and questions to other learners for response.

Point out that class members can find additional suggestions in "Conducting Discussions," pages 63–65 in this book.

Conclusion

Summary

Express your appreciation for the class members' demonstrations.

Remind class members that methods are important but that they should not be the focus of the lessons we teach. They are tools to help those we teach focus on the saving doctrines of the gospel and apply them in their lives.

Point out that our enthusiasm for teaching will increase as we continually seek to increase our ability to use a variety of methods. We may feel some fear and discomfort as we try new methods, but we can overcome those feelings.

Quotation

President Heber J. Grant often quoted Ralph Waldo Emerson, who said, "That which we persist in doing becomes easier for us to do; not that the nature of the thing itself is changed, but that our power to do is increased" (in *Gospel Standards*, comp. G. Homer Durham [1941], 335).

Testimony

Bear testimony as prompted by the Spirit.

Assignments

Encourage class members to:

1. Try new methods to teach gospel principles. Have them write about their experiences in their notebooks.

2. Come to class next week prepared to develop a plan for a lesson that they will soon teach. This lesson may be part of a family home evening assignment, a Church assignment, or another opportunity to teach. Bring lesson materials, such as the scriptures and lesson manuals.

Lesson
10

Prepare Every Needful Thing

Purpose	To help class members prepare effective lessons.

Note to the Teacher

Gospel teachers should ask themselves three questions as they prepare lessons:

1. What should happen in the lives of those I teach as a result of this lesson?

2. Which specific principles should be taught?

3. How should these principles be taught?

The first of these questions helps teachers focus the lesson on the needs of those they teach. With this in mind, teachers can decide what to teach. This is an important decision, especially since lessons often contain more material than teachers are able to cover in one class period. In deciding how to teach, teachers should select methods that complement the material, are in accordance with the Spirit, and invite diligent learning.

As you teach this lesson, help class members understand how to prepare lessons efficiently and under the direction of the Spirit. Remember that your preparation for this lesson can serve as an example to class members as they prepare to teach.

Preparation

1. Study the section of this book titled "Prepare Every Needful Thing" (pages 96–105).

2. Remind class members to come prepared to develop a plan for a lesson that they will soon teach. Encourage them to bring lesson materials, such as the scriptures and lesson manuals. (This assignment was given at the conclusion of lesson 9.)

3. Bring to class a copy of a current Church-produced lesson manual, such as a Primary manual or a Gospel Doctrine manual, in which the lessons contain purpose statements and suggested teaching methods.

4. Before class, write the following chart on the chalkboard:

1. What should happen in the lives of those I teach as a result of this lesson?	2. Which specific principles should be taught?	3. How should these principles be taught?

Suggested Lesson Development	**Personal preparation is essential for us to be able to teach the gospel.**
Quotation	Invite a class member to read the statement by Elder Dallin H. Oaks on page 96.
Chalkboard and Teacher Presentation	Direct class members' attention to the chart that you have written on the chalkboard. Have class members copy the chart in their notebooks.
	Explain that these are three important questions that we should ask ourselves as we prepare a lesson.
	Explain that during this lesson class members will answer these questions in relation to the lesson materials that they have brought.

1. Decide what should happen in the lives of those we teach as a result of the lesson.

Notebook Activity and Teacher Presentation	Ask class members to refer to the lesson materials that they have brought to class. Have them write the topic of their lesson at the top of the chart in their notebooks. If they are teaching from a block of scripture, have them write the chapter and verses.

Explain that with a topic in mind, we can decide how the lesson should influence those we teach. For example, in teaching a lesson about tithing, a Primary teacher may decide that the children should understand what tithing is and why we pay tithing. In teaching a lesson about the temple, parents may decide that their children should feel a desire to live worthy to be married in the temple. In teaching a lesson about family home evening, an elders quorum president may decide that the lesson should inspire quorum members to hold a meaningful family home evening every week.

Point out that many Church-produced lesson manuals include purpose statements with the lessons. Display the lesson manual that you have brought to class, and show class members the purpose statement in one of the lessons. Explain that we should use these statements as guides as we prepare lessons.

Invite class members to consider the needs of the people they teach. Then ask them the following question:

- What do you feel should happen in the lives of those you teach as a result of the lesson?

Explain that a teacher's answer to this question may include what people should understand, feel, desire, or do as a result of a lesson. Then give class members time to ponder the question. Have them write their answers on the chart in their notebooks.

Discussion	After class members have had time to write their answers, invite a few of them to share their responses and their reasons for giving those responses.

Emphasize that as we prepare a lesson, we should consider the needs of those we teach. Guided by the Spirit, we can know how the lesson should influence those we teach. This knowledge will help us decide what to teach and how to teach it.

2. Decide what to teach in the lesson.

Teacher Presentation

Point out that we often have more material than we are able to teach in the time we are given. This is true whether we teach from manuals with prepared lessons or from other resources, such as *Ensign* articles or general conference addresses. In such cases, we should prayerfully select the material that will be most helpful for those we teach.

Emphasize that when we teach the gospel, we should do more than simply present information. What matters most is not the amount of material covered but the influence the lesson has on those we teach.

Chalkboard and Discussion

- What can we do that will help us decide which specific points to teach? (Without erasing the chart, write class members' responses on the chalkboard. Note that some important points are listed below. Mention these ideas if class members do not mention them.)

    a. Prayerfully study the content of the lesson.
    b. Make a list of key principles covered in the lesson.
    c. Always keep in mind the needs and backgrounds of those you teach.
    d. Follow the guidance of the Spirit.

Encourage class members to begin preparing for a lesson at least a week before they teach it. This will give them time to ponder and pray about the material, understand it, and develop appealing ways to present it.

Notebook Activity

Have class members refer again to the lesson materials that they have brought to class. Encourage them to continue to consider the needs of those they teach as they answer the following question. Also encourage them to consider what the people they teach are prepared to receive.

- In this lesson, what are the most important ideas for the people you teach?

Give class members time to ponder this question. Have them write their answers on the chart in their notebooks under "Which specific principles should be taught?"

Discussion

After class members have had time to write their answers, invite a few of them to share their responses and their reasons for giving those responses.

3. Decide how to teach the lesson.

Discussion

Explain that after we have decided what to teach, we should decide how to teach it. This includes selecting methods that will help people understand the principles we teach.

- What are some methods we can use to teach the gospel? (Help class members recall the methods that were demonstrated in lessons 8 and 9. Also remind them of the list of methods on page 158 of this book.)

Remind class members that teaching methods should lift those we teach, invite diligent learning, and help class members understand and apply gospel principles.

Notebook Activity

Have class members look again at the chart in their notebooks. Ask them to consider one principle they have written under "Which specific principles should be taught?" Give them a few minutes to think of a method they might use to teach that principle and to include that method in their chart.

Display the lesson manual that you have brought to class. Point out that some lesson manuals include suggestions on how to teach certain principles. Teachers may use these suggestions, or they may think of their own ideas based on the needs of those they teach.

After class members have had time to write in their notebooks, invite a few of them to share their ideas.

Conclusion

Quotation

Read the following statement by President David O. McKay:

"There are three things which must guide all teachers: First, get into the subject . . . ; second, get that subject into you; third, try to lead [those you teach] to get the subject into them—not pouring it into them, but leading them to see what you see, to know what you know, to feel what you feel" (*Gospel Ideals* [1953], 424).

Encourage class members to apply the principles discussed in this lesson. Assure them that as they do so prayerfully, they will be able to plan lessons that will help others learn gospel doctrines and apply them in their lives.

Testimony

Bear testimony as prompted by the Spirit.

Assignments

Encourage class members to:

1. Complete the lesson preparation that they have begun in class. Write in their notebooks about their experience with preparing and teaching the lesson.

2. Review the principles taught in this lesson by studying the section of this book titled "Prepare Every Needful Thing" (pages 96–105).

3. Prepare for next week's lesson by studying Matthew 7:1–5. Consider if there is anything they are doing to contribute to the challenges they face as teachers. Think about changes they might make. As they do so, they should ponder the Lord's counsel in Ether 12:27, 37 about the blessings that can come as we humbly recognize our weaknesses.

Lesson

11

Improve upon Your Talents

Purpose	To help class members understand how to continually improve as teachers.

Note to the Teacher

As Enoch journeyed among his people, he heard a voice from heaven commanding him to preach repentance to the people. "When Enoch had heard these words, he bowed himself to the earth, before the Lord, and spake before the Lord, saying: Why is it that I have found favor in thy sight, and am but a lad, and all the people hate me; for I am slow of speech; wherefore am I thy servant?" (see Moses 6:26–31).

"And the Lord said unto Enoch: Go forth and do as I have commanded thee. . . . Open thy mouth, and it shall be filled, and I will give thee utterance. . . . Behold my Spirit is upon you, wherefore all thy words will I justify; . . . and thou shalt abide in me, and I in you; therefore walk with me" (Moses 6:32, 34).

Enoch went forth as he was commanded, and the Lord blessed him with the ability to teach with power.

Some class members may feel somewhat like Enoch did when he received his call to preach—aware of their weaknesses and unsure of their abilities. This lesson is designed to help them know how they can improve as teachers. The lesson focuses on the help available from resources such as Church curriculum materials, leaders' support, and teacher improvement meetings. However, it is important that you remind them that the Lord is their greatest source for help. As they humble themselves and exercise faith in the Lord, He will "make weak things become strong unto them" (Ether 12:27).

Preparation

1. In advance, ask a class member or a ward leader to prepare to read the statement by President Brigham Young on page 235. Also ask this individual to prepare to tell about an experience in which he or she has seen the truth of this statement.

2. Ask a teacher from one of the priesthood or auxiliary organizations to come to class and talk for three to five minutes about how support from a leader has helped him or her.

3. Ask a priesthood or auxiliary leader to come to the class and talk for three to five minutes about how leaders can support the work of teachers. Ask this person to base the presentation on the information on page 28 of this book. Ensure that this person prepares to discuss the importance of teachers contacting leaders in order to share experiences, discuss the needs of individuals in the quorum or class, and seek help and counsel. (It might be helpful to ask a leader who serves with the teacher who is giving the presentation outlined in item 2.)

4. Study the section of this book titled "Improve upon Your Talents" (pages 21–28).

5. Review the information about teacher improvement meetings on pages 7–9 in *Improving Gospel Teaching: A Leader's Guide.* Prepare to talk for three to five minutes about how teacher improvement meetings can help meet the needs of individual teachers. As part of this presentation, tell class members when the next teacher improvement meetings will be held and who should attend these meetings. (If you are not the teacher improvement coordinator, you may want to ask the teacher improvement coordinator to make this presentation.)

6. Prepare to share one or two things that you would include in the chart on page 25.

7. Before class, set up a display of current Church-produced teaching resources that are available in your area. Prepare to spend three to five minutes describing these materials. If the materials listed on page 105 are available, include them in the display.

Suggested Lesson Development	**In our efforts to reach each person we teach, we should continually strive to improve.**
Introduction	Have the assigned class member or ward leader read the following statement:
	President Brigham Young said that the Lord "gives a little to his humble followers today, and if they improve upon it, tomorrow he will give them a little more, and the next day a little more. He does not add to that which they do not improve upon" (*Discourses of Brigham Young,* sel. John A. Widtsoe [1941], 90).
	Ask the assigned individual to tell about an experience in which he or she has seen the truth of this statement.
Teacher Presentation	Point out that this principle taught by President Young applies to our efforts as gospel teachers. We receive the Lord's help as we continue to improve upon what He has given us. This lesson focuses on things we can do to improve our teaching. It also discusses the resources that are available in the Church to help us in these efforts.
	The Church provides resources to help us improve as teachers.
Reports	*Meetinghouse Library*
	Explain that the Church has produced materials that can help us teach effective lessons. Direct class members' attention to the display that you set up before class (see "Preparation," item 7). Spend a few minutes describing the materials, and give class members the opportunity to ask questions about them. Encourage class members to visit the meetinghouse library to learn more about these materials and other materials that might help them with their lessons.
	Explain that in addition to curriculum materials, the Church provides other resources to help us improve as teachers. Discuss these resources as shown below.
	Leader Support of Teachers
	Ask the assigned leader and teacher to share their presentations about leader support of teachers (see "Preparation," items 2 and 3).

After this presentation, invite class members to ask questions about leader support of teachers. Also invite them to discuss ways in which such support can help them improve as leaders and teachers.

Express your feelings about the importance of leaders supporting teachers.

Teacher Improvement Meetings

Tell class members about teacher improvement meetings (see "Preparation," item 5).

The Teaching the Gospel Course

Point out that this course is another resource that the Church provides to help us improve as teachers.

We should continually reflect on our effectiveness as teachers.

Notebook Activity

Explain that we should continually reflect on how our efforts are helping those we teach. Then ask class members to turn to the chart on page 25 of this book. Have them copy the chart in their notebooks.

Ask class members to think back over the weeks since the beginning of this course. Invite them to consider assignments from previous lessons. Then help them use the chart to briefly evaluate their progress as teachers. Have them write one strength that they have as teachers and one weakness. Encourage them to write one thing that they can do now to improve and one skill that they need to develop. (For an explanation of how to do this evaluation, see the example on page 25.)

Explain that this will help them get started. They should complete the chart on their own. As they do so, they may want to review "Making a Plan to Improve Your Teaching," on pages 24–27 in this book.

Teacher Presentation

After class members have had time to write in their charts, express your own desire to improve as a teacher. Share with class members one or two things that you would include for yourself in this chart (see "Preparation," item 6).

Quotation

Assure class members that the Lord will help them in their efforts to improve. Have a class member read the statement by President James E. Faust on page 21 of this book.

Conclusion

Teacher Presentation

Repeat the statement by President Brigham Young. Share your feelings about the importance of the principle. If time permits, share the account of Enoch as presented in the note to the teacher on page 234.

Testimony

Bear testimony as prompted by the Spirit.

Assignments

Encourage class members to:

1. Contact individual leaders in their organizations to share experiences, discuss the needs of individuals in the quorum or class, and seek help and counsel. (If class members do not have callings as teachers, encourage them to talk with a family member, with the teacher improvement coordinator, or with you to discuss what they have been learning in this course.)

2. Review the principles taught in this lesson by studying the section of this book titled "Improve upon Your Talents" (pages 21–28). Continue to work on their plan to improve.

3. Come to class next week prepared to make presentations on what they have learned or how they have grown in connection with this course. The presentations should be three to five minutes long, depending on the number of class members. They should include reports on *(a)* how they have changed as teachers because of the things they have learned and *(b)* what they plan to do to continually improve as teachers.

Lesson
12

Go Forth and Teach

Purpose	To give class members the opportunity to strengthen one another in their efforts to improve as teachers.

Note to the Teacher	The Lord taught an important principle of gospel teaching when He said, "Appoint among yourselves a teacher, and let not all be spokesmen at once; but let one speak at a time and let all listen unto his sayings, that when all have spoken that all may be edified of all, and that every man may have an equal privilege" (D&C 88:122).

Today's lesson, the final lesson in the Teaching the Gospel course, provides an opportunity for class members to teach and edify one another as they share their feelings about the doctrines, principles, skills, and methods that they have learned during this course. Structure the lesson carefully so that each class member has time to participate.

Preparation	1. In advance, remind class members of the assignment they were given to prepare for this lesson (see assignment 3 on page 237).

2. Consider how each class member has progressed during the course and what you have learned from each class member. Be prepared to share some of these thoughts as part of the lesson.

Suggested Lesson Development	Briefly share your testimony about the importance of teaching the gospel and about the privilege to serve as a teacher. Then read the statement below by Elder Jeffrey R. Holland, asking class members to listen carefully to see how the statement could serve as a summary for this course:

"Whether we are instructing our children at home or standing before an audience in church, let us *never* make our faith difficult to detect. Remember, we are to be teachers 'come from God.' Never sow seeds of doubt. Avoid self-serving performance and vanity. Prepare lessons well. Give scripturally based sermons. Teach the revealed doctrine. Bear heartfelt testimony. Pray and practice and try to improve. In our administrative meetings let us both 'instruct and edify' as the revelations say, that even in these our teaching may ultimately be 'from on high.' The Church will be the better for it, and so will you, for as Paul said to the Romans, 'Thou therefore which teachest another, teachest thou not thyself?' "(in Conference Report, Apr. 1998, 33; or *Ensign,* May 1998, 27).

Invite each class member, in turn, to make his or her presentation (see "Preparation," item 1).

Conclusion

Observations   As time permits, share your observations of class members' progress during the course (see "Preparation," item 2). Talk about some things you have learned from class members.

Testimony   Bear testimony as prompted by the Spirit. You might also include expressions of confidence, encouragement, and support as class members go forth to teach the gospel.

INDEX